# Redistricting

# Redistricting

## The Most Political Activity in America

### Second Edition

Charles S. Bullock III
*University of Georgia*

ROWMAN & LITTLEFIELD
*Lanham • Boulder • New York • London*

Published by Rowman & Littlefield
An imprint of The Rowman & Littlefield Publishing Group, Inc.
4501 Forbes Boulevard, Suite 200, Lanham, Maryland 20706
www.rowman.com

6 Tinworth Street, London SE11 5AL, United Kingdom

British Library Cataloguing in Publication Information Available

**Library of Congress Cataloging-in-Publication Data**

Names: Bullock, Charles S., 1942- author.
Title: Redistricting : the most political activity in America / Charles S. Bullock III.
Description: Second edition. I Lanham, Maryland : Rowman & Littlefield Publishing Group, 2021. I Includes bibliographical references and index. I Summary: "This authoritative overview of election redistricting at the congressional, state legislative, and local level provides offers an overview of redistricting for students and practitioners. The updated second edition pays special attention to the significant redistricting controversies of the last decade, from the Supreme Court to state courts"—Provided by publisher.
Identifiers: LCCN 2020050571 (print) I LCCN 2020050572 (ebook) I ISBN 9781538149652 (cloth) I ISBN 9781538149645 (paperback) I ISBN 9781538149638 (epub)
Subjects: LCSH: Apportionment (Election law)—United States. I Gerrymandering—United States.
Classification: LCC KF4905 .B85 2021 (print) I LCC KF4905 (ebook) I DDC 328.73/073455—dc23
LC record available at https://lccn.loc.gov/2020050571
LC ebook record available at https://lccn.loc.gov/2020050572

*To my grandsons:*
*Jason, Christopher, Daniel, and Matthew Fern*

# Contents

# Acknowledgments

This book is the result of teaching about redistricting—how it is done and its consequences—for five decades. Many people have contributed to my understanding of the topic. Most of those who have advanced my understanding were probably unaware of their role and none bear any responsibility for the lingering gaps in my knowledge. Much of my education has taken place in the context of the development of redistricting plans and then litigation challenging those plans. In some cases I have worked for the jurisdiction defending the plan while at other times I have helped those seeking to overturn the plan.

Those to whom I owe an intellectual debt include: John Alford, Steve Bickerstaff, Kim Brace, Kay Butler, Bruce Cain, David Canon, Dick Engstrom, the late Robinson Everett, Keith Gaddie, Bernie Grofman, Lisa Handley, Jerry Hebert, Sam Hirsch, the late Tom Hofeller, Bob Holmes, Trey Hood, Paul Hurd, Morgan Kousser, David Lublin, Susan MacManus, Doug Markham, Linda Meggers, Peter Morrison, Dick Murray, Dan O'Connor, Tim O'Rourke, Andy Taylor, Bryan Tyson, Dave Walbert, Ron Weber, and Steve Zack.

I appreciate the careful reading that my colleagues Trey Hood and David Cottrell gave to chapter 5. Trey brought his extensive experience as an expert witness in cases involving claims of partisan gerrymandering while David drew upon his work with Jowei Chen doing simulations to assess the likelihood that maps would have the level of partisanship observed by chance.

The maps that appear in this volume were prepared by two very talented individuals. Some were prepared by Kim Brace's Election Data Services that has been a major player in redistricting for decades. Maps showing the handiwork of those who made adjustments to reflect population shifts during the first decade of the twenty-first century were prepared by Mitchell Redd, who earned his master's degree in political science at the University of Georgia.

Completion of this manuscript would have taken much longer and might never have seen the light of day without the perseverance of my secretary Bridget Pilcher.

# Chapter 1

# Introduction

## Why Redistricting Is Important

The key concept to grasp is that there are no neutral lines for legislative districts.[1]

Gerrymandering is somewhat like pornography, you know it when you see it, but it's awful difficult to define.[2]

You can't take politics out of politics, and there is nothing more political than redistricting.[3]

In 2000, George Bush carried Texas by more than 1.3 million votes. The Bush victory sparked little surprise since Bush came from Texas and the Lone Star State had voted Republican for president since 1952 with four exceptions, in two of which another native son, Lyndon Johnson, was on the ballot. The Lone Star State voted for LBJ's former vice president Hubert Humphrey in 1968 and for southern Jimmy Carter in 1976. By 2000, Republicans filled 28 of the 29 statewide elective partisan offices. Republican candidates also took 50.8 percent of the congressional vote. At the onset of the twenty-first century, Texas seemed to be a red state. There was, however, a problem, at least from the Republican perspective. Although their nominees won most of the congressional votes cast in the state, this translated into only 13 of the 30 seats. The 2000 results continued a pattern that had begun with 1994 when Republican congressional candidates won a majority of the popular vote and yet failed to get even half of the state's congressional seats. The explanation for the failure of popular support to translate into a commensurate share of the congressional seats lay with the districting plan. After the 1990 census, Democratic Representative Martin Frost and a staffer devised a brilliantly effective gerrymander. Frost distributed Democratic supporters to maximize

1

the number of districts his party could win. For the next decade, Democrats received a substantially larger share of the seats than their share of the popular vote.

Elections are essential to the legitimacy of any democracy. However, as the Texas example demonstrates, and numerous other examples exist, the way in which votes translate into seats depends upon the districting format. A districting scheme can make some votes worth more than others. The party that gets fewer votes can win a majority of the seats if the districting plan packs supporters of one party into a minority of districts that are won by overwhelming majorities while carefully distributing the supporters of the other party so that they win a greater number of seats by narrower margins. By promoting or thwarting the ambitions of a political party, districting plans determine what interests in society will be best positioned to determine policy outputs. If the districting scheme favors rural voters, then the concerns of farmers may get more consideration than the needs of urban residents. A plan that gives Democrats a disproportionate share of the seats will likely enhance the influence of organized labor, environmentalists, and trial attorneys.

The impact of districting schemes is greatest in systems like those used in the U.S. House and most American state legislatures where each district chooses one representative. With only one representative per district, parties compete under winner-take-all rules, so that the seats in the legislature held by a party can be maximized under a plan that allows it to win consistently with small majorities. In the most extreme, hypothetical arrangement, if the majority party managed to win 51 percent of the vote in every district, then it would win all of the seats from a state even though it attracted barely half of the votes. Of course, any plan that distributes votes in anticipation that a party will narrowly win a number of districts runs the risk of losing those competitive districts should partisan preferences shift even slightly.

In contrast with the single-member, plurality elections widely used in the United States, many nations have electoral systems designed to promote proportionality. At one extreme the entire nations of Israel and the Netherlands serve as a single district and elect all members of their parliaments at-large with each party receiving a share of seats proportional to its share of the votes so that the ratio of seats to votes approximates 1:1. The approach used by the Dutch and Israelis eliminates any problem of one party designing a districting plan to the disadvantage of its opponents—although it would not necessarily prevent some areas of a country or interests being underrepresented. Most nations that use proportional representation have multi-member districts that represent states, regions, or other subdivisions within the nation. In these systems, districting can be important, as demonstrated in Japan where the party that has dominated its politics since World War II drew great support from rural areas and underrepresented urban interests.[4]

The debate over the way in which votes should translate into seats predates the Constitution. Supreme Court Justice Antonin Scalia referenced a concern in North Carolina that the governor might have manipulated boundaries in order to secure majority support in the lower chamber of the colonial legislature as early as 1732.[5] Even patriots of the American Revolution turned to gerrymandering, as when Patrick Henry sought to fashion a district to prevent James Madison's election to the First Congress.[6]

One of the most controversial issues at the Constitutional Convention involved the representation of states with populations of different sizes. The Great Compromise equalized state representation in the Senate regardless of population while representation in the House reflected population differences.

Using population to distribute seats in the U.S. House indicates a concern about fairness. Fairness has taken on many guises and is invariably invoked in the course of conflict over redistricting. While the Constitution is notable for its lack of specificity, which has allowed Congress and courts to expand federal authority through the necessary and proper clause, the document sets a lower limit with regard to the weighting of population in the House. Article 1, Section 2, specifies that "the number of representatives shall not exceed one for every 30,000 people." The Constitution also set the number of seats for each of the thirteen states in the First Congress. The Constitution called for a census within three years after Congress convened for its first meeting and then every ten years thereafter.

After the initial census, Congress adjusted the distribution of seats in the lower chamber. Following the first census in 1790, eleven states gained seats, with the New York, North Carolina, and Virginia delegations almost doubling in size. Delaware remained with a single seat while only Georgia lost a seat, declining from three to two. After each census, from 1790 through 1910 with one exception, the House expanded. Despite a growing number of seats available, reapportionment following the census resulted in some states, particularly those in New England, gradually losing representation.

Although redistricting and reapportionment are often used synonymously, they do have different meanings. Reapportionment is the redistribution of seats while redistricting involves the crafting of new districts from which those seats will be filled. Thus, reapportionment occurs following the census when seats in the U.S. House are allocated to states. When the states change their maps to reflect population shifts during the course of a decade, that is redistricting.

## SEAT ALLOCATIONS TO STATES

Until the 1960s, reapportionment and redistricting standards operated on very different bases. Except in 1920, reapportionment has followed each census, and while several different formulae have been used over time, the allocation of seats to states takes place with great precision. Redistricting, however, occurred infrequently even when rules were in place that called for it to be accomplished in order to reflect population shifts. Indeed the general practice was to redistrict only when *absolutely* necessary. While equally populated districts have been the standard for all collegial bodies beginning in the 1960s, for most of American history only the U.S. House reflected population changes among states, but even in that chamber, large population differences existed within states. We turn our attention now to the one instance in which population has always mattered, the distribution of congressional seats among states.

Table 1.1 shows the number of seats allocated to each state over time. The general trend has been for representation to move westward from the eastern seaboard. Another trend starting after World War II shifts seats from the North to the South.

A snapshot taken following the 1912 reapportionment, the last time the House was permanently expanded, shows the largest delegations to be New York (43 members), Pennsylvania (36), Illinois (27), Ohio (22), Texas (18), Missouri (16), Massachusetts (16), Indiana (13), and Michigan (13). A century later, California had the largest delegation (53 members), followed by Texas (36), New York (27), Florida (27), Pennsylvania (18), Illinois (18), Ohio (16), Michigan (14), and Georgia (14). Of the nine largest states in 1910, all except Texas and Michigan grew slower than the nation over the century and, consequently, lost seats. Pennsylvania, the nation's second largest state from 1820 until 1950, lost eighteen seats. Missouri also lost half its delegation during the century. While six of the nine largest states in 1910 remained in that exclusive category for a century, the two with greatest percentage increases were not among the top nine in 1912. California exploded from eight seats to fifty-three and Florida experienced comparable growth since the 1910 census allotted it only four seats.

California with fifty-three seats has the largest state delegation in the history of the nation, a distinction first achieved in 1992. Beginning with 1972, California has had more members of Congress than any other state. The Texas delegation overtook New York for second place with the 2002 reapportionment. Florida and New York each got twenty-seven members of Congress in 2012. Projections show Florida gaining at least one seat for the 2022 election and New York losing yet another seat in 2020. The 2020 census will allocate a fourteenth seat to North Carolina while Michigan and other Rust Belt states will continue experiencing losses. Texas is expected to add multiple seats, as it has following each of the four most recent reapportionings. A comparison of the nine largest delegations in 1910 and 2010 show the Northeast and North Central regions, which accounted for seven states in

**Table 1.1  U.S. House Apportionment, 1789–2002**

| State | 1789 | 1792 | 1802 | 1812 | 1822 | 1832 | 1842 | 1852 | 1862 | 1872 | 1882 | 1892 | 1902 | 1912 | 1932 | 1942 | 1952 | 1962 | 1972 | 1982 | 1992 | 2002 | 2012 |
|---|---|---|---|---|---|---|---|---|---|---|---|---|---|---|---|---|---|---|---|---|---|---|---|
| **Northeast** | | | | | | | | | | | | | | | | | | | | | | | |
| Connecticut | 5 | 7 | 7 | 7 | 6 | 6 | 4 | 4 | 4 | 4 | 4 | 4 | 5 | 5 | 6 | 6 | 6 | 6 | 6 | 6 | 6 | 5 | 5 |
| Maine | | | | | 7 | 8 | 7 | 6 | 5 | 5 | 4 | 4 | 4 | 4 | 3 | 3 | 3 | 2 | 2 | 2 | 2 | 2 | 2 |
| Massachusetts | 8 | 14 | 17 | 13 | 13 | 12 | 10 | 11 | 10 | 11 | 12 | 13 | 14 | 16 | 15 | 14 | 14 | 12 | 12 | 11 | 10 | 10 | 9 |
| New Hampshire | 3 | 4 | 5 | 6 | 6 | 5 | 4 | 3 | 3 | 3 | 2 | 2 | 2 | 2 | 2 | 2 | 2 | 2 | 2 | 2 | 2 | 2 | 2 |
| New York | 6 | 10 | 17 | 27 | 34 | 40 | 34 | 33 | 31 | 33 | 34 | 34 | 37 | 43 | 45 | 45 | 43 | 41 | 39 | 34 | 31 | 29 | 27 |
| New Jersey | 4 | 5 | 6 | 6 | 6 | 6 | 5 | 5 | 5 | 7 | 7 | 8 | 10 | 12 | 14 | 14 | 14 | 15 | 15 | 14 | 13 | 13 | 12 |
| Pennsylvania | 8 | 13 | 18 | 23 | 26 | 28 | 24 | 25 | 24 | 27 | 28 | 30 | 32 | 36 | 34 | 33 | 30 | 27 | 25 | 23 | 21 | 19 | 18 |
| Rhode Island | 1 | 2 | 2 | 2 | 2 | 2 | 2 | 2 | 2 | 2 | 2 | 2 | 2 | 3 | 2 | 2 | 2 | 2 | 2 | 2 | 2 | 2 | 2 |
| Vermont | | 2 | 4 | 6 | 5 | 5 | 4 | 3 | 3 | 3 | 2 | 2 | 2 | 2 | 1 | 1 | 1 | 1 | 1 | 1 | 1 | 1 | 1 |
| **North Central** | | | | | | | | | | | | | | | | | | | | | | | |
| Illinois | | | | | 1 | 3 | 7 | 9 | 14 | 19 | 20 | 22 | 25 | 27 | 27 | 26 | 25 | 24 | 24 | 22 | 20 | 19 | 18 |
| Indiana | | | | | 3 | 7 | 10 | 11 | 11 | 13 | 13 | 13 | 13 | 13 | 12 | 11 | 11 | 11 | 11 | 10 | 10 | 9 | 9 |
| Iowa | | | | | | | | 2 | 6 | 9 | 11 | 11 | 11 | 11 | 9 | 8 | 8 | 7 | 6 | 6 | 5 | 5 | 4 |
| Kansas | | | | | | | | | 1 | 3 | 7 | 8 | 8 | 8 | 7 | 6 | 6 | 5 | 5 | 5 | 4 | 4 | 4 |
| Michigan | | | | | | | 3 | 4 | 6 | 9 | 11 | 12 | 12 | 13 | 17 | 17 | 18 | 19 | 19 | 18 | 16 | 15 | 14 |
| Minnesota | | | | | | | | | 2 | 3 | 5 | 7 | 9 | 10 | 9 | 9 | 9 | 8 | 8 | 8 | 8 | 8 | 8 |
| Nebraska | | | | | | | | | | 1 | 3 | 6 | 6 | 6 | 5 | 4 | 4 | 3 | 3 | 3 | 3 | 3 | 3 |
| Ohio | | | | 6 | 14 | 19 | 21 | 21 | 19 | 20 | 21 | 21 | 21 | 22 | 24 | 23 | 23 | 24 | 23 | 21 | 19 | 18 | 16 |
| North Dakota | | | | | | | | | | | | 1 | 2 | 3 | 2 | 2 | 2 | 2 | 1 | 1 | 1 | 1 | 1 |
| South Dakota | | | | | | | | | | | | 2 | 2 | 3 | 2 | 2 | 2 | 2 | 2 | 1 | 1 | 1 | 1 |
| Wisconsin | | | | | | | | 3 | 6 | 8 | 9 | 10 | 11 | 11 | 10 | 10 | 10 | 10 | 9 | 9 | 9 | 8 | 8 |
| **Pacific** | | | | | | | | | | | | | | | | | | | | | | | |
| California | | | | | | | | 2 | 3 | 4 | 6 | 7 | 8 | 11 | 20 | 23 | 30 | 38 | 43 | 45 | 52 | 53 | 53 |
| Oregon | | | | | | | | | 1 | 1 | 1 | 2 | 2 | 3 | 3 | 4 | 4 | 4 | 4 | 5 | 5 | 5 | 5 |
| Washington | | | | | | | | | | | | 2 | 3 | 5 | 6 | 6 | 7 | 7 | 7 | 8 | 9 | 9 | 10 |
| Alaska | | | | | | | | | | | | | | | | | | 1 | 1 | 1 | 1 | 1 | 1 |
| Hawaii | | | | | | | | | | | | | | | | | | 2 | 2 | 2 | 2 | 2 | 2 |
| **South** | | | | | | | | | | | | | | | | | | | | | | | |
| Alabama | | | | | 3 | 5 | 7 | 7 | 6 | 8 | 8 | 9 | 9 | 10 | 9 | 9 | 9 | 8 | 7 | 7 | 7 | 7 | 7 |
| Arkansas | | | | | | | 1 | 2 | 3 | 4 | 5 | 6 | 7 | 7 | 7 | 7 | 6 | 4 | 4 | 4 | 4 | 4 | 4 |
| Florida | | | | | | | | 1 | 1 | 2 | 2 | 2 | 3 | 4 | 5 | 6 | 8 | 12 | 15 | 19 | 23 | 25 | 27 |
| Georgia | 3 | 2 | 4 | 6 | 7 | 9 | 8 | 8 | 7 | 9 | 10 | 11 | 11 | 12 | 10 | 10 | 10 | 10 | 10 | 10 | 11 | 13 | 14 |

*(Continued)*

**Table 1.1   U.S. House Apportionment, 1789–2002** (*Continued*)

| State | 1789 | 1792 | 1802 | 1812 | 1822 | 1832 | 1842 | 1852 | 1862 | 1872 | 1882 | 1892 | 1902 | 1912 | 1932 | 1942 | 1952 | 1962 | 1972 | 1982 | 1992 | 2002 | 2012 |
|---|---|---|---|---|---|---|---|---|---|---|---|---|---|---|---|---|---|---|---|---|---|---|---|
| Louisiana | | | | 1 | 3 | 3 | 4 | 4 | 5 | 6 | 6 | 6 | 7 | 8 | 8 | 8 | 8 | 8 | 8 | 8 | 7 | 7 | 6 |
| Mississippi | | | | 1 | 1 | 2 | 4 | 5 | 5 | 6 | 7 | 7 | 8 | 8 | 7 | 7 | 6 | 5 | 5 | 5 | 5 | 4 | 4 |
| North Carolina | 5 | | 12 | 13 | 13 | 13 | 9 | 8 | 7 | 8 | 9 | 9 | 10 | 10 | 11 | 12 | 12 | 11 | 11 | 11 | 12 | 13 | 13 |
| South Carolina | 5 | | 8 | 9 | 9 | 9 | 7 | 6 | 4 | 5 | 7 | 7 | 7 | 7 | 6 | 6 | 6 | 6 | 6 | 6 | 6 | 6 | 7 |
| Tennessee | | | 3 | 6 | 9 | 13 | 11 | 10 | 8 | 10 | 10 | 10 | 10 | 10 | 9 | 10 | 9 | 9 | 8 | 9 | 9 | 9 | 9 |
| Texas | | | | | | | | | 4 | 6 | 11 | 13 | 16 | 18 | 21 | 21 | 22 | 23 | 24 | 27 | 30 | 32 | 36 |
| Virginia | 10 | 19 | 22 | 23 | 22 | 21 | 15 | 13 | 11 | 9 | 10 | 10 | 10 | 10 | 9 | 9 | 10 | 10 | 10 | 10 | 11 | 11 | 11 |
| **Border South** | | | | | | | | | | | | | | | | | | | | | | | |
| Delaware | 1 | 1 | 1 | 2 | 1 | 1 | 1 | 1 | 1 | 1 | 1 | 1 | 1 | 1 | 1 | 1 | 1 | 1 | 1 | 1 | 1 | 1 | 1 |
| Kentucky | | 2 | 6 | 10 | 12 | 13 | 10 | 10 | 9 | 10 | 11 | 11 | 11 | 11 | 9 | 9 | 8 | 7 | 7 | 7 | 6 | 6 | 6 |
| Maryland | 6 | 8 | 9 | 9 | 9 | 8 | 6 | 6 | 5 | 6 | 6 | 6 | 6 | 6 | 6 | 6 | 7 | 8 | 8 | 8 | 8 | 8 | 8 |
| Missouri | | | | | 1 | 2 | 5 | 7 | 9 | 13 | 14 | 15 | 16 | 16 | 13 | 13 | 11 | 10 | 10 | 9 | 9 | 9 | 8 |
| Oklahoma | | | | | | | | | | | | | | 8 | 9 | 8 | 6 | 6 | 6 | 6 | 6 | 5 | 5 |
| West Virginia | | | | | | | | | | 3 | 4 | 4 | 5 | 6 | 6 | 6 | 6 | 5 | 4 | 4 | 3 | 3 | 3 |
| **Mountain West** | | | | | | | | | | | | | | | | | | | | | | | |
| Arizona | | | | | | | | | | | | | | 1 | 1 | 2 | 2 | 3 | 4 | 5 | 6 | 8 | 9 |
| Colorado | | | | | | | | | | | 1 | 2 | 3 | 4 | 4 | 4 | 4 | 4 | 5 | 6 | 6 | 7 | 7 |
| Idaho | | | | | | | | | | | | 1 | 1 | 2 | 2 | 2 | 2 | 2 | 2 | 2 | 2 | 2 | 2 |
| Montana | | | | | | | | | | | | 1 | 1 | 2 | 2 | 2 | 2 | 2 | 2 | 2 | 1 | 1 | 1 |
| Nevada | | | | | | | | | 1 | 1 | 1 | 1 | 1 | 1 | 1 | 1 | 1 | 1 | 1 | 2 | 2 | 3 | 4 |
| New Mexico | | | | | | | | | | | | | | 1 | 1 | 2 | 2 | 2 | 2 | 3 | 3 | 3 | 3 |
| Utah | | | | | | | | | | | | | 1 | 2 | 2 | 2 | 2 | 2 | 2 | 3 | 3 | 3 | 4 |
| Wyoming | | | | | | | | | | | | 1 | 1 | 1 | 1 | 1 | 1 | 1 | 1 | 1 | 1 | 1 | 1 |

1910, having five 100 years later, while the South, beginning with 2022, will account for four of the nine largest up from one in 1910.

In the wake of widespread availability of air conditioning, the South which, excluding Florida, Louisiana, and Texas, grew slower than the nation in the middle decades of the twentieth century, became a major gainer, increasing from 106 seats in 1962 to 138 in 2012. As in other regions, growth in the South has not been even. Growth has come to urban areas with cities and their suburbs in Florida and Texas experiencing some of the most rapid expansion. Atlanta, Austin, Asheville, Charlotte, Nashville, and Raleigh have an especial allure for well-educated, ambitious young adults who are transforming the politics of these metro areas. The more rural states, Alabama, Louisiana, Mississippi, and Arkansas, have seen their delegations shrink from a total of 31 seats in 1942 to 21 seats as of 2012, and the 2020 census may cost Alabama a seat, its third loss since 1962.[7] On the other hand, Florida, North Carolina, and Texas are expected to gain seats.

The other growth area in recent years has been the West, with California leading the way. As table 1.1 shows, at the end of World War II, California had twenty-three members of Congress, which tied it with Ohio as the fourth largest delegation. After gaining thirty seats, the 2010 census was the first in which the state's delegation did not expand. Other major postwar gainers in the West include Arizona, which has grown from two to nine seats, Colorado growing from four to seven, Washington from six to ten, and Nevada, the least populous state in 1940, now has four members of Congress. Over the last fifty years, only Montana among Mountain West and Pacific Coast states lost representation while eight of the thirteen states gained seats.

Major losses have come from the Rust Belt. New York, Pennsylvania, Ohio, Indiana, Illinois, and Michigan had a total of 155 representatives in 1942. After the 2010 census, these states' representation in the House had shrunk to 109 and additional losses will come after 2020. Every state in the North Central region has lost seats since 1942 and most have lost multiple seats. Since their high points early in the twentieth century, the delegations from Iowa, Kansas, Nebraska, and the Dakotas have each lost at least half their representation. The Ohio and Michigan delegations continued to grow until 1972 and 1982, respectively, but once their growth rate fell behind the national average, these states, like others in the region, have been unable to arrest the slide.

The shift in seats from the Rust Belt to the Sun Belt contributed to a loss of influence by organized labor. Unions had great strength in the heavy industries found in the band of states from New York westward to Illinois. The South has right-to-work laws and these make union organizing much more difficult. Moreover the independence of southerners has made them much less eager to join unions. The expansion of delegations from southern states has thus far strengthened opposition to various social programs, although that may be about to change as Democrats seem poised to make gains in the parts of the region experiencing growth.[8]

Taking seats away from the Northeast and industrialized North Central has reduced the strength of the Democratic Party while enhancing Republicans. Of the ten delegations that lost seats after the 2000 census, only three had GOP majorities in their delegations at that time. In five of the seven states that received additional seats following that census, a majority of the congressional delegation belonged to the GOP. The partisan split between winning and losing states following the 2010 census was not as stark, although Washington was the only Democratic state to gain seats. Among the losers were seven states that usually vote for Democrats in presidential elections.

The decennial reapportionment of House seats also adjusts the numbers of presidential electors states have. Had the post-2000 reapportionment been in place at the time of the 2000 presidential election, George Bush would have won the Electoral College vote by seven more electors. Had the 2000 election been run using the distribution of House seats in place for the election as of 1960, rather than for 2000, Al Gore would have become the nation's forty-third president even without the votes from Florida.

## STABILITY AND LEADERSHIP BEFORE THE REDISTRICTING REVOLUTION

As will be discussed in the next chapter, for decades, redistricting came infrequently and, in some states, almost never. As a consequence, legislative districts remained much the same for generations despite major population shifts. This continuity in district construction may help explain the startling phenomenon concerning the home districts of U.S. House leaders observed by Garrison Nelson.[9] In 1949, the Speaker of the House came from north Texas, the majority leader came from Boston, and the minority whip came from central Illinois. More than a generation later in 1976, the Speaker of the House came from Boston, the majority leader came from north Texas, and the minority whip came from central Illinois. More broadly, Nelson showed that more than 85 percent of the House leaders from the time of the Civil War until 1978 came from within five counties of another leader, indicating a remarkable continuity in the areas of the nation that produced the leadership of Congress, a phenomenon Nelson called "geographical propinquity."[10] As an explanation, Nelson hypothesized that these leaders sought to reproduce themselves by taking on as protégés individuals having similar backgrounds. The relevant background features were upward mobility, coming from a rural area, and having no sons. Although Nelson does not make this point, arguably the tendency to make few changes in district boundaries during most of the period he studied facilitated the desire of House leaders to pass on leadership positions to younger duplicates of themselves who were, to a degree, surrogate sons.

This phenomenon of House leaders sharing characteristics and coming from similar types of districts has now ceased and the change coincides with the increased emphasis on maximizing population equality among districts which dramatically reduced the number of rural districts. Also contributing to the end of the practice on the Democratic side was the decision to have the Caucus elect the party whip, who usually advances to become party leader, and still later, when Democrats organize the House, the Speaker. Until 1986 the majority leader in consultation with the Speaker tapped the new whip when that position became vacant, which made it easier to recruit replicas of the current leaders. Once the Democratic whip became an elected position, the entire Caucus made the decision and that has promoted variation in the geographic areas represented by Democratic leadership.

The recruitment of legislative leaders at the state level has not generated a study along the lines of Nelson's examination of House leaders. However, an example from one state indicates how a system where leaders are appointed helped rural interests maintain their influence even after redistricting reduced their numbers. As will be shown in chapter 2, Georgia had one of the most malapportioned legislatures in the nation. When the courts ordered that its districts be redrawn to reflect population, the makeup of the Georgia General Assembly underwent a major transformation as it welcomed Republicans and African Americans as members of much enlarged urban delegations. Even as more and more legislators came from urban and suburban areas, rural Democrats held on to a disproportionate share of the influence within the legislature for another four decades. Since the leadership appoints committee chairs in Georgia, rural Speakers promoted the careers of individuals who had similar backgrounds. In long-serving Speaker Tom Murphy's last term (2001–2002), no Democrats in major leadership positions came from metro Atlanta, although 45 percent of the Democratic legislators came from that part of the state.[11] Four years later, when Republicans won their first majority in the chamber in more than 130 years, the Speaker came from the Atlanta suburbs, as did the Speaker pro tempore and the chair of the powerful Rules Committee.

## WHO DOES THE REDISTRICTING?

In most states the legislature has primary responsibility for designing the districts of its members and the state's congressional districts.[12] As one

might expect, these decisions have become more controversial as the relations between Democrats and Republicans in Congress, in many state
legislatures, and the public have become increasingly testy. An extreme
partisan gerrymander is most likely when one party scores a trifecta, that is,
the party has majorities in both chambers and the governor in those states
where the governor can veto a plan.[13] Under a trifecta, the minority party
has little if any power to thwart the designs of the majority. Following the
GOP wave election in 2010, when it came time to draw new congressional
districts, Republicans had achieved a trifecta in seventeen states. In contrast,
Democrats had full control in five states. In nine states a court had to draw
the districts when the legislature deadlocked. Elsewhere redistricting was
done by a commission or the legislature under divided partisan control. In
five states, plans drawn by the legislature get reviewed by the state supreme
court before implementation.

Currently thirteen states have followed Ohio's lead and give sole responsibility for redistricting of state legislative districts to an independent commission as shown in table 1.2. Nine states assign responsibility for drawing
congressional boundaries to an independent commission. A few other states
circumscribe the role of the legislature, although it maintains responsibility
for approving plans for Congress and/or the state legislature. Some, but not
all, commissions seek to minimize partisanship. California has a detailed set
of conditions for selecting the fourteen commissioners who draw new districts. From a short list of sixty applicants, who submit four essays and then
undergo a ninety-minute interview, five Democrats, five Republicans, and
four Independents are selected. While the selection was designed to fence
out partisan considerations, Republicans believe that the 2011 congressional
plan favored Democrats. Supportive of those claims are calculations made by
the Center for American Progress that shows Democrats with six more seats
than might have been expected, the greatest advantage for either party in any
state, although there are other states in which the proportion of additional
seats gained exceeds the California figure.[14]

Republicans also believed that Arizona's independent commission favored
Democrats when redrawing congressional districts following the 2010 census. Republicans went to court questioning whether a ballot initiative could
be used to shift the authority for drawing districts from the legislature to a
commission. The GOP-controlled legislature contended that this method of
transfer violated the constitutional provision that the legislature determines
the times, places, and manner of holding elections. The Supreme Court interpreted the provisions as the authority to make laws and thus upheld the action
of the public voting on the initiative.[15]

Iowa, which is often pointed to as an example of a state where neither partisanship nor incumbent protection plays a role, has a unique approach with

a legislative agency drawing congressional districts. The legislature cannot amend the proposal, but it can reject the plan. Only if two proposals from the agency fail to gain acceptance can the legislature try its hand at redistricting.

The initiative process did not remove congressional redistricting from the Florida legislature, but it did impose limits on what the legislature could do. The initiative, approved in 2010, forbade the legislature from advantaging a party or incumbents when it drew new districts. Republicans, who had a trifecta in Florida in 2011, did not try to maximize their share of the seats as the GOP did in North Carolina, a story told in chapter 5. Under the new plan, Republicans won 17 of the 27 seats in 2012, a much weaker performance than under the previous plan when they took 19 of 25 seats in 2010. Nonetheless Democrats successfully sued, claiming that Republicans violated the terms of the constitutional amendment.

Ohio took another approach to limiting the ability of a legislative majority to enhance its prospects. An amendment to the state constitution specifies in precise order requirements for future congressional plans. The legislature retains the authority to draw maps but specifications as detailed in the insert seek to ensure that plans have bipartisan support, thereby neutralizing the power of a trifecta. The detailed process for drawing new congressional districts in Ohio requires the approval of the bulk of the minority party in the legislature.

## BOX 1.1  OHIO CONGRESSIONAL REDISTRICTING REQUIREMENTS

1. New maps must be approved by 60 percent of the membership of each chamber and that must include at least half the members of each party in each chamber.
2. If the legislature fails to produce a plan by September 30, a seven-person bipartisan commission will design the districts that must be approved by at least two minority party members.
3. If the bipartisan commission fails to produce an acceptable map by October 31, the legislature makes another effort and it must secure support from 60 percent of the members and include at least one-third of minority party members in each chamber.
4. If the legislature fails to meet the thresholds in item 3, a plan that passes each chamber with a majority goes into effect for four years. After four years, new maps must be drawn with the provisions in items 1 through 3 operable.
5. Redistricting plans adopted pursuant to items 1 through 3 cannot be changed until after the next census.

6. Plans shall not divide Cleveland or Cincinnati or 65 of the counties between congressional districts. Eighteen counties can be split between two districts and five counties can be split into three districts.

*Source*: "Overview: Ohio Redistricting Reform Proposal," Brennan Center for Justice (February 4, 2018).

In Category F of table 1.2 are states with backup commissions. These become active only if the legislature fails to act, elsewhere a legislative deadlock would shift responsibility for new maps to the courts. The backup commission membership consists either of officeholders or individuals named by elected officials like leaders of the legislature and, therefore, may have levels of partisanship comparable to that found in legislative chambers. For example, in 2001 the Texas legislature deadlocked since each party controlled one chamber and, as a consequence, the five-member Legislative Redistricting Board redrew boundaries for the state House and Senate. Four board members were Republicans and, not surprisingly, the plan they devised enabled their fellow partisans to seize control of the House.

In the past, the Census Bureau has released the information needed for redistricting at the end of the year ending in zero. As discussed in chapter 7, the COVID-19 pandemic may delay the collection and release of census data into 2021. States that hold state elections in even-numbered years have more than a year in which to redistrict; the few states that choose their legislators in odd-numbered years must work under a tighter schedule. Excepting states in Category F, if the legislature fails to act because it is riven by internal partisan rivalries or by partisan differences between the legislature and the governor, courts carry out the task. Court-drawn maps remain in effect unless the legislature replaces them. After Republicans took control of the Texas House in 2003, they drew a controversial plan that netted them six congressional seats. Courts can also get brought into the redistricting process when the party that has lost in the legislature asks a state court, federal court, or both to replace the map.

While federal law usually takes precedence over state law, when it comes to redistricting, the state has the first opportunity to complete the process. Federal courts will not interfere with the state legislatures' efforts so long as it appears that the legislature will complete the task in time for the next election, nor can a federal court block the activities of a state court that is making adequate progress toward the development of a new plan.[16] As will be described in chapter 5, state courts now have the primary responsibility for adjudicating claims of partisan gerrymanders.

**Table 1.2   States That Limit Legislative Control of Redistricting**

| *Congressional Districts* | *State Legislative Districts* |
| --- | --- |
| A. Independent Commissioners | |
| Arizona | Alaska |
| California | Arizona |
| Colorado | Arkansas |
| Hawaii | California |
| Idaho | Colorado |
| Michigan | Hawaii |
| Montana | Idaho |
| New Jersey | Michigan |
| Washington | Missouri |
| | Montana |
| | New Jersey |
| | Ohio |
| | Pennsylvania |
| | Washington |
| B. Legislative Services Agency | |
| Iowa | Iowa |
| C. Limits on Use of Partisan and Incumbency Data | |
| Florida | Florida |
| D. Requiring Bipartisan Support for Plans | |
| Ohio | |
| E. Map Drawn by Governor, Legislative Approval Necessary | |
| Maryland | |
| F. Backup Commissions | |
| Connecticut | Connecticut |
| Indiana | Illinois |
| Ohio | Mississippi |
| | Oklahoma |
| | Texas |

*Sources*: "Redistricting Commissions: Congressional Plans and State Legislative Plans," National Conference of State Legislatures for A.

If a judicial challenge to an existing districting plan succeeds, the legislative body or commission responsible for redistricting has the first opportunity to take corrective action. Especially if an election is in the offing, the court may set a deadline for adoption of a new plan. If the deadline is not met, then the court will draw a map on its own or, more likely, employ an outside expert to help with the process. Or the court may adopt a plan offered by the plaintiff. When Florida failed to come up with a congressional plan in 1992, a law professor serving as consultant to the federal judge who heard the case stitched together a map using parts of plans urged by three different parties in the litigation.

Members of Congress have no direct control over redistricting. About half the members of Congress have previously served in their state legislature and may be able to convince former colleagues to provide them with a secure district. However, when the majority of the legislature does not belong to the same party as the member of Congress, pleas from the Washington representative may go unheeded. In a worst-case scenario, a House member may become the victim of an ambitious state legislator who connives to redesign the district in hopes of unseating the incumbent. Especially vulnerable are members of Congress in states that lose seats. To win favor with state legislators, members of Congress host fundraisers for state legislators, attend meetings of the National Conference of State Legislatures, and will quickly return the phone calls of state legislators in the year or so leading up to a redistricting.[17]

In preparation for the 2010 census and redistricting, both parties created organizations to promote their interests. Both of these organizations helped fund state legislative elections in critical states in the hopes of either winning complete control and therefore dominating redistricting or by controlling at least one legislative chamber so they could block partisan plans coming from the other side. Republicans were much more aggressive than Democrats in working to elect state legislators in 2010. The first goal of these efforts was to ensure that a party controlled at least one chamber of the legislature, since doing so could check the ambitions of the opposition. A more ambitious objective would be to achieve a trifecta. The Republican State Legislative Committee's (RSLC) expenditures on state legislative contests leading up to the 2010 election exceeded the Democratic Leadership Campaign Committee's (DLCC) investment by a margin of $31.7 million to $10.9 million.[18] The massive spending advantage, coupled with Tea Party anger fueled in part by the passage of Obamacare, resulted in Republicans gaining about 700 state legislative seats on the way to winning majorities in twenty legislative chambers in the 2010 wave election.

Democrats, who have had a decade to ponder the bitter lesson taught by stern Republican taskmasters in 2010, approached the 2021 redistricting with plans to turn the tables on the GOP. The DLCC in conjunction with the National Democratic Redistricting Committee (NDRC), led by President Obama's attorney general Eric Holder and assisted by failed billionaire presidential candidates Michael Bloomberg and Tom Steyer, launched their effort to flip legislative chambers controlled by Republicans in 2017 when Holder's NDRC spent $1.2 million in Virginia and gained fifteen seats. Two years later Democrats secured majorities in Virginia's House of Deputies and Senate by gaining six and two seats, respectively. In the Senate, two of six candidates endorsed by the NDRC won, as did six of eleven House endorsees.[19] The NDRC built on its 2017 Virginia success and, boosted by a $35 million budget, targeted 230 state legislative seats in 2018, winning 60 percent of them.[20]

Hoping to repeat their success in Virginia, Democrats targeted six states in 2020 where Republicans had trifectas: Florida, Georgia, North Carolina, Pennsylvania, Texas, and Wisconsin. These states, along with Ohio, were also singled out for attention by the GOP. Note that four of the states are in the Growth South where demographic change is reducing GOP margins.[21] Pennsylvania and Wisconsin were two of the Midwest States critical for Trump's 2016 Electoral College victory. The DLCC is targeting opportunities such as the nine Texas legislative districts that voted for Beto O'Rourke in his bid to unseat Senator Ted Cruz. It has budgeted $50 million to break GOP control in at least one chamber of the trifecta states, where flipping as few as forty-two seats could shift partisan fortunes.[22]

Republicans worry that they are off to a slow start in defending the states in which they have trifecta status. Warned Adam Kincaid, executive director of the National Republican Redistricting Trust, "If Republicans don't start investing in state legislative races and the litigation and data needed to secure our majorities to the same extent the Democrats are, the GOP will see our legislative majorities erased and it will take decades to rebuild them."[23] To avert that consequence, Kincaid's group set a goal of $35 million for its 2020 election activities.[24] The RSLC pointed out in 2019 that forty-nine seats across a dozen state senates could determine which party would be positioned to design maps in 2021.[25] Republican fears proved unfounded as Democrats failed to gain majorities in any legislative chambers.

In recognition that redistricting battles will increasingly be fought in state rather than federal courts, a topic covered in chapter 5, both parties have taken an unprecedented interest in elections of state supreme court justices. The maneuvering around the 2020 election for a seat on the Wisconsin Supreme Court saw parties investing heavily in what is technically a nonpartisan position with almost $5 million spent above and beyond what the candidates raised.[26] In 2019, the NDRC spent $350,000 in another Wisconsin judicial contest but was outbid by the RSLC's $1.3 million, which reelected the Republican by 6,000 votes.[27]

## WHEN IS REDISTRICTING DONE?

As will be explained in the next chapter, the Redistricting Revolution of the 1960s has required jurisdictions that elect representatives from districts to redraw the boundaries to reflect population shifts after each census. This is a marked departure from the past where district lines usually remained unchanged for generations.

Because getting approval for a new set of districts often inflames controversy, requires a great deal of time, and may leave deep wounds that are slow to heal, most states undertake the process only when necessary. That has meant that even after the Redistricting Revolution, states usually redo their congressional and state legislative districts only once in a decade. The major exception to this once-a-decade norm comes in the wake of a success-ful judicial challenge to the existing plan. Correcting problems identified by the courts may necessitate remapping the entire jurisdiction, although under some circumstances a less dramatic remedy may be possible. In both the mid-1990s and then a decade later after the Supreme Court identified problems with the Texas congressional districts, the legislature responded by redrawing only enough of the state to correct the concerns raised by the court.

In a break with tradition, the first decade of the new century saw three states redraw their congressional districts even though the current plans had *not* run afoul of a judicial decision. In the most controversial of these, U.S. House Majority Leader Tom DeLay convinced the Texas legislature to imple-ment changes designed to defeat his Anglo Democrat colleagues.[28] DeLay hoped that eliminating these Texas Democrats would increase the narrow Republican majority in the House.

The 2000 census gave Colorado a seventh district. The new map, which was drawn by a judge, sought to create a Denver-area district in which Democrats and Republicans would have equal strength. The judge displayed a keen eye for political strength, coming up with a district that gave Al Gore a victory margin of less than 2,000. In the first congressional election, the district performed as expected, yielding the nation's most competitive result with Republican Bob Beauprez eking out a 121-vote victory. Republicans sought to make Beauprez safer by removing some Democrats.

The third example of a midterm redistricting not necessitated by a court order came in Georgia. Democrats had executed a viciously partisan ger-rymander in an effort to increase their share of the congressional delegation from three to seven. After Republicans achieved a trifecta, they created a new map to solidify the position of a junior Republican who had managed to win a district designed to elect a Democrat.

Democrats launched court challenges to all three of these plans, arguing in part that since the state had a legal plan in place changes could not be made until the next census. This argument prevailed in Colorado because the state constitution permits only one districting plan per decade unless a second one becomes necessary to meet court objections. Neither Texas nor Georgia had state laws or constitutional provisions banning a new mapping effort and federal judges found nothing in federal law that prevented drawing a new map. Critics worried that every time control of the redistricting forces in a state changed partisan hands, the victors would impose a new set of maps, what Engstrom calls "unprompted redistricting" and which occurred thirty-two times during the latter half of the nineteenth century.[29] These fears have proven baseless and no state has significantly altered its congressional districts voluntarily since Georgia did so in 2005.

Not surprisingly, the party that gets to draw district lines usually comes out ahead. This is especially true if reapportionment gives the state an additional congressional seat.[30] In states that lose seats, the party drawing the districts traditionally has done little better than hold its own. While it is not surprising that legislators will take care of their fellow partisans when drawing new maps, it may come as a shock to learn that judges also reveal partisan preferences when reviewing new maps. In an analysis of the plans drawn in the 1960s, Cox and Katz write: "Democratic dominance of the federal judiciary, combined with court decisions in deciding which plans were adequate in terms of malapportionment, meant that the pattern of reversions greatly facilitated, indeed, pushed, the adjustment of plans in a pro-Democratic direction."[31] While judges may have revealed partisan preferences in striking down existing plans, it is rare for a federal judge to come up with a blatantly partisan replacement plan. When judges must draw new districts, they rely heavily on the last legal plan rather than starting de novo. They may employ experts to help with the task. In explaining maps produced by or for courts, judges stress that they have sought to act in a nonpartisan manner.

## CONSEQUENCES OF DISTRICTING DECISIONS

The distribution of seats in the legislative chamber goes a long way toward determining policy outcomes. Groups that are underrepresented have poorer prospects for setting the agenda and securing the policies that they prefer. The disadvantages of the minority have become more pronounced in Congress and state legislatures where partisanship has become more toxic, making bipartisan coalitions infrequent. In most legislatures, the majority party exercises disproportionate control over the issues that come to the floor and the timing for issues to be considered. Some legislatures, like Tennessee and Texas, have a tradition of allowing members of both parties to chair committees, but many other states follow the practice in Congress where majority-party members chair all committees.

Districting plans affect not only the representation of parties but also the extent to which minorities serve in the legislature, and diversity in a chamber can affect the agenda. Research has shown that having members of racial and ethnic minorities in a collegial body results in more race-related issues being introduced and explored more extensively in committees.[32] David Canon reports that African Americans in Congress are more likely than white legislators to introduce legislation that has a racial component, even when the white legislator represents a district with a sizable minority population.[33]

According to Canon, black members are more likely to put out press releases dealing with racial issues and to insert racially oriented materials into the Extension of Remarks portion of the *Congressional Record* than are white legislators.

As they have accrued seniority, African American state legislators have achieved leadership positions in the Democratic Party. In chambers in which Democrats have majorities, African Americans increasingly chair committees and fill chamber leadership posts like California's former Speaker Willie Brown and North Carolina's former Speaker Dan Blue. Case studies of black influence in southern state legislatures report variation in the success of legislative black caucuses in achieving their policy objectives, but the mere presence of a black caucus ensures that African Americans' concerns get aired.[34]

Case studies at the local level also document the ability of minorities to at least inject their concerns into the policy debate. Success in achieving minorities' objectives hinges on the ability of minorities to form coalitions with the dominant group on the governing body.[35] Districting practices that ensure the presence of minorities on governing bodies result in decisions that distribute a larger share of public benefits to the minority community.[36]

## GERRYMANDERING TECHNIQUES

Until the 1960s, many of the inequities within legislative chambers stemmed from what might be called sins of omission rather than sins of commission. Differences in district populations resulted largely from inaction or what has been labeled the silent gerrymander. Seats in the U.S. House got redistributed after each census, but states that maintained the same number of seats rarely altered their congressional districts. Those favoring changes found it impossible to overcome inertia. Incumbents, not surprisingly, liked the arrangement under which they had succeeded. As has become readily apparent in the wake of the Redistricting Revolution, when changes have to be made, they unleash frenetic political ambitions that can divert the attention of the legislature from all other tasks and inflict wounds that may never heal. Therefore, during the first six decades of the twentieth century, unless necessary, legislatures usually thought it far better to leave existing congressional districts in place even as populations among the districts became increasingly unequal. Changing districts' boundaries occurred even less often for state legislatures where the number of seats rarely changed, and counties usually served as the basis for representation. Legislatures failed to reallocate their seats even as the population of states underwent dramatic changes, a topic to be explored in detail in the next chapter.

Once the Supreme Court mandated adjustments of legislative district lines after each census in order to reflect population shifts, gerrymandering became increasingly a "sin" of commission rather than omission. Legislators have used four tactics extensively to secure a disproportionate share of the legislative seats. These tactics have disadvantaged political parties as well as racial and ethnic minorities.

One tactic is to *crack* the opposition by dividing a population that if put into a single district would be sufficient to determine the outcome of elections in that district. Dividing a group into two or more districts so that it is less than a majority in any district denies the party or group an opportunity to elect its preference. Figure 1.1 shows Mississippi's congressional districting plan adopted in the immediate aftermath of the Voting Rights Act of 1965. Historically the majority-black counties along the state's western boundary from Issaquena north to the Tennessee border had constituted a single district, the Delta District. Every county in the Delta District, which existed from 1882 until 1956, had a black majority, and once African Americans could vote without impediment, they would be able to send their preferred candidate to Congress. The cracking of the African American population displayed in figure 1.1 put portions of the old Delta District in three different districts. As a consequence, in none of Mississippi's districts did blacks constitute as much as 45 percent of the adult population.[37] As a result of cracking the black population, Mississippi, the state with the highest black percentage in the nation, did not send an African American to Congress until 1986, following the creation of a 58 percent black district.

The second technique *packs* a district when the minority is too large to be denied any representation. Those in charge of redistricting set out to minimize the number of seats that the minority can win by placing as many members of the minority as possible into a single district as shown in table 1.3. Although Party B accounts for 48 percent of the votes in the community, the packed plan gives it only a single seat, District 3, which it wins with 90 percent. To the right of table 1.3 is an alternative plan in which Party B's supporters have been unpacked. Party B still wins District 3 comfortably and under a more equitable plan would also win District 1. Party A continues to have commanding margins in Districts 4 and 5 and has a slight advantage in District 2, although Party B is competitive in that district under the unpacked plan. Packing has become increasingly common as the party in charge of a redistricting seeks to limit the seats likely to be won by the opposition. The minority party wins a few seats with overwhelming majorities while the dominant party wins many more seats with relatively narrow margins.[38]

*Stacking*, the third tactic, involves including the minority party or ethnic group as part of a much larger district that elects multiple legislators.

**Figure 1.1 Cracking Mississippi's Black Vote in the 1966 Congressional Plan.** *Source:* Frank R. Parker, *Black Votes Count: Political Empowerment in Mississippi after 1965* (Chapel Hill: University of North Carolina Press, 1990), 49.

Table 1.3  **Example of an Effective Plan to Pack One Party into a Single District and an Alternative**

|  | Packed | | Unpacked | |
|---|---|---|---|---|
|  | *Party A* | *Party B* | *Party A* | *Party B* |
| District 1 | 600 | 400 | 425 | 575 |
| District 2 | 600 | 600 | 525 | 475 |
| District 3 | 100 | 900 | 350 | 650 |
| District 4 | 650 | 350 | 650 | 350 |
| District 5 | 650 | 350 | 650 | 350 |
| Total Votes | 2600 | 2400 | 2600 | 2400 |

If single-member districting were used, the minority party or group could dominate one district but by including it in a district that elects multiple members, its preferences can be voted down by the predominate party or ethnic group. Figure 1.2 provides an example of stacking carried out by the Georgia General Assembly in 2001. As part of an effort by Democrats to maximize the number of seats they could control in the state House, they combined single-member districts to form multi-member districts. In the example in figure 1.2, Districts 70 and 73 in DeKalb County, which had elected black Democrats before redistricting, got combined with District 108 in Henry County, which had elected a white Republican. The new district, number 60, had three seats and in 2002, African American Democrats won all three, thereby eliminating one Republican.

A fourth gerrymandering technique disadvantages incumbents of the opposing party. This can be done by separating incumbents from the population that they have represented. Incumbent members of Congress whose districts get redrawn by legislatures dominated by the opposition party more frequently face competition when seeking reelection and more often retire than sitting members given new districts by fellow partisans.[39] In more extreme cases, multiple incumbents are forced to compete against each other. One type of incumbency gerrymandering pairs an incumbent of the majority party with one of the minority party in a district in which the electorate favors the majority party. This may be done to punish a member of the minority party who has been a particularly aggressive partisan. In some instances, the new map places two or even more incumbents from the same party in a single district. Figure 1.3 shows a corner of southwest Georgia. The only two Republicans from this part of the state in 2001 represented Districts 163 and 180. District 163 contained the white, Republican-leaning population of northwest Dougherty County. Fifty miles and two intervening districts to the south lay District 180 in Thomas County. The new map managed to combine the homes of the representatives of these two districts. Republican

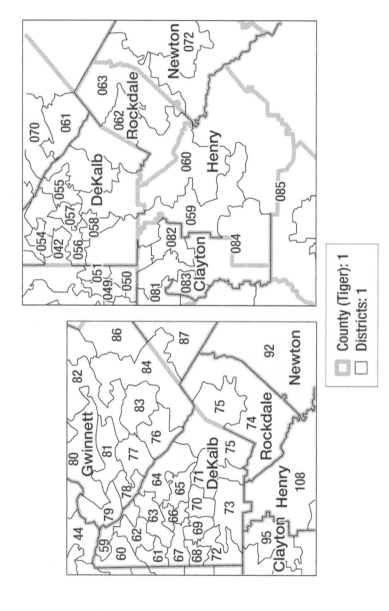

**Figure 1.2  Example of Stacking. Districts 70 and 73, which elected black Democrats, are configured with District 108, which elected a white Republican, to form District 60, which elected three black Democrats.** *Source:* Prepared by the Carl Vinson Institute of Government, University of Georgia.

## Old (Pre-2002) Georgia House Districts

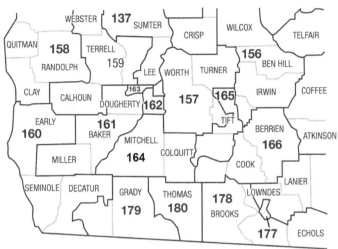

## New (2003) House District 137
## in Southwest Georgia

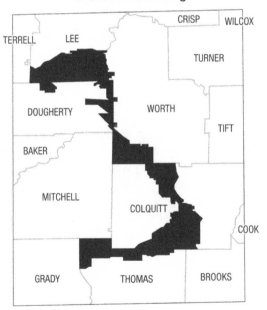

**Figure 1.3   Maps Showing How the Houses of Republicans in Old Districts 163 and 180 Were Combined in New District 137.** *Source*: Prepared by the Carl Vinson Institute of Government, University of Georgia. Plaintiff's demonstrative exhibits *Larios v. Cox* 300 F Supp. 2d 1320 (N.D. Ga. 2004).

areas of Dougherty County were extracted as was the northern portion of Thomas County. Uniting this district shaped something like a seahorse were the suburban Republicans in southern Lee County and then selected precincts in Worth and Colquitt counties. By combining the homes of the Republicans representing Districts 163 and 180, one would surely lose. Since southwest Georgia had grown very slowly, the area was scheduled to lose a seat, and by combining the two Republicans into a single district, Democrats ensured that the loss came from the opposition party.[40] Another benefit for the majority from eliminating some members of the minority party is to remove minority leaders who have the experience, skill, relationships, and insight to maximize their party's influence within the legislature.

## Wasted Votes

Each of the first three tactics identified above is sometimes discussed in the context of "wasted votes." The idea behind wasted votes is that the disadvantaged group will get less in return for its votes than does the majority group. For example, in cracking, the minority group may win as much as 49 percent of the vote in multiple districts and yet none of its nominees win. For example, consider a chamber that included ten seats and the majority party won each of these by a 51–49 percent margin. Obviously, the majority made very efficient use of its votes, while the minority party won nothing despite attracting almost half the votes. In stacking, like cracking, the minority group party wins no seats despite having a substantial share of the vote.

With packing, wasted votes works in the following fashion. Since all that it takes to win is a majority, by concentrating the minority in a district that it wins, it spends far more votes by, for example, winning the district with 80 or 90 percent of the vote where only 50.1 percent would be necessary, and even with a comfortable margin of 55 percent of the vote, the district contains far more of a party's supporters than necessary. In the hypothetical packed example in table 1.2, Party B wins District 3 with 90 percent of the vote, far more than needed, and loses the other four districts. The concept of wasted votes will be revisited in chapter 5 since it is one of the measures suggested for identifying unacceptable partisan gerrymanders.

## MAJORITY PARTY PAYOFF

Single-member districts are not designed to achieve proportional representation of political parties. The winner-take-all nature of single-member districts makes it extremely unlikely that each party will get a share of seats proportional to its share of the votes. Systems designed to achieve proportional representation use multi-member districts for at least some of the seats, and the designers of these systems want to see parties achieve a proportion of the seats roughly equal to their share of the vote.[41] Even in the absence of aggressive gerrymandering, single-member district systems typically reward the majority party with a larger share of the seats than its share of the vote. The majority party is more likely than the minority party to have districts in which its electors have a slight advantage, and therefore the majority party will have fewer wasted votes. The advantage enjoyed by the majority party has been dubbed the Matthew Principle, based on the New Testament passage, "For whosoever hath, to him shall be given, and he shall have more abundance: but whosoever hath not, from him shall be taken away even that he hath."[42] In a similar vein, the advantage of the majority party has also been referred to as the Sheriff of Nottingham phenomenon after the sheriff, who, in contrast to Robin Hood, stole from the poor to give to the rich.

In a single-member plurality system the relationship between votes and seats is not a straight line running at about a 45 degree angle, as one might expect in a proportional representation system. Instead, in an unbiased single-member system, the relationship between votes and seats will be curvilinear with the line passing through the point at which 50 percent of the vote translates into half of the seats. The mere fact that the majority party gets more seats than its vote share need not indicate a gerrymander. Andrew Gelman and Gary King explain that an apportionment scheme is free of *bias* if the reward given to one party should it achieve a majority of the vote is comparable to the bonus given to the other party should it receive the same share of the vote.[43] Thus if Democrats get 57 percent of the legislative seats when they poll 52 percent of the vote in the state, the system would be free of bias if Republicans also won 57 percent of the seats in return for a 52 percent vote share. Gelman and King developed a free software program that assesses the degree of bias in an apportionment system.[44]

A phenomenon related to bias in a districting plan is *responsiveness*, which refers to the degree to which changes in the partisan preferences of the electorate result in changes in the makeup of the legislature. Many criticize the current congressional districting schemes for reducing responsiveness by making most districts either safely Democratic or overwhelmingly Republican. When districts have been packed with members of a particular party, then even if a substantial minority of the population changed its preferences and voted for the opposing party that would fail to shift partisan control of many districts. For example, in the packed arrangement in table 1.3, even if Party B gained an additional 9 percent of the vote in each district, it would still win only in District 3. The unpacked plan has greater responsiveness; if Party B won an additional 3 percent of the vote in District 2, it would gain another seat.

Since incumbents are unlikely to change their policy preferences dramatically, getting a legislature to adopt different policies requires the replacement of incumbents with new members who have different preferences. The greater the number of marginal districts, the greater the potential for achieving policy change. The smaller the shift in the electorate needed to replace one party with another, the more responsive the system.

Journalists and academics have long argued the desirability of having competitive districts. About the only dissenters were incumbents who, not surprisingly, preferred electoral systems that returned them to office with comfortable margins. One political scientist, Thomas Brunell, has presented the case for having legislators represent districts comprised overwhelmingly of supporters of one party.[45] Brunell relies on survey data showing that individuals who support winning congressional candidates are more likely to approve of the job being done by Congress and to believe that their representative attends to the needs of the constituency. Additionally, voters whose choice won the election have a greater sense of political efficacy. Based on these findings, Brunell argues that districts should pack in voters of the district's majority party to eliminate competition, since in competitive districts greater numbers of voters will have backed the unsuccessful candidate. Brunell's recommendation therefore is to draft a plan in which Democrats have overwhelming majorities in some districts while Republicans enjoy insurmountable majorities in the remaining districts.

## IMPORTANCE OF THE CENSUS

Since the apportioning of seats in the Congress and the distribution of benefits under some programs rest on the census, states have become increasingly interested in ensuring an accurate count. States join the Census Bureau in sponsoring public service announcements to encourage residents to complete the census forms. Census takers are trained to go to out-of-the way homes to tally as many people as possible and to seek out the homeless by going to shelters and checking under bridges, in wooded camps, and abandoned buildings. No matter how conscientious census takers and local communities are in encouraging a full count, some people, such as undocumented aliens, do not want to be found and counted. The undocumented have been particularly difficult to enumerate since, despite promises from the Census Bureau that they will not be reported to the Immigration and Naturalization Service, those who are in the country illegally fear that federal agents may report them and they will be deported. President Trump, from the launching of his presidential campaign, has railed against individuals who entered the nation illegally. He has fired up his rallies and knocked heads with Congress over building a wall along the border with Mexico to prevent people slipping into the country. He claimed, without supporting documentation, that he lost the popular vote to Hillary Clinton due to ballots cast illegally by non-citizens.

In 2018 Commerce Secretary Wilbur Ross announced that in response to a request from Attorney General Jeff Sessions, a question would be added to the 2020 census asking about the citizenship status of everyone in each household. The rationale for the citizenship question, a topic last included in the Census of 1950, was that having these granular data would help the office of the attorney general when dealing with cases under Section 2 of the Voting Rights Act.[46]

Civil rights groups objected to inclusion of this question, asserting that it would make the count less accurate. They claimed that despite assurances that other government officials do not get to see census forms, some households containing individuals not legally in the country would fail to return the census form or exclude undocumented family members resulting in an undercount in the millions.[47] Estimates placed the number of individuals who might not be counted if a citizenship question were included as high as 6.5 million.[48] Since immigrant populations tend to be greater in Democratic than Republican areas, if the citizenship question lowered participation in the census, it would advantage the GOP when legislative seats were allocated. Widespread reluctance to complete the census by households having non-citizens might cost states like California, Florida, and Texas seats in Congress.

Suspicions about partisan motivations were confirmed in 2019 when computer files of the late GOP redistricting mastermind, Thomas Hofeller, came into the hands of Common Cause. Among Hofeller's thousands of computer files were his projections that asking about citizenship would reduce the count of minorities and in doing so advantage the GOP when it came to apportioning congressional seats among the states and distributing legislative seats in a jurisdiction. Hofeller had shared his thoughts with the Trump transition team immediately after the 2016 election.[49]

Multiple lawsuits challenged the inclusion of the citizenship question. The courts, including ultimately the U.S. Supreme Court, sided with the plaintiffs. The Trump administration's position was undermined upon a showing that Commerce Secretary Wilbur Ross, who was responsible for implementing the 2020 census, had suggested including this question rather than responding to a request for the data coming from the Department of Justice. Ross's office prompted DOJ to ask that the question be included. Initially, President Trump threatened to delay the census in order to try to find a way around the Supreme Court ruling but soon backed off so that citizen status was not part of the 2020 questionnaire.

It is true that information on citizenship is needed to satisfy the first *Gingles* prong, as discussed in chapter 3, but civil rights groups contend that the information gathered by the American Community Survey suffices. Each year the ACS surveys 3.5 million households, in the course of which it asks about citizenship status, where respondents were born and, for non-natives, when they came to the United States. Aggregating data from five years of surveys allows for the estimation of citizenship at the block group level and block groups can be aggregated to form legislative districts.

Critics of relying on the ACS estimates point out that they are not coterminous with the census. For example, the five-year ACS data available when the 2020 census figures are released will be for 2015–2019. The ACS data, being a sample rather than a full count, might be less accurate, especially when assessing a districting plan that relied in part on individual census blocks rather than block groups.[50]

In July 2020, with the census count well under way, President Trump ordered the exclusion of noncitizens from the Bureau's determination of how many House seats each state would receive.[51] Critics challenged the constitutionality of this novel approach. Since the census did not include a question about citizenship, it would be necessary to rely on ACS estimates. Implementation of the Trump order would likely result in one fewer seat for California, New York, and Texas with Alabama, Minnesota, and Ohio being the beneficiaries.

At the margins, it may not take too many individuals to win or lose a seat for a state. In 2000, Utah failed to get an additional seat by a margin of 857 individuals.[52] In 1981, poor jobs of counting residents cost Georgia and Indiana seats that went to California and New York.[53] A more accurate count might have netted California, Georgia, and Montana each an additional congressional seat following the 1990 census while Oklahoma, Pennsylvania, and Wisconsin would have each received one fewer seat.[54]

The other side of the coin for achieving accurate enumeration is overcounting some people. This tends to involve the more affluent who may have multiple homes but can also involve students counted both at their parents' home as well as at their campus address.

Even though states have become increasingly concerned about getting a full count, critics contend that an accurate count is impossible. The American Statistical Association and the Census Bureau itself both recommend sampling to ensure a more accurate enumeration of the population rather than actually trying to locate every person living in the United States. The supporters of sampling note that despite efforts at encouraging a full count, the numbers of households failing to return the census forms has increased. With the 2020 census due to be conducted largely online, there may be new problems in getting a full count. With the census under way in the midst of the coronavirus pandemic, it became especially challenging to track down the poor and often minority households that failed to respond electronically. Retirees, who in the past have often taken the temporary jobs as census enumerators, hesitated to risk their health to do the face-to-face contact involved in going door-to-door tracking down non-respondents.

Since some $900 billion a year in federal programs is allocated based on population, having a more complete count also advantages states where finding all of their residents may be particularly difficult. The Census Bureau estimates that the undercount in Georgia in 1990 amounted to 142,425 people, which cost Georgia $2 billion in federal dollars over the decade.[55] One estimate put New York City's loss at $850 million because of the undercount in 2000.[56] The loss of federal funds because of an undercount becomes especially painful as states try to balance their budgets during an economic downturn.

Arguments over the advantages of sampling versus a census quickly took on partisan overtones in the late 1990s. Democrats believed that since the census disproportionately misses the poor while double counting the wealthy, a more accurate figure would increase the number of people who could be used to draw Democratic districts while reducing the number of Republican districts. In the course of drawing new plans, some individuals in Democratic districts would be shifted to those represented by Republicans, which might result in Democrats winning some of what had been Republican districts.[57] This explains why the Republican Speaker of the U.S. House characterized sampling as "a dagger aimed at the heart of the Republican majority."[58]

Resolution of this partisan debate fell to the Supreme Court, which required the use of the census counts and not sample estimates to apportion seats among the states.[59] Since the Constitution designates the census as the basis for allocating seats, the Court rejected arguments that it could be done using a sampling technique even if statisticians were correct in their contention that a sample would be more accurate. The Court did say, however, that the estimates based on sampling could be used for other purposes such as allocation of funds or the actual drawing of districts. The data on the citizen adult population that is used to assess whether a majority-minority district can be drawn (a topic in chapter 3) comes from the sample drawn for the American Community Survey.

## PLAN OF THE BOOK

The next four chapters examine items that influence the drawing of district maps. Chapter 2 focuses on what has become the most important criterion and that is equalizing populations among districts. Chapter 3 looks at the second most important factor, which is treating ethnic minorities fairly. Chapter 4 considers multiple traditional districting principles, such as compactness and respect for existing political boundaries.

Partisanship is the topic for chapter 5. The initial gerrymander sought to disadvantage a political party and much of today's gerrymandering is designed to enhance the strength of one party at the expense of the other. After more than a generation of debating when a partisan gerrymander becomes so egregious that courts should invalidate a plan, the Supreme Court ruled this to be a political question and therefore not in the purview of federal courts. A few state courts have been less timorous and acted so that if partisan gerrymanders are to be challenged in the future, it will be before state judges.

One of the states that has experienced repeated challenges both in the courts and in its dealings with the Department of Justice is Georgia. Chapter 6 provides a case study of the application of districting standards to this state.

Chapter 7 looks forward to the changes that the 2020 census may provide for the apportionment of congressional seats. We also review the rules likely to guide the redistricting that will take place early in this decade.

*Chapter 2*

# Population Equality

## *How Equal Must Districts Be?*

To the extent that a citizen's right to vote is debased, he is that much less a citizen.[1]

In a democracy as practiced still in a few New England towns, the citizenry comes together and sets policy for the community. Each participant has a single vote. In representative democracies, citizens choose representatives who make decisions for them. Each representative has one vote. But what if the representatives come from constituencies that have dramatically different numbers of people? The idea behind a citizen democracy suggests that these representatives who have equal votes should represent roughly equal numbers of constituents.

Questions about the weight to be given the population go back to the earliest days of the Republic. A stumbling block at the Philadelphia convention which drafted the federal Constitution involved allocation of representatives. The larger states thought their greater population entitled them to more influence in the legislature. The less populous states, fearing that their interests would be made subservient to those of the more populous states, wanted equal representation for each state as had existed under the Articles of Confederation. The Great Compromise provided something for both the large and the small states with each state having equal representation in the Senate in order to address the concerns of the small states, while the House allocated representation on the basis of population as demanded by the larger states.

The Constitution established each state's initial representation in the U.S. House. The two smallest states, Delaware and Rhode Island, each received one representative. The most populous states got greater numbers of seats with Virginia receiving ten, while Massachusetts and Pennsylvania got eight each. These allocations based on best guesses as to relative population size

31

got adjusted after the first census, taken in 1790. The Constitution under-scored the importance of linking representation to population since it pro-vided for a decennial census and reassessment of a state's number of House seats following the census.

The early interest in linking population to seats in the House did not extend to concern about the population per seat in state delegations. In 1872 Congress admonished states to strive for equal populations among districts but no steps were taken to achieve this goal. Not until the 1960s did courts review population deviations and strike down plans that allowed vast dispar-ities in the number of people per district. Until the Supreme Court held that population deviations in congressional districts violated Article I, Section 2, states rarely redrew district lines unless the size of their delegation changed. And even a change in a state's number of seats did not always immediately lead to new maps. The failure to address population deviations also char-acterized state legislatures and local collegial bodies. Even when the state constitution called for periodic adjustments to reduce population deviations, the legislators responsible for drawing new maps often ignored the require-ment, since reallocation would result in some of their number losing their seats. Not until the second half of the twentieth century did districts with equal populations become the most important requirement when creating a new plan.

America began as an agrarian nation with cities developing slowly. Shifts in population resulted in urban districts having far more people than rural districts and rural legislators saw no reason to cede influence to their urban rivals, especially if giving cities and suburbs more seats would strengthen the opposition party.

## A HISTORY LESSON

The concerns of rural America were so great that after the first census report-ing that most Americans no longer lived in rural communities, Congress failed to reapportion its seats. Following the 1920 census, Congress declined to increase the number of seats as it had done after every census except for 1840, when it eliminated ten seats. With the size of the House fixed, Congress ignored the census rather than reduce the representation of rural states located primarily in the Midwest and South. Had reapportionment occurred, ten rural states would have lost representation. Some rural legislators questioned the accuracy of the census and hoped that dislocations caused by World War I were temporary, with people returning to rural communities.[2] For the first and only time in history, the size of a state's congressional delegation was divorced from the state's share of the national population.

Rural members of Congress ultimately acknowledged that those who enjoyed the amenities of city life were not going to return to the uncertainties of farming and the absence of electricity and indoor plumbing and bowed to the constitutional directive that "Representatives . . . shall be apportioned among the several states . . . according to their respective numbers." Recognizing its own weakness in failing to carry out its duty, Congress passed the Permanent Apportionment Act that transferred responsibility for determining each state's number of seats to the Census Bureau. Not surprisingly, after congressional failure to reallocate seats following the 1920 census, the reapportionment carried out in the next decade had a dramatic impact. Almost half of the states, 21 of the 48, lost seats following the 1930 census. While most only lost a single seat, Missouri, which had been the seventh largest state in the nation in 1910, saw its delegation shrink from 16 to 13 members.

The trauma of losing seats proved so great that Missouri along with Kentucky, Minnesota, and Virginia failed to adopt plans for their shrunken delegations and instead elected all members at-large in 1932. In each of these states except Minnesota, statewide elections coupled with Franklin Roosevelt's coattails resulted in the defeat of Republican incumbents so that the entire delegation became Democratic. Alabama adopted the same ostrich-like approach when it lost a seat following the 1960 reapportionment. In each of these instances, before the next election, the state drew single-member districts around the homes of the surviving legislators.

Reluctance to draw new maps was not limited to states that experienced loss. At times, states reacted slowly to the good fortune of gaining a second seat. Idaho, Montana, and Utah, each of which gained a seat following the 1910 census, elected both of their members at-large in 1912 before creating single-member districts prior to the 1914 election. When Arizona received a second seat following the 1940 census, it did not get around to drawing single-member districts until the 1946 election. After gaining seats in 1932, 1952, and 1962, Texas filled the new seats through at-large elections before creating a new district around the home of the winner. Following the 1940 reapportionment, three of seven states that gained seats did not redistrict in time for the 1942 election. From 1912 when Illinois gained two seats until 1942 when it lost a seat, it elected two at-large members. Four states that gained seats following the 1932 reapportionment were slow to draw districts. Both Ohio and New York elected some members at-large throughout that decade and the Connecticut delegation had one at-large seat up until the Redistricting Revolution hit in 1964. Following the 1930 reapportionment, 12 of 42 states with multi-member delegates elected at least one at-large member.

Prior to the 1960s, the U.S. House was the one institution in which an attempt was made to base representation on population—and even there the

1920s constituted a notable exception. While each state's House delegation reflected its share of the national population, states made little effort to see that each of their members of Congress represented roughly equal constituencies. Indeed the condition under which each member of a state's House delegation had constituencies of the same size occurred in the anomalous situation of electing all members at-large. In those few situations, each of the state's representatives had exactly the same number of constituents since each represented the state's entire population. While some people who lived in districts where the member of Congress had far more constituents than the representatives from other parts of the state fretted that they were underrepresented, no serious challenge to the status quo came until the 1940s.

## UNSUCCESSFUL CHALLENGE TO
## POPULATION DEVIATIONS

The 1940 census showed Illinois to be the third most populous state, a position it had held for half a century. Most of the population lived in Chicago, which accounted for 51.5 percent of Illinois's population. In apportioning its twenty-five districts for the 1940s, six districts wholly lay within the city of Chicago with another six partially in the city.[3] Of these dozen districts, all but three had more people than the average for the state. Of the thirteen districts that did not include part of Chicago, all but three were underpopulated, and one of the overpopulated districts, while it did not include any of Chicago, was in suburban Cook County where Chicago is located. Illinois's district lines had not changed since 1901. Over the next four censuses, populations shifted so that after the 1940 census, the least populous district had 112,116 people, only one-eighth the number in the most populous district. Seven districts had fewer than 200,000 people. The ideal (or average) population for an Illinois district based on the 1940 census was 303,740.

The state legislature's persistent failure to address the underrepresentation of the Windy City prompted a judicial challenge that reached the Supreme Court. Chicago residents wanted more influence in the congressional delegation and that could be achieved if their share of seats approximated their share of the state's population. In the opinion of the court, which attracted only two other justices, Felix Frankfurter dismissed the complaint because of a lack of justiciability. That is, the Court said it lacked jurisdiction over what it saw as a political question.[4] According to Frankfurter, Congress, and not the courts, had the authority to supervise the districting policy of states. Frankfurter saw the question presented to the court in *Colegrove v. Green* as a political thicket which he warned the judiciary not to enter. Frankfurter naively observed that "Of course no court can affirmatively re-map the

Illinois districts so as to bring them more in conformity with the standards of fairness for a representative system." As we shall see, courts now regularly carry out redistricting when legislatures fail to act. Frankfurter recommended that the plaintiffs turn to the legislature, advice which had already proven fruitless. He also observed that Congress has responsibility for overseeing the makeup of its membership and therefore could intervene—another suggestion that has never helped those aggrieved by an unequal districting system.

The Supreme Court had also indicated its unwillingness to become embroiled in challenges to the districting arrangements of state legislatures. It refused to overturn the arrangement used by Georgia, which severely limited the influence of urban areas by restricting even the most populous counties to no more than three seats in the State House, while even the least populous counties each had one representative.[5] Under an arrangement somewhat analogous to the Electoral College, this weighting gave an urban county no more than 6 of the 410 unit votes used to determine winners in statewide Democratic primaries, a topic revisited in chapter 6.

## CONDITIONS ON THE EVE OF THE REVOLUTION

Justice Frankfurter's advice that those unhappy with population inequalities should look elsewhere for help did nothing to improve the situation for underrepresented portions of states. Table 2.1 shows several measures of population inequality for state legislative chambers calculated shortly before the Supreme Court launched the Redistricting Revolution. With rare exceptions, the districts within each chamber had wide differences in their populations.

The first measure, calculated by Paul David and Ralph Eisenberg, presents the ratio of the population for the most and least populous districts within a legislative chamber.[6] In state lower chambers, the most extreme values come from New England states, which gave representation to every township. Districts in the larger cities had hundreds of times more people than did the districts of tiny rural townships. Two of the states, Connecticut and Vermont, also had the oldest plans in place with Vermont not having redistricted since it became a state in 1793, while the most recent map for the Connecticut House dated from 1876.[7] Outside of New England, the Florida and Georgia Houses had the largest values with some districts having populations approximately 100 times greater than the least populous district.[8] Even in the most equitably apportioned chambers, the most populous House districts had three, four, or five times the population of the smallest districts. Hawaii, the nation's newest state, had the least skewed districting arrangement, but even there some districts had more than twice as many people as others.

**Table 2.1 Measures of Malapportionment Prior to the Redistricting Revolution**

| State | David and Eisenberg* | | 1955 Apportionment** | | Measuring Malapportion.*** Schubert-Press |
|---|---|---|---|---|---|
| | Lower | Upper | Lower | Upper | |
| Alabama | 15.6 | 41.2 | 27.15 | 28.26 | 13.8 |
| Alaska | 6.4 | 10.8 | NA | NA | 41.5 |
| Arizona | 5.3 | 85.8 | NA | 19.3 | 27.2 |
| Arkansas | 6.4 | 2.3 | 37.52 | 46.95 | 66.1 |
| California | 6.2 | 422.5 | 44.7 | 11.88 | 20.2 |
| Colorado | 8.1 | 7.3 | 34.67 | 36.12 | 45.5 |
| Connecticut | 424.5 | 6.4 | 9.59 | 36.5 | 27.1 |
| Delaware | 35.4 | 16.8 | 19.4 | 22.7 | 50.6 |
| Florida | 108.7 | 98 | 17.19 | 17.67 | 10.2 |
| Georgia | 98.8 | 42.6 | 26.3 | 26.89 | -4 |
| Hawaii | 2.2 | 5.9 | NA | NA | 48.9 |
| Idaho | 25.5 | 102.1 | 41.53 | 19.05 | 50.1 |
| Illinois | 3.6 | 9.4 | 46.02 | 29.42 | 47.2 |
| Indiana | 5.4 | 4.4 | 36.95 | 39.25 | -4.3 |
| Iowa | 17.8 | 15 | 29.34 | 33.94 | 7.8 |
| Kansas | 33.2 | 21.3 | 22.59 | 33.67 | 10.9 |
| Kentucky | 6 | 2.9 | 37.59 | 45.19 | 13.9 |
| Louisiana | 17.4 | 8 | 25.61 | 34.07 | 40.9 |
| Maine | 6.6 | 2.8 | 39.12 | 37.91 | 80.3 |
| Maryland | 12.5 | 31.8 | 27.57 | 15.52 | 29.8 |
| Massachusetts | 13.9 | 2.3 | 42.15 | 48.76 | 96.3 |
| Michigan | 4 | 12.4 | 42.29 | 32.34 | 43.7 |
| Minnesota | 13.3 | 5.8 | 31.56 | 35.93 | 1.3 |
| Mississippi | 16.7 | 8.8 | 32.67 | 34.59 | 42.1 |
| Missouri | 22.2 | 2.8 | 23.71 | 47.37 | 46.2 |
| Montana | 14 | 88.4 | 40.8 | 18.4 | 44.7 |
| Nebraska | unicameral | 2.7 | NA | 41.88 | 80.9 |

| State | | | | | |
|---|---|---|---|---|---|
| Nevada | 31.4 | 223.6 | 28.82 | 12.36 | 16.6 |
| New Hampshire | 1081.3 | 3 | 37.4 | 44.75 | 71 |
| New Jersey | 4.6 | 19 | 43.95 | 17.01 | 58.9 |
| New Mexico | 15.5 | 139.9 | 35.67 | 20.07 | 23.2 |
| New York | 14.8 | 4 | 37.06 | 40.91 | 69.2 |
| North Carolina | 19 | 6 | 30.16 | 40.09 | 56.6 |
| North Dakota | 7.5 | 9.9 | 39.02 | 35.36 | 41.8 |
| Ohio | 14.5 | 2.2 | 29.19 | 20.68 | 81.2 |
| Oklahoma | 14 | 26.4 | 33.38 | 29.45 | 9.5 |
| Oregon | 3 | 3.5 | 45.42 | 42.18 | 86.5 |
| Pennsylvania | 31.1 | 10.7 | 41.63 | 35.44 | 70.8 |
| Rhode Island | 39 | 141 | 34.17 | 13.53 | 42 |
| South Carolina | 3.1 | 25.1 | 46.72 | 26.57 | 55.6 |
| South Dakota | 4.7 | 5.8 | 38.73 | 40.85 | 44.2 |
| Tennessee | 23 | 6 | 30.13 | 33.26 | 11.8 |
| Texas | 6.7 | 9.4 | 39.85 | 36.8 | 26.6 |
| Utah | 27.8 | 6.9 | 38.99 | 26.75 | 43.2 |
| Vermont | 987 | 6.4 | 12.58 | 45.67 | 44.8 |
| Virginia | 7.1 | 5.5 | 43.69 | 43.93 | 47.6 |
| Washington | 4.6 | 7.3 | 33.87 | 35.44 | 62.6 |
| West Virginia | 9 | 3.4 | 38.87 | 45.68 | 65.2 |
| Wisconsin | 3.9 | 2.8 | 38.87 | 46.53 | 58.5 |
| Wyoming | 3.4 | 9.8 | 39.92 | 28.77 | 62.3 |

*Sources:* Paul T. David and Ralph Eisenberg, *Devaluation of the Urban and Suburban Vote* (Charlottesville: Bureau of Public Administration, University of Virginia, 1961), 3; Gordon E. Baker, *Rural versus Urban Political Power* (New York: Random House, 1955), 16–17; Glendon Schubert and Charles Press, "Measuring Malapportionment," *American Political Science Review* 58 (June 1964), 325–326.

* David and Eisenberg measure calculates the ratio in the population in the most and fewest people represented by a member in the legislative chamber at the time of the 1960 census.

** Minimum percentage of the population needed to elect a majority of the chamber using the apportionment plan in place following the 1950 census. "Unrepresentative States," *National Municipal Review* (1955), 571–575, 587.

*** These data show the underrepresentation of the most urban areas in the state. Only in Massachusetts and Wisconsin do the shares of seats given to urban areas equal the urban area's share of the state's population. In all other states the urban areas have a smaller share of the legislators than of the state's population.

**** This measure is the Schubert and Press measure of apportionment fairness based on skewness and kurtosis of the distribution of legislators.

In state senates, the upper range was not as great as in the House, although in five states some districts had more than a hundred times as many people as others with California being the least equitably apportioned; Los Angeles County had a senator for its 6,000,000 people while at the other extreme one rural district had only 14,000 people. Eight states apportioned their senators in such a way that the range between the largest and smallest districts was less than a factor of three with Ohio having the fairest distribution, although even there the largest district had more than twice the population of the smallest district.

The second measure in table 2.1 reports the smallest share of the state's population that could elect a majority within a legislative chamber. For example, in the Alabama House if one began with the least populous district and then added the next least populous until the 53 least populous of the 105 districts in the House had been aggregated, based on the apportioning system used in the 1950s, this would account for just over 27 percent of the state's population. In a perfectly apportioned legislative chamber, it would take just over 50 percent of the population to elect a majority of the chamber. In the most extreme situation, less than 10 percent of the population of Connecticut could elect a majority of that state's lower chamber. In four states, less than 20 percent of the population could elect a majority of the House. In eleven states which had the most equitable systems it would require more than 40 percent of the state's population to elect a majority of the chamber. In South Carolina 46.72 percent of the population would be the minimum to elect a majority in its House, while in Illinois just over 46 percent of the population provided the minimum to elect a majority of that state's lower chamber.

In nine states, a majority of the Senate could be elected by less than 20 percent of the population. In California and Nevada approximately 12 percent of the population sufficed to elect a majority of the Senate, while in Rhode Island, as little as 13.5 percent of the population could elect a Senate majority. At the more equitable end of the distribution, it would take the districts accounting for almost 49 percent of the Massachusetts population to elect a majority of the Senate in the Bay State. Seats in the upper chambers were more equitably distributed than in lower chambers with at least 40 percent of the population required to elect a majority of the senators in fourteen states. In seven of these states it would have required more than 45 percent of the population to elect a majority of the Senate.

The final equality measure which was developed by Glendon Schubert and Charles Press is a more sophisticated effort and looks at the shape of the distribution of legislative districts in terms of population using two measures of distribution, skewness and kurtosis.[9] Unlike the other measures that provide a separate score for each chamber, Schubert and Press calculate a single score for a state. On their measure, a perfectly apportioned legislative chamber in which areas got a share of seats equal to their share of the population would score 100. While no state achieved perfect proportionality, Massachusetts with a score of 96.3 comes closest. Maine, Nebraska, Ohio, and Oregon each received scores above 80. At the other extreme, Georgia and Indiana had negative scores while Oklahoma, Iowa, and Minnesota each had positive scores of less than 10.

## BACK TO COURT

Early in the 1960s the Supreme Court received another invitation to enter the political thicket and this time the court accepted the challenge. A 1960 voting rights case served as a bridge. *Gomillion v. Lightfoot* challenged an action by the Alabama legislature that transmogrified Tuskegee from a square to a twenty-eight-sided polygon in order to remove all but a few African American voters.[10] Justice Frankfurter, who wrote the majority opinion, strove to distinguish the plan from this city from the one the court avoided in *Colegrove v. Green.* While the *Colegrove* plaintiffs complained of vote dilution, the new maps *denied* most Tuskegee blacks a vote in municipal elections. The racial discrimination here made this case appropriate for relief under the Fifteenth Amendment rather than it being a political issue which Frankfurter would not have touched. Coming to the aid of the *Gomillion* appellants in a complaint about district fairness served as a halfway step toward repeal of *Colegrove.*

*Baker v. Carr* involved the Tennessee state legislature which, like the Illinois congressional districts, had not been redrawn since 1901.[11] As a result of legislative inaction, often called the silent gerrymander, by the 1960s, huge disparities in representation existed among Tennessee's counties which, as in most states, provided the basis for legislative seats. These disparities existed even though the state constitution required that counties' representation in the legislature be based on the number of registered voters. As an example of the inequity, two counties had two representatives each even though one county had more than ten times the population of the other. As the measures of equality presented in table 2.1 show, Tennessee does not score well. On the Schubert and Press Index, it scored 11.8 and the majority of the House could be elected by less than a third of the population. The range between the largest and smallest districts in Tennessee was a factor of twenty-three. While the state did not score well, it was far from the worst apportioned state in the Union.

Brushing aside Justice Frankfurter's concerns, the Court plunged into the "political thicket" and cited the Equal Protection Clause of the Fourteenth Amendment as the basis for requiring greater equality in the population of the districts. The Fourteenth Amendment, ratified in the immediate aftermath of the Civil War, focuses on the actions of states with its admonition that "No state shall . . . deny to any person within its jurisdiction the equal protection of the laws." The Court perceived denial of equal protection in districts that had differences in their populations. Voters in overpopulated districts had less influence in the political system than did those living in districts with fewer people. The court did not indicate how much variation would be tolerated in district populations, but in a concurring opinion, Justice Clark observed that "No one . . . contends that mathematical equality among voters is required by the Equal Protection Clause." As we shall see, Justice Clark failed to anticipate subsequent pressures that have prompted ever smaller deviations in the populations of a jurisdiction's districts. The Clark concurrence did, however, demonstrate greater political sophistication than Frankfurter had in *Colegrove*. Clark recognized that the plaintiffs had no other recourse since the legislature and the governor of Tennessee had ignored calls for adherence to the requirement of the state constitution.

The Supreme Court ruling in the Tennessee case resolved the issue of justiciability of equal population challenges in state legislatures and within a year, thirty-six similar suits challenged legislative plans across the nation.[12] These challenges prompted many states to redraw districts to eliminate the grossest inequalities. Relying on the federal analogy, states initially took steps to equalize district populations in only one chamber. Since every state has two U.S. senators, states assumed that if the seats in one chamber reflected population differences, seats in the other chamber could be based on other considerations such as geography, which might allow them to continue allocating one seat per county or some other geographic grouping.

Two years after *Baker*, the Supreme Court addressed the federal analogy and found it inappropriate for states. Seats in the Alabama legislature had not been reallocated since the beginning of the twentieth century despite a requirement in the state constitution for a decennial redistricting. Birmingham and other cities were underrepresented while rural areas had more seats than their population would justify. Jefferson County (Birmingham) had 600,000 people; Bullock County had 13,000. Both had one senator. In requiring population as the basis for seat distribution in *both* chambers, the Court observed that "people, not land or trees or pastures, vote." Chief Justice Earl Warren saw the right to an equally weighted vote as a critical right of citizenship. To the extent that some people's votes had greater influence than others, it amounted to a form of disenfranchisement. Voters who lived in overpopulated districts had less opportunity to shape the makeup of the government which in turn might mean less opportunity to influence its policy decisions. As in *Baker*, the *Reynolds v. Sims* decision did not require exact equality in the population of districts but speculated that:

> So long as the divergences from a strict population standard are based on legitimate considerations incident to the effectuation of a rational state policy, some deviations from the equal-population principle are constitutionally permissible

with respect to the apportionment of seats in either or both of the two Houses of a bicameral state legislature.[13]

The *Reynolds* decision set off another round of litigation. By the mid-1960s, cartographers were busy redrawing legislative chambers in forty-seven states.[14]

Shortly before rejecting the federal analogy, the Supreme Court had revisited the question of congressional districting which had lain dormant since 1946. While the Court relied on the Equal Protection Clause to require that states equalize populations among their legislative districts, that portion of the Constitution could not be used to challenge disparities in congressional populations. Despite the inapplicability of the Equal Protection Clause to the federal Congress, the Supreme Court extended its call for greater population equity to congressional districts. To justify its congressional ruling, the Court turned to Article I, Section 2, of the Constitution, which states that "The House of Representatives shall be composed of members chosen every second year by the people of the several states, and the electors in each state." The court interpreted this provision as banning irrational population differences among a state's congressional districts. The leading case, *Wesberry v. Sanders*, involved Georgia's congressional districts redrawn when the state lost two seats in the 1930 reapportionment.[15] By 1960 the 5th District had the nation's second largest population with more than 800,000 people. At the other extreme, the 9th District had fewer than a third as many people.

As table 2.2 shows, when *Wesberry* was filed only three of Georgia's ten congressional districts were overpopulated (had populations more than 100

Table 2.2  Population of Georgia Congressional Districts Before and After *Wesberry v. Sanders*

| District | Before | | After | |
|---|---|---|---|---|
| | Population | % of Ideal | Population | % of Ideal |
| 1 | 379,933 | 96 | 420,354 | 107 |
| 2 | 301,123 | 76 | 358,133 | 91 |
| 3 | 422,198 | 107 | 340,110 | 86 |
| 4 | 323,489 | 82 | 424,917 | 108 |
| 5 | 823,489 | 209 | 398,763 | 101 |
| 6 | 330,235 | 84 | 455,575 | 116 |
| 7 | 450,740 | 114 | 450,740 | 114 |
| 8 | 291,185 | 74 | 338,948 | 86 |
| 9 | 272,154 | 69 | 329,738 | 84 |
| 10 | 348,379 | 88 | 408,823 | 104 |

*Sources*: U.S. Bureau of the Census, *Congressional District Data Book (Districts of the 88th Congress)*. (Washington, DC: U.S. Government Printing Office, 1963); *Congressional Directory*, 89th Congress, 1st Session (Washington, DC: U.S. Government Printing Office, 1965).

percent of the ideal)[16] with the range being from a low of 69 percent of the ideal in the 9th District to 209 percent of the ideal in the 5th District. After the state redrew its districts following the *Wesberry* decision, six districts were overpopulated while four remained underpopulated. While the range had been from 69 percent up to 209 percent of the ideal before redistricting, after redistricting the least populated had 84 percent of the ideal while the most populous was 116 percent of the ideal. This amounted to a difference of about 125,000 people. The new plan divided the 5th District and the part that remained in the 5th District came closest to having the ideal population with a score of 101 percent. The remainder of the old 5th District became the new 4th District, which had a population 108 percent of the ideal. The mountainous 9th District remained the most underpopulated with only 84 percent of the ideal population. While Georgia's ten districts came nowhere close to having exactly the same number of people, redistricting substantially reduced the range.

As happened with state legislative districts, once the courts demanded equal populations in congressional districts, similar challenges became widespread. In the first two years after *Wesberry*, congressional districts in twenty-six states got challenged.[17] Another seventeen suits were filed during the next biennium and in 1969–1970 six more suits were filed. As we will see shortly, some states had to defend not only their old plans, which suffered from the silent gerrymander, but also some of the corrective efforts that they took.

In time, the Supreme Court extended its ruling involving state legislatures to include local collegial bodies that elected representatives from districts.[18] Members of school boards, county commissions, city councils, and other local bodies elected by districts must be chosen from districts with equal populations. The sole exception to the requirement that legislative districts have equal populations remains the United States Senate. To change the districting arrangement for the Senate would, of course, require a constitutional amendment.

## EQUALITY REQUIREMENTS BECOME MORE PRECISE

The Supreme Court follows a minimalist approach and decides only what it must in order to resolve the specific fact situations in the cases before it. While the three decisions discussed above made quite clear that the status quo would no longer be tolerated, the Court did not provide precise details for what would be necessary to meet the "one person, one vote" standard first enunciated by Justice William Douglas.[19] Although these decisions became characterized as requiring population equality among districts, perfect equality was not Clark's standard in the *Baker* concurrence. The amount of acceptable variation gradually became clearer and narrower as courts ruled on additional challenges and struck down smaller and smaller deviations between the most and least populous districts.

## The Congressional Standard

The Supreme Court's reluctance to establish a precise guideline for congressional districts resulted in states having to pay repeated visits to the cartographers. Hiring mapmakers was not the only cost. Since the maps go a long way toward determining who will continue to serve in the legislature, the fights over redistricting are some of the most vicious and evoke some of the most duplicitous behavior. Moreover, frequent shifting of district lines can cause confusion among voters and weaken their relationships with their legislators.

The lack of clarity over acceptable population deviations exacted the highest price in Missouri. The "Show Me State" had to redraw its districts three times between 1960 and 1970. The plan in place after the 1960 census had districts that ranged in population from 378,499 to 506,845 as reported in table 2.3. Obviously, districts in Missouri were not as unequal as those in Georgia had been. While the largest Georgia district had about 550,000 more people than the smallest, in Missouri, the largest district had only 128,000 more people than the smallest. Nonetheless, Missouri like Georgia placed its largest city at a disadvantage. The three most overpopulated districts in 1962 contained St. Louis and its immediate suburbs. In terms of deviations from the ideal population, the range extended from 88 to 117 percent.

In the first remap (1966), Missouri reduced the range in populations to 390,240 to 475,667. Note that the deviations in the 1966 plan for Missouri are smaller than in the post-*Wesberry* plan for Georgia. Nonetheless, the Missouri plan included a 10 percent overpopulated district and another one that was 10 percent underpopulated. This triggered a second challenge, which the state also lost, and led to the 1968 map that had a range in populations of 420,180 to 453,000. The second remap reduced the population deviations in eight districts, added fewer than 1,000 people to the 8th District, and left the 7th District further from the ideal than it had been. The range in population as measured in terms of the ideal had now been narrowed to 97 to 105 percent. The St. Louis districts were no longer the most overpopulated in the state, although each had slightly more people than the ideal for Missouri. The range in population which had been 128,000 in 1963 had been reduced to 33,000.

Despite these improvements, urban residents prevailed on yet another challenge which prompted the state to devise a plan that reduced the population range of 1,357 people. The third redistricting done in time for the 1970

**Table 2.3  Population of Missouri Congressional District in Plans from 1962 to 1970**

| District | 1962 Plan | | 1966 Plan | | 1968 Plan | | 1970 Plan | |
|---|---|---|---|---|---|---|---|---|
| | Pop. | % of Ideal | Pop. | % of Ideal | Pop. | % of Ideal | Pop. | % of Ideal |
| 1 | 466,482 | 108 | 475,667 | 110 | 439,648 | 102 | 431,210 | 99.8 |
| 2 | 506,854 | 117 | 460,501 | 107 | 437,456 | 101 | 432,535 | 100.1 |
| 3 | 480,222 | 111 | 469,888 | 109 | 449,743 | 104 | 432,449 | 100.1 |
| 4 | 418,981 | 97 | 402,526 | 93 | 420,180 | 97 | 432,254 | 100.1 |
| 5 | 378,499 | 88 | 406,067 | 94 | 430,412 | 100 | 431,178 | 99.8 |
| 6 | 388,486 | 90 | 394,236 | 91 | 440,145 | 102 | 432,130 | 100.0 |
| 7 | 436,933 | 101 | 425,820 | 99 | 453,000 | 105 | 432,215 | 100.1 |
| 8 | 452,385 | 105 | 443,747 | 103 | 444,695 | 103 | 431,630 | 99.9 |
| 9 | 409,369 | 95 | 451,121 | 104 | 427,841 | 99 | 431,811 | 100.0 |
| 10 | 381,602 | 88 | 390,240 | 90 | 423,868 | 98 | 432,007 | 100.0 |
| Range | 88–117 | | 90–110 | | 97–105 | | 99.8–100.1 | |

Sources: U.S. Bureau of the Census, Congressional District Data Book (Districts of the 88th Congress) (Washington, DC: U.S. Government Printing Office, 1993); Supplement to Congressional District Data Book: Missouri (Washington, DC: Bureau of the Census, August 1966); Congressional Directory, 91st Congress, 1st Session (Washington, DC: U.S. Government Printing Office, 1969); Congressional Directory, 92nd Congress, 1st Session (Washington, DC: U.S. Government Printing Office, 1971).

election had almost completely eliminated population deviation, bringing it down to 0.3 percent based on the 1960 census. The 1970 plan that reduced the population deviations did so by breaking with tradition and splitting counties other than those in the St. Louis and Kansas City areas.

Of course, a critic might look at the figures used to assess the 1970 plan and point out that this plan was drawn a decade after the population enumeration on which it was based. Consequently the effort at eliminating population deviations had something of an artificial ring to it. Indeed the best estimates suggested that the range in the 1970 populations in these districts went from 380,047 in Kansas City's 5th District to 576,117 in the 8th District, extending from the Missouri River to the Arkansas border.[20] Consequently while the plaintiffs in the prolonged litigation could take pride in having achieved almost absolutely equal populations in Missouri's districts based on the 1960 census, in reality the deviation in these new districts exceeded that for the state in the 1962 plan. Of course, Missouri along with other states redrew its congressional districts prior to the convening of the 93rd Congress in 1973. The new plan had a total range in population of 2,109 based on the 1970 census.

By the time states adjusted their congressional districts to reflect the population shifts during the 1960s, most had brought the range in their populations down to less than 1 percent. Almost 300 congressional districts had population deviations within 1 percent of the ideal for their state, a dramatic change from a decade earlier when only nine districts in the entire nation came that close to the ideal population.[21]

After almost a generation of ever-constricting limitations on population deviation, the Supreme Court enunciated what has become its final statement on population variations in a state's congressional districts. *Karcher v. Daggett* involved the New Jersey redistricting following the 1980 census. In the challenged plan, the range between the largest and the smallest districts was just under 0.7 percent or 3,674 people. Nonetheless, when confronted with a plan that had even smaller deviations, the Court rejected the state's plan, observing that "there are no de minimis population variations, which could practically be avoided, but which nonetheless meet the standard of Article I, Section 2 without justification."[22] Justice William Brennan recognized the artificiality of the push for absolute equality since the census undoubtedly fails to count some people, and even if absolutely accurate when taken, by the time that a legislature draws districts and the court rules on a challenge, population shifts will have occurred. Nonetheless, Brennan pushed for equality in district populations since he feared that setting an acceptable standard as anything other than absolute equality would be treated by states as a license to have that much deviation. He feared that what a court might think of as a ceiling for acceptable deviation states would treat as the floor.

States learned through bitter experience and at the cost of millions of dollars in litigation fees that a plaintiff who produces a map with less population deviation than that adopted by the state usually wins in court and has the cost of litigation absorbed by the state. In 2002, a federal court struck down Pennsylvania's congressional map that had a population range of only nineteen people when plaintiffs provided a map that zeroed out the differences.[23]

By 2001, a number of states had taken the *Karcher* ruling to heart and, hoping to stave off delays and costly litigation, produced plans that reduced population deviation to the absolute minimum of one person.[24] Seventeen states achieved minimum deviations and another six reduced the range in population to less than ten people. The largest range was right at 1 percent.

Eliminating all deviations has become feasible thanks to geographic information system software (GIS) which links population to geography. These computer programs facilitate drawing numerous alternative plans in quick succession. In the past, redistricting involved drawing lines on large maps and then calculating district population by manually adding up figures for numerous counties, precincts, and census blocks. With this labor-intensive procedure, time constraints limited the number of iterations that a map could be put through and, consequently, mapmakers worked with larger geographic units, concentrating on counties in most states, in order to make their tasks manageable. In larger cities, mapmakers in the days before GIS would work with precincts, the smallest political units, which frequently contain 1,000 to 2,000 voters.

With GIS software, the population for a proposed district can be obtained with a few clicks of a mouse by indicating which counties, precincts, or census blocks to include. This allows cartographers to work quickly, trying alternatives with smaller and smaller pieces of geography as they seek to eliminate population differences among a state's districts. The census block is the smallest available unit and typically contains less area than an electoral precinct. In an urban area, a census block is usually defined by four streets, and by what one generally thinks of as an urban block. In a rural area, a census block may contain many square miles and might be defined by highways, railroad tracks, rivers, streams, or political boundaries like state, county, or city lines. Census blocks must have visible boundaries except when relying on a political boundary, as when a portion of a block is in a city and the other part lies outside of the corporate limits. In those instances, the city boundary divides a block often along lines not visible to the naked eye. When trying to even out the population of a district, mapmakers will frequently have to go census block by census block, making slight adjustments in the district's population as they substitute a block with slightly more or less population as needed to eliminate population deviations.

A consequence of demanding smaller population deviations is to split a larger number of cities and counties. Working with smaller bits of geography can also make it easier to gerrymander.

Note that the quote from *Karcher* above suggested that states might be able to justify deviations from absolute equality. One potentially acceptable factor would be to minimize splitting precincts or counties. Iowa law prohibits splitting counties when drawing congressional districts. Nonetheless its five-district plan for 2001 had a range in populations of only 134 people. The largest deviation in the post-2000 plans also occurred in a state that did not split any counties. The Arkansas plan had a total deviation of 1 percent.

## Population Deviations below the Congressional Level

Courts have viewed the constitutional basis for requiring equality among congressional districts as setting a more demanding standard than the Equal Protection Clause establishes for other collegial bodies. At about the same time that the Supreme Court concluded that states should aim for zero deviation in congressional plans, it seemingly gave the nod to permitting a 10 percent total deviation in plans for other jurisdictions.[25] Following numerous cases in which the courts required smaller and smaller population deviations, the Supreme Court adopted a standard widely interpreted as permitting deviations of 5 percent above and below the ideal population for a jurisdiction. For the next twenty years, the plus and minus 5 percentage point deviation rule was widely accepted as a safe harbor. If a jurisdiction devised a plan in which no districts fell outside of the plus-minus 5 percentage point range, many doubted whether the plan could be successfully attacked on population grounds. Numerous states specify that no district's population be outside the +/- 5 percent deviation from the ideal population. Iowa limits deviations to +/- 1 percent. Deviations from the ideal population smack of partisanship. The party drawing plans underpopulates districts it expects to win while overpopulating districts it anticipates will go for the opposition.[26] In so doing the mapmakers maximize the number of districts they hope to win while packing the opposition. Both parties are guilty of the practice.

The Georgia General Assembly was among those that accepted the +/- 5 percent rule as a safe harbor. As will be described in greater detail in chapter 6, the Georgia legislature devised plans in 2001 in which the range in population from the ideal totaled 9.98 percent. In a desperate effort to maintain their legislative majorities, the Democrats overpopulated Republican districts by 4, 4.5, and even 4.99 percent while underpopulating Democratic districts by comparable amounts.

When Republicans challenged the Democratic gerrymander, the state answered that since all districts conformed to the +/- five percent rule, they were not subject to attack. The trial court rejected the idea that plans which limited deviation to +/- five percent enjoyed some kind of immunity.[27] Witnesses for the state justified the House and Senate plans explaining that they underpopulated districts in south Georgia and Atlanta in order to maintain more seats in these slow growing portions of the state. In striking down the plans, the court pointed back to the *Reynolds* decision handed down forty years earlier, which had banned giving disproportionate influence to certain parts of states. The Supreme Court upheld the decision of the lower court.[28]

When the Georgia legislature failed to come up with new plans, the three trial court judges who had heard the case employed law professor and redistricting expert Nathaniel Persily to produce new maps.[29] The court's plan reduced the range in population to less than 2 percent in each chamber.

While the Georgia court plan has little deviation in district populations, it remains possible for states and localities to have plans with more variation if they provide an acceptable explanation. For example, a state might justify population deviations as necessary to avoid splitting racial groups, counties, precincts, or communities of interest between districts or to avoid pairing incumbents. Another possible rationale would be that the deviations resulted from drawing districts that followed natural boundaries such as rivers or mountain ranges. Yet another justification for a plan would be that it produced more compact districts. The Georgia defendants cited none of these possible explanations.

Pressures to draw districts likely to elect members of a minority group—a topic explored in detail in the next chapter—may spur efforts to underpopulate a district. To pass muster under Section 2 of the Voting Rights Act, it must be shown that a minority group is large and compact enough to constitute a majority of the adult population in a district. It becomes easier to satisfy that expectation the smaller the population thus an incentive to underpopulate the district by as much as 5 percent. In a challenge to Alabama legislative districting plans, among plaintiffs' objections was that the state had limited the population range to +/- 1 percent.[30]

## PROBLEMS WITH THE EQUAL
## POPULATION STANDARD

Critics of the emphasis on having equal populations point out that equalizing populations among districts need not produce the one person, one vote called for by Justice Douglas. If the objective is for each *vote* to have equal weight, registered voters or at least perspective voters rather than population should be equalized among districts.[31] After all, children cannot vote nor can noncitizens or those in prison. Nonetheless, the courts have focused on the total population counts and sought to equalize those numbers. As a consequence, the voters in districts with large numbers of children and/or non-citizens have a greater influence in the policy process than do voters living in districts with few children and/or non-citizens.

An effort to equalize numbers of registrants would exclude non-citizens, children, and others who had not registered to vote when designing districts. Even equalizing numbers of registrants would leave voters in some districts with greater influence than in others because of differences in turnout rates. If the standard really became equal numbers of voters, then districts comprised of low income areas or heavily populated by young adults would have far more people than districts in affluent areas or having an older population.

Political scientist James Campbell has demonstrated that the differences in participation rates bear a relationship to partisanship with districts that elect Democrats frequently, having far fewer active participants than districts that elect Republicans.[32] Campbell shows that during the 1990s, the ratio between the most and fewest votes in a congressional district went as high as 8.48 to 1. Ronald Weber, in an extensive analysis of differences in turnout in state legislative elections from 1968 through 1998, finds ratios for the most to least votes in a state legislative district as high as 20 to 1.[33] A quick look at the David and Eisenberg ratios in table 2.1 shows that the disparity in numbers of actual voters exceeds the differences in districts' total population in many states prior to *Baker*. Weber finds that districts having the lowest turnout are ones with heavy concentrations of African Americans or Latinos and that it is in these districts that competitive elections least often occur. In the absence of uncertainty about the electoral outcome, fewer voters bother to turnout.

Texas has a large non-citizen population, which is disproportionately concentrated along the border with Mexico and in large cities. As a consequence of the state's large numbers of non-citizens, legislative districts that have equal populations have unequal numbers of electors. Plaintiffs living in the two Senate districts with the largest numbers of voting age citizens challenged the districting plan, asking the court to require that districts have equal citizen voting age populations (CVAP). Plaintiffs pointed out that in one district the CVAP numbered 573,895, over 200,000 more than in the district with the smallest CVAP. The range in the population across Senate districts was an acceptable 8.04 percent while the disparity in the CVAP exceeded 40 percent. If one person, one vote were taken literally, then like before the Redistricting Revolution, some districts' voters had much greater weight than voters in districts with large CVAPs. The ratios of the largest to the smallest districts based on turnout in 2010 exceed the population ratios as of 1962 in at least nine states. In California, for example, the most populous 1962 district had 195 percent of the population of the smallest district. In 2010, the congressional district with the most voters had 340 percent the turnout in the least active district. For New York, the comparable figures are 135 percent for 1962 population compared with 343 percent for 2010 turnout.[34]

The Supreme Court noted the universal practice of using population and not CVAP in explaining that Texas was not obligated to use CVAP.[35] The Court left open the question whether a state might opt to substitute CVAP for population. A consequence of using CVAP or some measure of participation would be to shift seats from urban to rural areas and from Democratic to Republican areas. Using some measure other than total population, such as adults, registrants or voters would have similar political implications.

While equalizing voters among a jurisdiction's districts might be more in keeping with the one person, one vote concept, it would introduce another set of problems. First, turnout at least partially is driven by competition with more voters mobilized by interest in the outcome of a high-profile election. While interest in the result of a presidential or statewide contest for governor or senator may push up turnout, a fiercely contested congressional seat or even sheriff's office can also bring voters to the polls. Consequently, if turnout became the basis for drawing districts, there might be an accompanying obligation to make districts equally competitive.[36]

Second, as the enthusiasm surrounding Barack Obama's candidacy demonstrated, numbers of registrants and turnout can increase dramatically in a short period of time. Figures from the 2009 New Jersey and Virginia elections show that participation rates can also fall precipitously as African Americans and young voters inspired by Obama failed to turn out for state contests. In light of the political bloodletting that invariably accompanies redistricting and the time often required to pass a plan, legislators would hate to have to redistrict after each election, or at least after each presidential election, to adjust for variations in participation. If adjustments came only once a decade, as they currently do, then (to return to the first point) districts that had hotly contested elections—perhaps triggered by the death or retirement of the incumbent—in the election year used as the basis for redistricting would be advantaged (be drawn to include fewer people), while those in which an established incumbent ran unopposed would be penalized as they expanded to include more people.

## ALLOCATION OF PRISONERS

For the most part, when it comes to redistricting, people are allocated to the places where they voluntarily have chosen to live. As an exception to this rule, most states count prisoners where their cells are even though no one could contend that the incarcerated have chosen their place of residence. As the numbers of individuals held in state and federal prisons have risen, the distortions caused by prison gerrymandering have increased.

Critics have challenged the practice of allocating prisoners to the counties in which they are housed as a violation of the one person, one vote precept of the early 1960s redistricting decisions. In some states the practice seemingly violates state law, which considers a person's place of residence as dictated by a voluntary choice so that even living somewhere else is not the official residence if the absence is temporary and the person intends to return to the previous address.

The problem with counting inmates where they are held rather than where they last lived when free is twofold. Specifically, for redistricting, it transfers population from urban to rural areas since most new prisons have been built in rural communities where land acquisition costs less and the prison may provide an economic stimulus. In the short run, there will be construction jobs associated with the building of the facility, but in the longer run, there will be jobs for guards and other support staff. Once operational, the prison population will bolster communities that have seen young people leaving for the improved job prospects offered by cities. Most of the inmates, like disproportionate shares of the population, come from cities and, upon release, will return. In much of the country, counting prisoners at the site of incarceration bolsters Republican areas at the expense of Democratic ones. In large metropolitan areas, the loss of the prison population may cost the community one or more seats in the legislature.[37]

Accompanying the loss of representation in the legislature is the loss of a share of the billions of dollars in federal revenues distributed on a per capita basis. The rural communities that house the prisons need the funds just as do the urban areas from which prisoners tend to come, but prisoners reap no benefits from money going to local governments just outside the walls that confine them. In light of the urban–rural nature of the issue, it is not surprising that this issue is often seen through a partisan lens, with Republicans preferring to count prisoners where they are incarcerated and Democrats wanting them allocated to their address prior to the cell block.

The potential for distortions that extend from using prison populations for apportioning seats is especially great when it comes to districts for city councils, county commissions, school boards, and other local bodies. Instances in which prisoners constituted the bulk of a local district's population have existed, with the extreme case coming in a district in an Iowa town where 96 percent of the population was incarcerated.[38]

Recognizing the potential distortion of having a prison dominate a district, hundreds of local governments have opted not to count the imprisoned population when drawing districts. Several states beginning with Maryland and New York in 2011 have now followed suit. The U.S. Supreme Court

allowed Maryland's No Representation without Population Act that awards
the prison population to the jurisdiction from which the inmates came to
stand.[39] Other states that count prisoners where they came from include New
York, California, Colorado, Delaware, Nevada, New Jersey, Virginia, and
Washington.


## CONSEQUENCES ON ONE PERSON, ONE VOTE

As noted at the outset of this chapter, the Illinois plaintiffs' brought the
*Colegrove* case because voters living in different parts of a state had unequal
influence. Those who lived in underpopulated, rural districts had greater
influence than those who lived in overpopulated, urban districts since each
vote in an underpopulated district had more weight in determining electoral
outcomes. Overpopulated urban districts elected fewer legislators than under
a fairly apportioned plan and therefore had less ability to pass legislation that
would benefit cities and their suburbs.

An important consequence of urban underrepresentation was thought to
be receipt of state funds. A leader in the Florida House, which for decades
was run by and for the benefit of the rural, north Florida Park Chop Gang,
justified his legislature's allocation formula. "I believe in collecting taxes
where the money is—in the cities—and spending it where it's needed—in
the country."[40]

The requirement that states equalize populations among districts after
what had frequently been decades of inaction produced dramatic changes in
the makeup of most legislatures. Immediately following the early redistricting decisions of the 1960s, the number of rural legislators declined while
those from urban areas increased. Now, suburban areas increasingly benefit
from decennial redistricting, with rural areas continuing to lose representation and many cities also getting fewer legislators. Those changes have
resulted in fewer farmers and small town merchants serving in the legislature often being replaced by owners of small businesses and community
activists.

Critics of the inequities that resulted from the silent gerrymander had
high expectations for the Redistricting Revolution. They anticipated that as
metropolitan areas gained seats, legislatures would pass more progressive
legislation. Early research done on the consequences of equalizing populations among legislative districts threw cold water on those hopes. Studies
that used equity of apportionment as an independent variable generally
found that a fairer distribution of legislative seats did not correlate positively
with more spending on public schools or welfare programs or the needs of
large cities.[41]

While the general thrust of the early research suggested that equitable apportionment had little effect, some researchers did identify consequences of redistricting. Not surprisingly, reapportionment increased the frequency with which urban legislators appeared on the winning side of roll calls.[42] States with more equitably apportioned legislatures tended to spend more on higher education and housing programs.[43] Redistricting resulted in legislatures becoming more supportive of consumers, the environment, and civil rights.[44]

A correlate of more equal distribution of representation was a more equal distribution of state funding. Not surprisingly, before the Redistricting Revolution, rural counties overrepresented in the state legislature received a disproportionate share of state funding as the Florida legislator cited above believed they should.[45] Scholarship has shown that following redistricting, counties that received additional representation began getting a more proportionate share of the state's dollars. The amount of money redistributed was far from trivial. "The cumulative effect was to shift approximately $7 billion annually towards counties that had been under-represented prior to the imposition of the one-person, one-vote."[46] Not only did redistricting shift the allocation of state funds, federal funds also flowed more generously to urban areas at the expense of rural areas.[47] McCubbins and Schwartz summarized, "Equal votes produced equal distribution of money." Crop supports for farmers became less of a congressional priority, while Congress increasingly turned its attention to the concerns of consumers and environmentalists. The authors emphasize that "In transferring political power from rural to metropolitan areas, redistricting was the enzyme for the organization of consumer and environmental interests."[48]

In the South, shifting seats from rural counties to urban areas opened the way for the election of the first African American legislators in decades. When legislators had represented entire counties, urban voters sent whites to fill their few seats, while in rural areas, obstacles to participation such as literacy tests, poll taxes, and intimidation sufficiently reduced the black electorate so that, even in majority-black counties, whites won the legislative seats. But when urban areas got their proportionate share of the seats in single-member systems, African Americans dominated some districts and, with fewer obstacles to participation in urban areas, they began to win seats.

Note that the Voting Rights Act, initially passed in 1965, coincides with the onset of the Redistricting Revolution. The protections extended by the federal government in much of the South removed the literacy, good character, and understanding tests that had minimized black registration. Once African Americans could register and vote, they began to translate their new political power into legislative seats. The last struggle in the effort to secure fair representation for urban areas often involved a switch to single-member districts rather than electing all legislators from multi-member, countywide districts. That issue got resolved at different times in different southern states, with Mississippi being the last state to make single-member districts widespread and, once it did so, black members in the state House jumped from four to fifteen.[49]

The introduction of minorities into state legislatures resulted in new issues appearing on the policy agenda. Even if minority legislators could not attract enough allies to adopt their preferences, their views and concerns often differed from those of the white, frequently rural legislators of the past.[50]

A third change from redistributing seats to reflect population promoted the political party which had greater strength in the cities than the countryside. Redrawing congressional districts outside the South eliminated what had been a Republican bias. The causes for this change were twofold. First, Democrats enjoyed exceptional political success in winning state legislative seats in 1964 when Barry Goldwater's presidential bid proved unpopular even with many traditional Republican voters. Thus the legislatures responsible for reacting to suits filed pursuant to *Wesberry* were much more likely to be Democratic than if the Redistricting Revolution had come earlier.[51] Second, the courts that passed on the constitutionality of districting plans disproportionately had judges with Democratic leanings and the partisan orientation of the judge influenced how the jurist reacted to challenges to the existing plans.

While the 1964 election with the Lyndon Johnson coattails helped Democrats win state legislative seats, two years later a reaction favoring Republicans occurred. The swing back toward the GOP in 1966, along with continued redrawing of state legislative districts, resulted in the 1966 elections recording the greatest number of state legislative chambers changing partisan hands at least since 1940.[52] Thirty of seventy-seven non-southern, partisan legislative chambers underwent a change in their majority. Outside the South, increasing representation for urban areas frequently advantaged Democrats but not in all states, as Persily and his collaborators point out.[53] In the North and West, farmers and small town merchants tended to vote Republican. While Republicans might also have substantial strength in urban areas, Democrats were relatively stronger there than in the rural parts of the state and consequently benefited from the new urban districts.

In the South, Republicans tended to be the beneficiaries. While Democrats maintained overwhelming majorities in southern legislatures into the 1990s and well beyond in some states, Republican presidential candidates began attracting urban voters in the 1950s. With reappointment, additional seats went to suburbs where a white-collar labor force fresh from the Midwest or Northeast had recently settled. These imported voters, who had brought their

Republican loyalties along with their household goods, enthusiastically sent Republicans to the legislature.

The *Reynolds* decision that both of a state's chambers must be based on population eliminated an alternative rationale for legislative districts. Indeed some states nested House districts within Senate districts. As Persily and his colleagues show, following implementation of *Reynolds* changes, the legislative chambers within a state came to look much more alike in terms of their partisan composition.[54]

## CONTROVERSY

In this and the next three chapters, each of which deals with standards considered for redistricting, the chapter concludes with continuing arguments over the standards that have been adopted. To some extent this reviews the reason for the standards that have been imposed by courts and juxtaposes against those rationales the arguments that have come from opponents.

### Arguments For

Population equality has been the foremost consideration in redistricting ever since the federal judiciary stepped in to regulate what had been exclusively a matter for state legislatures. Ensuring that each voter has an equal influence in selecting legislators has an obvious appeal. Each vote counts equally when electing executives from president or governor and down to mayor, so why should votes not count equally when selecting those who pass the laws?

Requiring that congressional districts zero out population differences or come very close to doing so may seem ridiculous in light of the acknowledged failure to count everyone. However, setting tolerances for population deviations can, as Georgia demonstrated when redistricting its state legislative districts, result in many districts being at the upper limits of the acceptable deviations, as show in figure 6.3.

The consequences of the silent gerrymanders that distorted most state's congressional delegations and state legislatures resulted in rural areas exercising inordinate influence. Rural dominance meant that urban and suburban interests got short shrift even as they became home to increasing shares of states' populations and had growing needs for state and federal aid.

Using some basis other than total population as the basis for allocating legislative seats fails to recognize the relationship between non-voters and the government. Children don't vote, but they rely on public support for education. An apportionment scheme that utilized adults or registrants would likely result in less representation for areas with larger shares of school kids and consequently less support for education funding. Retirees in some communities have been less willing to vote for school funding. If state or federal funding formulae were to be linked to an apportioning scheme that used something other than population, less money would go to some of the poorest districts.

The practice of counting prisoners where they are serving time deprives the communities from which they came, to which they hope to return, and which they consider their home of political influence, and dollars distributed on a per capita basis. Many local governments do not consider prisoners temporarily confined in their jurisdiction as citizens when drawing districts. States should adopt the same practice when designing congressional and state legislative district.

While the drafters of the federal Constitution had to allow small states greater influence than large states in the Senate in order to devise a plan acceptable as a replacement for the Articles of Confederation, no such compromise had been required in the individual states. Consequently the Supreme Court could assert that all state legislators should represent people and not acres, trees, or farm animals.

## Arguments Against

If the objective is for each district to have equal influence, then focusing on populations misses the mark. Because of differences in the concentrations of non-citizens, children, felons, and the politically apathetic, voters in some districts have much greater influence than in other districts even after equalizing populations among districts. For example, in 2018 in Texas congressional elections, the number of votes cast ranged from just under 117,000 in two districts to 353,617 in the 21st District. Similar ranges occurred in other large states with, for example, as few as 113,616 votes cast in California-21 to 340,654 in the Golden State's 4th District. Alexandria Ocasio-Cortez's district had 129,520 votes, the second lowest in New York, while in the 19th District, 280,746 votes were tallied. If the objective is for voters to have equal influence then at a minimum it is citizen, voting-age populations and not total populations that should be equalized. Drawing districts with equal numbers of registrants would come still closer to equalizing the weight of each vote. The closest approximation might come from drawing districts with little deviation in the numbers of votes cast in the most recent presidential election.

The *Karcher* decision's push for minimal population deviations among a state's congressional districts rests on an untenable assumption. The failure to count all Americans with the poor and minorities especially likely to be overlooked means that districts actually lack equal numbers of people even in plans that have zeroed out population differences. Even if districts have equal numbers of people when counted in the census, by the time states get the census data and draw districts, the figures are outdated as new housing has sprung up on what had been vacant lots or farmland at the time of the census and some dwellings inhabited at the time of the census have been abandoned. Think of the devastation wrought by Hurricane Katrina on the housing stock of New Orleans and other low-lying areas along the Gulf Coast.

Judicial demands for miniscule population deviations have an artificial ring and carry costs. Efforts to eliminate population deviations prolong redistricting sessions, and when even the smallest population differences provide the basis for judicial challenges that can cost jurisdictions millions of dollars in attorney's fees.

The demand that plans zero out population differences creates new opportunities to gerrymander. The emphasis on eliminating trivial population differences necessitates dividing counties, cities, and communities of interest that would much prefer to remain united in a single district. Splitting a community among two or more districts may reduce its influence in the legislature as it plays a smaller role in the electoral fortunes of the legislators who represent parts of it than it would in one legislator's constituency. An alternative argument that a community split between two legislators may have two people who will promote its interests may be correct for populous cities or counties but unlikely to hold true for small communities.

Prisoners are like college students in that they are temporarily living in a community that they may not consider to be their permanent address. For this reason prisoners should be allocated to the jurisdiction where they find themselves when the census is conducted.

At least during the early days of the Redistricting Revolution, people living in counties that no longer had a local resident representing them expressed alienation and frustration.[55] They doubted whether their new legislator who lived in a neighboring county would look out for their interests and they began plying the governor with requests for assistance. Residents of small counties who can never send one of their own to the legislature because of the electoral dominance of a larger neighbor may be more likely to question whether the government responds to the needs of people like them.

## CONCLUSIONS

In two generations, the population standards for districting plans have gone from tolerating as wide a variation in district populations as a state chose to permit to pressing toward zero deviation. The gross disparities such as those cited early in this chapter gave rural voters a disproportionate influence in legislatures and over the shaping of public policy.

Courts gradually forced jurisdictions to minimize the deviations in district populations. For congressional districts, the perspective of the high court has been that all citizens should have equal representation and that value has made it increasingly difficult to justify deviations from absolute equality. Courts have pressed toward this standard of absolute equality even while acknowledging that problems in getting a full and accurate census count coupled with population shifts make absolute equality more myth than reality. The problem of the census missing some residents, particularly poorer ones, is widely acknowledged. The explosive growth in some suburban areas means that from the taking of the census in April until legislatures get around to drawing districts more than a year later will likely result in underrepresentation of some suburban voters in the new plans.

The courts have continued to accept more population deviation for collegial bodies below the U.S. House. For years it appeared that these districts could deviate from the ideal population by as much as +/- 5 percent. Drawing districts with that level of population deviation, however, does not make them immune to a challenge, as Georgia learned in 2004.

# Chapter 3

# Minorities and Redistricting

A redistricting plan violates the Voting Rights Act if it simply has a discriminatory result.[1]

Within the Division, the failure to maximize came to be regarded as evidence of purposeful discrimination.[2]

We do not insist that a legislature guess precisely what percentage reduction a court or the Justice Department might eventually find to be retrogressive. The law cannot insist that a state legislature, when redistricting, determine precisely what percent minority population §5 demands. The standards of §5 are complex; they often require evaluation of controverted claims about voting behavior; the evidence may be unclear; and, with respect to any particular district, judges may disagree about the proper outcome. The law cannot lay a trap for an unwary legislature, condemning its redistricting plan as either (1) unconstitutional racial gerrymandering should the legislature place a few too many minority voters in a district or (2) retrogressive under §5 should the legislature place a few too few.[3]

The consequences of districting plans for minorities and their reactions to the districting process have varied greatly over time. This chapter takes a largely chronological approach to organize the materials relating to the relationship between minorities and districting plans. In the days before the one person, one vote court decisions, plans in most states, especially in the South, disadvantaged minorities. In some instances the disadvantage was not based on an intention to discriminate against minorities but stemmed from the failure to adjust boundaries to reflect population shifts. As America became less reliant

on agriculture for its economic success, the nation's black population moved
to the cities. Some share of this migration combined a move to the city with
a departure from the Jim Crow South to Detroit, Chicago, New York, and
other northern cities that provided greater opportunities for better jobs, better
schools, and a better life. To the extent that districting plans disadvantaged
urban America, they resulted in fewer districts in the areas where minorities
concentrated.

In the wake of *Baker v. Carr, Wesberry v. Sanders,* and the one person, one
vote, requirements placing more seats in urban areas witnessed the election of
the first blacks to southern state legislatures in decades. In large urban areas
with substantial minority concentrations, single-member district plans produced majority-black districts and these elected African Americans. Change
did not always come early as some southern legislatures and communities
cracked minority concentrations in an effort to eliminate or at least minimize
the likelihood that a black could be elected. Some jurisdictions that had utilized single-member districts shifted to at-large elections at the local level to
make it harder for minorities to win office.

Implementation of Section 5 of the Voting Rights Act ensured that districts
which had become majority black would not be redrawn to eliminate the
black majority. Later, this provision, which until 2013 covered all of nine
states and portions of seven others, forced the creation of additional minority districts. In the early 1990s, the Department of Justice demanded that
jurisdictions subject to Section 5 maximize the number of districts in which
a racial minority would constitute a majority of the electorate. Affirmative
action gerrymandering generated an unprecedented number of new majority-minority districts. These new districts sent record numbers of African
Americans to Congress.

By the turn of the twenty-first century, a number of black political leaders
had embraced new objectives. Into the 1990s their top priority had been to
maximize the number of districts likely to be won by a minority candidate.
In 2001, the top priority in some states shifted to protecting the Democratic
majority in the legislature, even if that meant reassigning minority voters
to bolster the electoral prospects of white Democrats. In the 2010s, African
American plaintiffs in areas where a Democrat could expect to attract sufficient white votes alleged racial gerrymanders as they sought to reduce black
concentrations below those set when the state redistricted.

## IMPACT OF ONE PERSON, ONE VOTE

For decades African Americans left the South for the greater freedom and
opportunities in northern cities. In 1960, the black population had reached

23 percent in Chicago, 14 percent in Los Angeles, 29 percent in Detroit, and 14 percent in New York. Among African Americans who remained in the South, many had sought better paying jobs in cities. The 1960 census showed Atlanta to be 38 percent black, while New Orleans was 37 percent black and Birmingham's black population approached 40 percent.

The pervasive underrepresentation of urban areas reduced the number of legislative seats that might be placed in heavily black neighborhoods, and, consequently, reduced opportunities—in the South it eliminated opportunities—for African American representation in the state legislature. While the Latino population in 1960 was heavily concentrated along the Mexican border and still largely rural, had the Redistricting Revolution not taken place, this group would in time also have suffered from the failure to redraw legislative districts to reflect urbanization.

Shifting legislative seats to metropolitan areas provided the first opportunities for African Americans to elect members of their race to southern legislatures since the massive disenfranchisement that took place around the turn of the twentieth century.[4] While each southern state had one or more majority black counties, meaning that a county-based apportionment scheme might result in the election of black legislators, Jim Crow barriers proved so insurmountable that no rural blacks had won legislative seats in half a century. Conditions in the rural South prior to the Civil Rights Revolution fit with the "black threat hypothesis" from V. O. Key.[5] Based on his extensive study of southern politics in the middle of the twentieth century, Key observed that white resistance to black political and economic progress varied directly with the proportion of blacks in the local population, so that African Americans had the fewest rights in the most heavily black areas. Consequently it was in the majority-black counties where barriers to political participation proved most impenetrable. White opposition stemmed from a realization that, should political rights be extended to African Americans, the jurisdiction would likely be governed by blacks or at least by the candidates for whom blacks voted. With blacks barred from polling places, the county-based districting schemes saw overwhelmingly black counties elected white legislators.

With the onset of equally populated districts, minorities faced new challenges. The same tactics used to disadvantage a minority party can be and have been employed to limit the influence of racial or ethnic minorities. District lines can split or crack minority concentrations so as to deny them any representation.[6] Alternatively, where minority concentrations are too large to deny them any representation, the number of legislative seats they are likely to win can be reduced by packing the minority population into one or a few districts rather than adopting alternative plans that, by distributing the minority population more broadly, would likely result in a greater number of seats being controlled by those voters. Finally, the widespread use of multi-member plans at the time of the Redistricting Revolution often stacked the decks against the minority population, so that its candidates lost in each of a series of head-to-head contests where, if single-member districts were drawn, the minority population would stand a good chance of electing its preferred candidate in at least one of those districts.

An early challenge to multi-member districts involved Marion County, Indiana, which includes Indianapolis. The eight senators and fifteen representatives from Marion County all ran countrywide, resulting in twenty-three head-to-head contests forcing each candidate to campaign throughout the county. This arrangement frequently resulted in a one-party sweep. Although the county had a substantial black population, African Americans rarely won seats to the legislature because they ran as members of the minority (Democratic) party, which consistently lost countywide.[7] A single-member system would have anchored some seats in black neighborhoods where black Democrats could have won. While the trial court found for the plaintiffs and threw out the multi-member plan, the Supreme Court allowed it to stand because partisanship and not race explained the electoral outcomes. The Supreme Court acknowledged that when racial or partisan minorities compete countrywide, they were less likely to win than if the county had a series of single-member districts, some of which would be dominated by the minority.

A couple of years later, in another opinion written by Justice Byron White, the Supreme Court reached a very different conclusion from its Indiana holding.[8] The high court upheld a lower court decision that required replacing at-large districts in two Texas counties with single-member districts. The Court pointed to the infrequency of victories by African Americans in Dallas County or Latinos in Bexar County. The opinion reviewed examples of discrimination that had confronted blacks and Latinos in these counties before concluding that while partisanship accounted for the defeat of African Americans in Indianapolis, discrimination thwarted minorities' political ambitions in Texas.

At almost exactly the same time the Supreme Court launched the Redistricting Revolution, Congress passed the Voting Rights Act. This 1965 legislation, which was renewed four times, authorized federal officials to serve as guardians of black political interests during redistricting in selected states. Amendments to the VRA in 1975 extended protections to language minorities as will be described later. A subsequent amendment to the Voting Rights Act in 1982 broadened the scope of the federal protection against racial gerrymandering so that it applies nationally. The next section explores how federal law has invalidated efforts to minimize minority influence through redistricting.

## SECTION 5

The 1965 Voting Rights Act followed three attempts to facilitate black registration. The Civil Rights Acts of 1957, 1960, and 1964 had produced modest improvements in black registration rates in the region so that in 1964, only 43 percent of the South's black adults had registered to vote.[9] A frustrated President Lyndon Johnson directed his attorney general, Nicholas Katzenbach, to draft "the goddamndest, toughest voting rights law you can devise."[10] Katzenbach's design froze existing practices relating to registration and participation in selected states and required that any changes in the laws regulating registration or voting in those jurisdictions receive federal approval before implementation. He anticipated that requiring federal pre-approval for changes would prevent southern jurisdictions from designing new obstacles to black participation, thus avoiding the dilatory practices that had thwarted school desegregation during the previous decade.

The Voting Rights Act (VRA) involved an unprecedented intervention of the federal government in what had been exclusively a state responsibility. Aside from the constitutional guarantees of the right of women and African Americans to vote, conduct of voter registration activities had been left to the states and, in reality, typically to local officials in county registration offices. Given the intrusion of federal authority into what had been a local responsibility, the scope of jurisdictions to be covered was carefully drawn. The jurisdictions that would need federal approval prior to implementing changes in their registration or voting laws, a procedure called *preclearance*, had long records of discriminating against prospective black voters. The preclearance provision is also frequently referred to as Section 5 because it appears in that part of the VRA.

Section 4 of the VRA set forth a two-part test to identify jurisdictions needing preclearance. Jurisdictions had to obtain preclearance if less than half of their voting age population had registered or voted in the 1964 presidential election *and* they had a test or device as a prerequisite for voter registration. The tests or devices included a literacy test, an understanding test, or a good character test. The legislation did not include poll taxes as a test or device. The two-part test made Alabama, Georgia, Louisiana, Mississippi, South Carolina, Virginia, and a little more than a third of North Carolina's counties subject to preclearance.

Preclearance of laws relating to voting or registration could be pursued in either of two ways. A jurisdiction could submit proposed changes to the attorney general, who had sixty days in which to review the matter. If the attorney general objected to the proposal, the jurisdiction had to go back to the drawing board and redesign the proposal to meet the federal objections. The alternative approach allowed jurisdictions to ask the district court of the

District of Columbia for a declaratory judgment that the proposed change did not discriminate against African Americans. If the attorney general rejected a jurisdiction's proposal, it could appeal to the court in the District of Columbia. No changes could be implemented until approved through one of these two approaches.

During the latter half of the 1960s as the one person, one vote revolution got under way, the need for preclearance did not apply to redistricting. The covered jurisdictions and, seemingly, the DOJ, applied the preclearance requirement only to proposals that changed the conditions under which prospective voters went about registering or voting and, since drawing districts did not directly affect registration or turnout, jurisdictions did not need to secure preclearance for their new plans.

The DOJ became more aggressive after 1969 when the Supreme Court gave a broad interpretation to the Voting Rights Act preclearance requirement. In *Allen v. State Board of Elections*, the Court held that Mississippi jurisdictions needed to secure preclearance before changing the electoral structure of county supervisors from districts to at-large, before making the position of county superintendent of education an appointive rather than an elective office, and before changing the criteria that must be met for a candidate to run as an Independent.[11] None of these changes related to requirements for individuals seeking to register or cast votes and, therefore, the Mississippi jurisdictions had not sought preclearance. These changes did, however, affect the ability of minorities to elect their preferred candidates. In explaining its decision, the Court took language from the redistricting cases that had discussed the importance of having a "meaningful" vote. Drawing on *Reynolds v. Sims*, the Court observed that "The right to vote can be affected by dilution of voting power as well as by the absolute prohibition on casting a ballot." The court took an expansive view of Section 5 observing that

> We must reject a narrow construction that appellees would give to Section 5. The Voting Rights Act was aimed at the subtle, as well as the obvious, state regulations that have the effect of denying citizens their right to vote because of their race.

While the *Allen* decision broadened the scope of the VRA, it did not specifically address the issue of redistricting which came up in 1973. DOJ rejected Georgia's initial state House plan and found a remedial effort inadequate. At that point, Georgia refused to submit any further plans, arguing that Section 5 did not apply to redistricting since the legislation made no mention of that activity. Moreover, the state contended that even if Section 5 did apply to redistricting, a plan could be rejected only if DOJ found it to be discriminatory and DOJ had not reached that conclusion. The Supreme

Court rejected Georgia's contentions.[12] The Court referred back to *Reynolds v. Sims* which had discussed vote dilution in the context of urban votes often having less weight or influence than those of rural voters. Moreover, the court pointed out that Congress had not objected to the Supreme Court decision in *Allen* when renewing Section 5 in 1970 and thus had given tacit consent to the Supreme Court's ruling broadening the applicability of Section 5. The Court also rejected the state's claim that a plan had to be approved unless DOJ showed it to be discriminatory. The Court noted that had Georgia followed the judicial route and sought a declaratory judgment from the court in Washington, D.C., the state would have had the burden of proof. This burden of proving that its actions did not discriminate also extended to administrative submissions to DOJ.

## Retrogression

The Supreme Court set forth the standard for assessing the impact of new plans on minority political strength. The Court clarified that while Congress designed Section 5 to prevent harm to minorities, it could not be used as an affirmative tool. DOJ had rejected a plan for New Orleans that made two districts majority black by population where previously there had been none. DOJ objected to the new plan because blacks did not constitute a majority of the registered voters in both of these districts. The Supreme Court held that Section 5 prohibits only *retrogression*, meaning that as long as a new plan did not leave black voters worse off than the status quo, DOJ must approve the proposal.[13] Even though an alternative plan might result in African Americans having greater political influence, *Beer v. U.S* held that Section 5 created no obligation to maximize the political influence of minorities. In the 1980s, the first redistricting round after *Beer*, efforts to protect seats currently held by minorities frequently helped the Democratic Party.[14]

## Consequences of Early Redistricting

Even though jurisdictions had no obligation to draw additional minority districts, the consequences of the initial implementation of districting plans equalizing populations had a dramatic impact on black representation in most southern legislatures. After decades of failing to adjust for population shifts, the first equal-population plans often increased black representation. Placing additional seats in urban areas promoted black office holding because some of the new urban districts had black population majorities. In states subject to Section 5 a dramatic increase occurred as the number of blacks serving in lower chambers more than tripled from nineteen to sixty, as shown in table 3.1. Excluding Georgia, where Atlanta's black concentration coupled

Table 3.1 The 1970s Redistricting and the Increase in the Numbers of African Americans Elected to Lower Chambers of Southern Legislatures

| State | 1969 | After 1970 Redistricting |
|---|---|---|
| **Section 5 States** | | |
| Alabama | 2 | 13 |
| Georgia | 12 | 19 |
| Louisiana | 1 | 8 |
| Mississippi | 1 | 4 |
| North Carolina | 1 | 3 |
| South Carolina | 0 | 12 |
| Virginia | 2 | 1 |
| Total | 19 | 60 |
| **Non–Section 5 States as of 1972** | | |
| Arkansas | 0 | 3 |
| Florida | 1 | 3 |
| Tennessee | 6 | 9 |
| Texas | 2 | 8 |
| Total | 9 | 23 |

*Source*: Author.

with the region's largest legislature and adoption of single-member districts in urban areas facilitated the election of African Americans in the previous decade, the increase in Section 5 states is even more impressive. In the Alabama House the number of black legislators jumped from two to thirteen following redistricting. Redistricting saw the first dozen African Americans elected to the South Carolina House, and in Louisiana the number grew from one to eight. In states not subject to Section 5 as of 1972, the number of black representatives grew from nine to twenty-three. The need to secure preclearance also increased black representation on many city and county collegial bodies.[15]

Section 5 of the VRA came up for renewal in 1975. Latinos, who had monitored the effectiveness of Section 5 in increasing the numbers of black officeholders, used the opportunity for renewal to press Congress to expand the scope of the legislation to include language minorities. The 1975 amendments to the VRA included a new trigger that extended coverage to jurisdictions in which less than half of the voting age citizens had registered or participated in the 1972 presidential election and in which registration and election materials had been available only in English where at least 5 percent of the adult citizens belonged to a single language minority group. Thus, for example, if at least 5 percent of the adult citizens in a county or state primarily spoke Spanish and the election-related materials had not been published in Spanish, and fewer than half of the adults had voted in 1972, the jurisdiction now had to comply with Section 5 preclearance. This amendment extended Section 5 coverage to all of Alaska, Arizona, and Texas along with five Florida counties, two New York counties, three California counties, and selected counties in South Dakota and Michigan. Jurisdictions covered by the 1965 trigger continued to have to secure preclearance.

Once jurisdictions with substantial Latino populations subject to Section 5 had to secure preclearance, the numbers of districts likely to elect Hispanics increased. In the Texas House, immediately following the 1982 redistricting, the number of Latino members rose from seventeen to twenty-one.

## SECTION 2

In 1982, in addition to extending Section 5 for a quarter of a century, Congress added a new provision to the VRA that applied nationwide. Congress rewrote Section 2, which had previously been nothing more than a restatement of the Fifteenth Amendment. The objective of the rewrite reduced the evidentiary burden on plaintiffs challenging *existing* electoral systems. Recall that Section 5 applied only to selected jurisdictions seeking to make changes and, consequently, when no changes were attempted, Section 5 had no role. For example, Section 5 did not help minorities unable to elect their preferred candidates in a city that had used at-large elections prior to congressional adoption of the VRA. Of course if plaintiffs could prove that a jurisdiction had intended to discriminate against minorities, then the jurisdiction could prevail either under the Fourteenth or Fifteenth Amendments to the Constitution. Section 2 eliminated the requirement that plaintiffs prove an intent to discriminate in order to force a change in an existing electoral structure. All that plaintiffs needed to demonstrate under Section 2 was that an electoral system provided minorities less opportunity to participate in the political process and to elect their preferred candidates than whites had. While a caveat warned that Section 2 did not require that minorities be represented on governing bodies in proportion to their share of the population, wide disparities between the minority percentage in the electorate and holding elective office frequently triggered litigation.

The impetus for rewriting Section 2 came from a Supreme Court decision that allowed Mobile, Alabama, to elect all commissioners citywide.[16] Although Mobile's population was almost 40 percent black, no African American had won a seat on the city commission. The Supreme Court ruled against the plaintiffs because they failed to prove that the at-large electoral system, which dated from 1911, had been adopted or maintained for discriminatory purposes.

Since the jurisdiction had no obligation to have minorities serving in roughly the same proportion as in the population, Congress identified a set of factors for judges to consider when hearing suits brought under Section 2.

These elements came from problems uncovered in voting rights litigation. The seven major factors and two subsidiary ones constituted what became known as the totality-of-the-circumstances test. The seven elements of the totality of the circumstances are:

(1)  Has there been a history of official discrimination in the jurisdiction that makes it harder for minorities to register or vote?
(2)  Is there evidence of racially polarized voting?
(3)  Have members of the minority community won elections in the jurisdiction?
(4)  Have slating groups discriminated against minorities when backing candidates?
(5)  Are there lingering consequences of past discrimination such as school segregation?
(6)  Have candidates made racial appeals in previous elections?
(7)  Has the jurisdiction made use of factors that may have enhanced the impact of other elements and made it harder for minorities to succeed politically? Among the enhancing factors are unusually large electoral districts, a majority vote requirement, and a prohibition on single-shot voting.

Two secondary factors that the courts might consider in a Section 2 suit are:

(1)  Whether local elected officials had been responsive to the policy requests coming from the minority community.
(2)  Whether the political practice being challenged is standard for the state or is something extraordinary.

Congress specified that judges should not simply count up the number of items on which the plaintiffs prove their case and the number on which the defendants' evidence is more compelling. Nor need the courts give equal weight to each of the items. Finally, courts could also consider additional evidence; the items in the totality-of-the-circumstances test should not be considered exhaustive.

Immediately after the enactment of Section 2, voting rights attorneys began challenging at-large and multi-member electoral systems across the nation. In *Thornburg v. Gingles*, the first case to work its way through the judicial system and come before the Supreme Court, the majority opinion established a three-part test that plaintiffs must meet in order to prevail.[17] The first prong of the *Gingles* test requires that plaintiffs demonstrate that the minority group seeking relief is sufficiently large and compact to form a majority of the adult population in a single-member district that could be carved out of the existing arrangement. In meeting this test, the plan offered by the plaintiffs can have no more districts than the number of officials currently elected at-large or from a multi-member district.[18] If it is impossible to create a district in which the minority group would dominate, then the court saw no way in which relief could be provided. The second prong requires that the plaintiffs prove political cohesion, which means that the group bringing the suit usually unites behind the same candidates. If the plaintiff minority group is not politically cohesive, then it may be losing elections because it fails to coalesce behind particular candidates. The third prong requires a showing that when the minority group has united behind candidates, those individuals usually lose as a result of a bloc vote by whites. If the plaintiffs successfully meet the three prongs of *Gingles* test, then the court will review the factors in the totality of the circumstances test.

The Supreme Court set forth the three-prong *Gingles* test in a challenge to North Carolina's multi-member legislative districts. Seven years later, the Court extended the test to efforts to reconfigure existing single-member arrangements.[19] As a consequence of the literally hundreds of challenges filed pursuant to Section 2, the number of local collegial bodies that have single-member districts has increased, which necessitates adjusting their boundaries to equalize population after each census. Multi-member districts that once dominated state lower chambers have now become rare and except in areas where minorities are too scarce to be able to meet the first *Gingles* prong have disappeared altogether.[20]

## SECTION 2 AND SECTION 5 REVIEWS

Section 2 proved useful beyond challenging at-large and multi-member districting systems. DOJ incorporated Section 2 into reviews of plans submitted by jurisdictions subject to Section 5 following the 1990 census. With Section 2 available, DOJ could enforce affirmative action gerrymandering designed to promote descriptive representation, that is, creating heavily black districts that would be represented by an African American. The Justice Department reasoned that it made no sense to approve a plan that might later be attacked under Section 2 for not providing an equal opportunity for minorities to elect their preferred candidates. Avoiding retrogression no longer sufficed to secure DOJ approval. DOJ even rejected plans that increased the number of majority-minority districts, if additional minority districts could be drawn. Section 2 gave DOJ the leverage to force the creation of majority-minority districts (districts in which most adults belonged to a minority group). The approach adopted by DOJ became known as MAXBLACK since it sought to maximize the number of majority black districts. It often involved pushing jurisdictions to adopt plans prepared by black legislators or groups.

David Lublin demonstrated the link between racial concentrations and the election of minorities to Congress. From 1972 to 1994, African Americans won all but 19 of 219 elections in majority-black districts but only 72 of 5,079 in districts lacking a black majority.[21] Latinos had won 82 of 105 contests in districts in which they constituted a majority but only 29 of 5,190 in districts where they were in the minority. While Lublin's book appeared after DOJ's push for majority-minority districts, it had long been recognized that these offered the surest way to increase the minority presence in legislative bodies.

White southern Democrats objected to the creation of majority black districts. While some of the opposition may have stemmed from racism, white and black Democratic politicians often found themselves competing in a zero-sum game. As conservative, southern, white voters defected to the GOP, white Democratic politicians became increasingly dependent on black votes. As the black percentage in a district's electorate declined, so did prospects for a Democratic victory. Since majority black districts almost always elect African Americans while overwhelmingly white districts in the South elect Republicans, the most optimal districts for white Democrats were in the 30–50 percent black range.[22]

North Carolina illustrates what happened in the early 1990s when DOJ incorporated Section 2 into Section 5 reviews. North Carolina, which had not elected a black member of Congress since 1898, created a majority black district in its 1991 the plan. Despite the absence of retrogression, DOJ refused to preclear the plan because the state could have drawn a second majority black district. While not guilty of retrogression, one black district among a dozen fell far short of the 22 percent black in North Carolina's population and alternative plans contained two majority-black districts.

Georgia and Louisiana encountered similar rejections from DOJ, even though in Georgia's case the plan enhanced black representation by creating a second majority-black district. With two majority-black districts among eleven, African Americans would be in a good position to elect 18 percent of Georgia's members of Congress. However, by forcing Georgia to develop a plan with three majority-black districts, the potential to elect 27 percent of the delegation would match the black percentage in the state's adult population.

Relatively early in the redistricting process, DOJ warned jurisdictions that did not have to get preclearance that they must now comply with the Department's interpretation of Section 2. The assistant attorney general for civil rights announced, "We plan to exercise our authority under Section 2 and examine plans adopted in states not subject to Section 5 review."[23]

In order to maximize the number of majority-minority districts, jurisdictions often had to link geographically separated minority concentrations. The requirement that districts have equal populations meant that a cartographer connecting pockets of minority voters would have to avoid including too

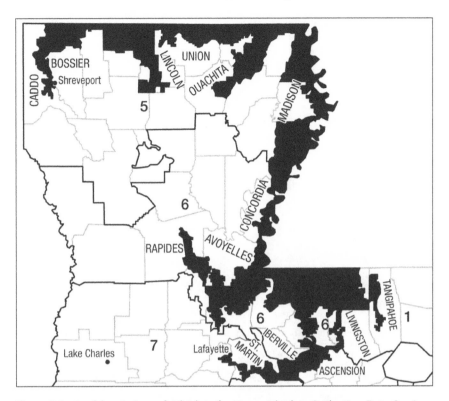

**Figure 3.1 Louisiana's Second District, the Zorro District.** © Election Data Services, Inc. (www.electiondataservices.com)

many whites lest the population become too large. These plans produced some exceptionally convoluted districts, as shown in figure 3.1 where a 620-mile long Louisiana congressional district combined black populations in five urban areas along with majority black rural parishes bordering the Mississippi River. The weirdly shaped 4th District followed the entire length of the Mississippi River as it separates Louisiana from Mississippi, and almost the entire state boundary between Louisiana and Arkansas to the north. This district became christened the "Zorro" District after a 1950s television show featuring a Robin Hood–type character named Zorro whose trademark was a "Z" slashed with a sword on a piece of fabric that somewhat resembled the district.

Once DOJ had established its expectation that jurisdictions submit plans designed to maximize the number of districts likely to elect minorities, other states took the cue and submitted plans that enhanced minority representation. The affirmative action gerrymanders that resulted from DOJ's incorporation of Section 2 expectations into its Section 5 reviews produced the first majority-black district in Alabama, South Carolina, and Virginia. North

**Table 3.2   New Majority-Minority Districts Created in Section 5 States After the 1990 Census**

|  | Before 1992 | In 1992 | After Challenge |
|---|---|---|---|
| *Black Districts* | | *Percent Black* | |
| AL – 7 | 33 | 67 | unchallenged |
| FL – 3 | 27 | 55 | 50 |
| FL – 17 | 27 | 59 | unchallenged |
| FL – 23 | New | 52 | unchallenged*** |
| GA – 2 | 37 | 57 | 39 |
| GA – 11 | New | 64 | 37 |
| LA – 4 | New | 67 | 31* |
| NC – 1 | 35 | 57 | 50 |
| NC – 12 | New | 57 | 36 |
| SC – 6 | 41 | 62 | settled** |
| TX – 30 | New | 50 | 45 |
| VA – 3 | 28 | 64 | 54 |
| *Hispanic Districts* | | *Percent Hispanic* | |
| FL – 21 | New | 70 | unchallenged |
| NY – 12 | New | 57 | 49 |
| TX – 28 | New | 60 | unchallenged |
| TX – 29 | New | 60 | 45 |

*Sources*: Racial percentages for the districts used in 1992 come from Michael Barone and Grant Ujifusa, *The Almanac of American Politics, 1994* (Washington, DC: National Journal, 1993). The before 1992 racial figures come from Alan Ehrenhalt, ed., *Politics in America, the 100th Congress* (Washington, DC: CQ Press, 1987). The racial figures for districts redrawn after successful challenges come from Michael Barone and Grant Ujifusa, *The Almanac of American Politics, 2000* (Washington, DC: *National Journal*, 1999).
* When redrawn following a successful challenge, this became LA – 5.
** SC – 6 was challenged but resolved before a trial and was not redrawn.
*** Challenge dismissed for being filed too late.

Carolina drew two and Florida created three black districts. Georgia added two majority-black districts, raising its number to three, while Louisiana and Texas each added a second black district. As table 3.2 shows, each of the new black districts drawn in Section 5 states had a black majority population. Districts in Alabama, Louisiana, South Carolina, Virginia, and Georgia's 11th District all had populations more than 60 percent black.

The DOJ reviews in the early 1990s prompted Florida to create a second Latino congressional district, while Texas added two districts with heavy Latino concentrations as shown in table 3.2. New York added a 57 percent Hispanic district that sent the state's second Latino to Congress. Illinois, although not subject to Section 5, drew a 64 percent Latino Chicago district dubbed the "Earmuff District" because of the shape it took to link two Hispanic neighborhoods separated by a black concentration—a design that persists in 2020.

The 1992 elections produced results in line with DOJ expectations. The number of African American members of Congress from the South increased from five to seventeen and Latinos won House seats in three of the four new

Hispanic districts. The one exception, Texas 29, saw an Anglo Democrat defeat a Latino in a contested runoff that featured racially polarized voting.[24] Although Latinos constituted 55 percent of the adults in Texas 29, only 31 percent of the voters had Spanish surnames, indicating that efforts to mobilize Latinos met with little success. Ben Reyes, the first Latino to represent a Houston district in the Texas House, led in the initial primary but lost the runoff when the eventual winner, Gene Green, made an issue of Reyes's bankruptcy and failure to pay taxes. Reyes failed to consolidate the supporters who had backed the Latino candidates eliminated in the first primary.

Some of the gains by minority candidates came at the expense of Anglo incumbents. In Alabama, South Carolina, and North Carolina long-time white representatives chose not to run. Another white Democratic incumbent lost a renomination bid in Georgia-2. In New York, Stephen Solarz, a leading House foreign policy expert who had the largest campaign war chest of any House member, nonetheless lost the Democratic primary to Nadia Velazquez in the new Hispanic district.

## Impact below Congress

Each round of redistricting has facilitated the election of African Americans to southern state legislatures and DOJ's standards for the early 1990s made an additional contribution. Table 3.3 shows pickups by African Americans of southern state House seats in the elections held immediately after a state adopted new maps. While more intensive research would be required before attributing all of these gains to the new maps, the table reports a striking coincidence. In every state except Virginia more than half the number of seats held by blacks in 2017 were initially won in the immediate aftermath of a

Table 3.3    Increases in African-American House Members Following Redistricting

| | 1963 | 1973 | 1983 | 1993 | 2003 | 2013 | Black Members 2017 |
|---|---|---|---|---|---|---|---|
| AL | 0 | 13* | 6* | 8 | 0 | 0 | 27 |
| AR | 0 | 3 | 0 | 5* | 0 | 2 | 12 |
| FL | 1 | 1 | 7 | 0 | 0 | 4 | 20 |
| GA | 7 | 6* | 0 | 4 | 3 | 5 | 47 |
| LA | 1 | 7 | 3 | 9 | 1 | 5 | 24 |
| MS | 1 | 14* | 3 | 9 | 1 | 0 | 36 |
| NC | 1 | 1 | 8 | 4 | 0 | 4 | 24 |
| SC | 0 | 9* | 0 | 7* | 1 | -1 | 28 |
| TN | 6 | 1 | 1 | 2 | 1 | -1 | 14 |
| TX | 2 | 6 | 0 | 1 | 0 | 0 | 16 |
| VA | 2 | 0 | 0 | 0 | 1 | 0 | 13 |

*Source*: Author.
* Figures from two redistrictings during the decade are combined.

redistricting. The numbers of black-held seats in 2017 does not constitute the high water mark in all states and, following the 2010 census, two states saw their number of black legislators decrease while another four states experienced no increases. On the other hand, four states saw black legislators' ranks increase by at least four.

DOJ's demands that states create more black districts in the early 1990s led to additional black-held seats in nine states. Arkansas and Louisiana experienced their greatest increases in African American representatives in that decade. Five other states had their second largest post-redistricting boost in the 1990s. The 1990s saw major increases even in states that had sizable black caucuses. Mississippi, South Carolina, and Alabama, which follow Georgia in terms of numbers of black representatives, each elected at least seven additional African Americans under the 1990s plans. Nationwide the number of black legislators grew from 438 to 523 between 1991 and 1993. The new plans sent one more Latino to the Texas Senate and four to the House while Florida Latinos added two state House seats.

The number of blacks serving on county commissions jumped by more than 10 percent while the number serving on city councils increased by approximately 200 following the 1990 round of redistricting. While it would be inaccurate to attribute all of the increase in minority public officials to redistricting, rearranging boundaries to form majority-minority districts played a major role. In the early 1990s, DOJ rejected 183 redistricting plans,[25] and while the cause for some of these may have been retrogression, the problem with others was their failure to increase the number of districts likely to elect minorities.

## Courts React to DOJ's Use of Section 2

Some observers found the emphasis on creating heavily minority districts offensive. Robinson Everett, a Duke University law professor, went to court challenging North Carolina's 12th District. That district, which appears in figure 3.2, stretched from Gastonia, west of Charlotte, then northward in an arc through High Point and Greensboro to Durham with an arm extending up to the northwest to include the black population of Winston-Salem. Connecting the black neighborhoods in seven cities made a 57 percent black district possible. As it went about linking black concentrations, at some points the district narrowed to include only I-85, thereby avoiding whites and giving the district its popular name, the "I-85 District." As a black legislator observed, the district was so narrow that if someone drove the length of that interstate highway with doors open on both sides of the car it might kill a large share of the district's population. As shown in chapter 4, at several points the I-85 District had only touch-point contiguity.

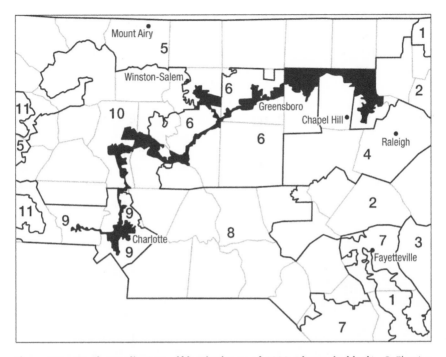

**Figure 3.2  North Carolina's Twelfth District as of 1993 (shown in black).** © Election Data Services, Inc. (www.electiondataservices.com)

Although the trial court in North Carolina dismissed Everett's complaint, the North Carolina map troubled five members of the Supreme Court. Justice Sandra Day O'Connor's opinion for the court in *Shaw v. Reno* observed that

> We believe that reapportionment is one area in which appearances *do* matter. A reapportionment plan that includes in one district individuals who belong to the same race, but who are otherwise widely separated by geographical and political boundaries and who may have little in common with one another but the color of their skin, bears an uncomfortable resemblance to political apartheid. It reinforces the perception that members of the same racial group—regardless of their age, education, economic status, or community in which they live—think alike, share the same political interests, and will prefer the same candidates at the polls. We have rejected such perceptions elsewhere as impermissible racial stereotypes.[26]

The *Shaw* decision focused on how North Carolina-12 looked. In subsequent decisions the Supreme Court clarified when efforts to create a majority-minority district went too far. In *Miller v. Johnson* challenging Georgia's 11th District that, like General Sherman, went from Atlanta to the sea, and *Bush v. Vera*, a challenge mounted by Edward Blum to three

Texas districts, the court provided a test when affirmative action gerry-mandering was alleged.[27] In keeping with the Voting Rights Acts and the non-retrogression test, jurisdictions had to consider race when drawing new maps. However, building on earlier cases that found race to be a suspect category, the court applies strict scrutiny. To withstand a challenge, the jurisdiction must prove that the plan was narrowly tailored and furthered a legitimate state interest. Absent such a showing, the map would fail as a violation of the Equal Protection Clause previously used to invalidate racial segregation in the workplace, schools, and public facilities generally. Since DOJ had led jurisdictions to believe they must draw predominately minority districts, those who challenged the districts had no difficulty demonstrating that considerations of race dominated the mapping decisions.

## BOX 3.1   EDWARD BLUM

Edward Blum had a good life as a stockbroker but then he stepped out of his comfort zone and ran for Congress. As a novice politico, Blum ran as a Republican in an overwhelmingly Democratic Houston district, a district in which Bill Clinton beat George Bush by a 3:1 margin. Texas-18, which appears in figure 3.3, was one of the least compact districts in the nation. It took its shape as the legislature tried to separate blacks, who went into District-18 from Hispanics who went into the majority-Hispanic 30th District. As Blum visited 20,000 households with an enlarged map to ensure that he was campaigning in the district, he found that many voters did not know that they lived in the misshapen district.

After losing to the incumbent by forty points, Blum decided to challenge the racially gerrymandered district in court. He paid for the attorneys and experts who succeeded in getting the U.S. Supreme Court to strike down the 18th and 30th districts and a majority-black Dallas district as racial gerrymanders.[1] He next sponsored the successful challenge to racially gerrymandered district of Virginia, New York, and South Carolina.

In time, Blum left the steamy Gulf Coast for the increasingly politically hot Washington, DC. Based on his court success, Blum, who is not an attorney, has succeeded in getting wealthy conservatives to fund his Donors' Trust. Those funds pay Blum a modest salary but also allow him to challenge aspects of laws that he believes violate the Equal Protection Clause. He has been especially successful in getting the U.S. Supreme Court to hear the cases he has sponsored.

Arguably Blum's most significant success came in 2013 when the Supreme Court found that the triggers written into Voting Rights Acts passed in 1965, 1970, and 1975 which relied on electoral data from 1964, 1968, and 1972 were outdated. While *Shelby County v. Holder* did not invalidate the preclearance requirement that applied to all or parts of sixteen states, striking down the triggers in Section 4 rendered preclearance a dead letter.[2] No longer must jurisdictions get federal approval for new maps or other changes affecting elections.

Blum had less success in the *Evenwel* case that challenged reliance on total population when drawing districts rather than using citizen population.[3] He did, however, succeed in getting the case before the Supreme Court.

Voting rights is not the only sphere in which Blum has challenged what he considers to be illegal affirmative action. He successfully challenged the selection process for honors programs in Houston school districts. Continuing his amazing success at getting cases before the Supreme Court, the high court agreed to hear a case in which a white girl challenged the University of Texas's selection practice that she claimed rejected her but accepted African-American students who had weaker records.[4] Blum was also behind the suit filed by Asian Americans that claimed that prestigious institutions, including Harvard, were rejecting Asian-American students who had stronger records than some of the minorities who were admitted.[5] Thus far his challenges to university admission practices have not succeeded.

[1]*Bush v. Vera*, 517 U.S. 952 (1996).
[2]*Shelby County v. Holder*, 570 U.S. 18 (2013).
[3]*Evenwel v. Abbott*, 136 S. Ct. 1120 (2016).
[4]*Fisher v. University of Texas*, 136 U.S. 2198 (2016).
[5]*Students for Fair Admissions v. Harvard*, 261 F. Supp. 3d 99 (D. Mass., 2017).

North Carolina-12, which touched off challenges to racially gerrymandered districts in *Shaw*, continued to be litigated throughout the decade. A new version drawn in 1997 extended no further east than Greensboro and no further west than Charlotte. This shorter district, nonetheless, reached out to pick up the black population of Winston-Salem for an overall black percentage of 47. This district was challenged for giving predominance to racial considerations. The state responded that in drawing this district the legislature had relied primarily on party voting preferences and not race. To counter the state's claims, plaintiffs introduced an e-mail sent from the staff member responsible for the new districts to the chair of the Senate redistricting committee. The staffer explained, "I have moved Greensboro Black community into the Twelfth District and now I need to take bout [*sic*] 60,000 out of the twelfth. I await your decision on this."[28]

While that e-mail convinced the trial court that race remained the primary consideration in drawing the new version of the district, the Supreme Court disagreed and upheld the legality of the district.[29] By accepting the state's claim that partisan considerations, in this case the effort to draw a district likely to elect a Democrat, had guided its actions, the Supreme Court sent a clear signal to jurisdictions preparing to equalize populations following the 2000 census. The court acknowledged that the most heavily Democratic districts would also often be the ones with the largest concentrations of African Americans. Nonetheless so long as most of the rationales offered for a map emphasized partisanship and not race, the Supreme Court seemed likely to uphold the plan.

When plaintiffs proved that plans had been drawn predominantly on the basis of race, jurisdictions had to redesign their maps and invariably this lowered minority concentrations. The final column in table 3.2 shows the percentage of relevant minorities in new districts following successful challenges to the racially gerrymandered districts created at the beginning of the decade. The least change in a black composition occurred in Florida's 3rd District and Texas's 30th District where the black percentage fell five points. Both districts in Georgia, North Carolina-12, Louisiana-4, and Texas's 30th ended up with black percentages below 40 percent.

Voting rights attorney Laughlin McDonald expressed the fears of many in the civil rights community when he said about *Miller v. Johnson,* "I really fear this court is sending us back to the dark days of the 17th century."[30] Despite concerns that adding whites to these districts would make it impossible for the minority legislators to win reelection,[31] only one black legislator left Congress following successful *Shaw* challenges. Cleo Fields (LA-4), believing that with a population less than one-third black and having to compete against a Republican incumbent he had such poor prospects for winning, instead ran for governor. Although he made it into the runoff, he polled only 37 percent of the vote in the second round against Republican Mike Foster.[32] In the other redrawn districts, black incumbents continued to win until retiring. Black incumbents' ability to replace black supporters removed from the districts with white votes indicates that growing numbers of southern whites support the candidacy of a minority candidate.[33]

The one Latina whose district got changed, Nydia Velázquez, won additional terms with overwhelming majorities even though the Hispanic percentage in her district declined by eight points. In Texas's 29th District, the Anglo Democrat continued to win as the district lost a quarter of its Hispanic population.

Toward the end of the 1990s, the Supreme Court addressed DOJ's requirement that jurisdictions making Section 5 submissions devise plans that would withstand a Section 2 challenge. The police jury (the equivalent of county commission in other states) of Bossier Parish, Louisiana, submitted a new plan for its twelve districts in 1991. DOJ approved the plan even though none of the districts had a black majority. About fifteen months later the Bossier Parish school board submitted a plan identical to that of the police jury, but by this time the local chapter of the National Association for the Advancement of Colored People had come up with an alternative that had two majority-black districts. DOJ rejected the school board plan citing the new information provided by the NAACP chapter. The school board challenged DOJ's authority to reject a plan that was not guilty of retrogression. The previous plan had no majority-black districts and neither did the new one. When the case got to the Supreme Court, it reasserted the *Beer* non-retrogression standard from a generation earlier.[34] All that jurisdictions needed to do to secure preclearance was to avoid making the situation for minorities any worse in the new plan. Congress had not added Section 2 considerations to Section 5 reviews when it renewed the Voting Rights Act in 1982, which led the court to believe that the standard from *Beer* remained unchanged. The DOJ argument that it made no sense to approve a plan that could then be successfully challenged under Section 2 did not convince a majority of the court.

## IS PROPORTIONALITY SUFFICIENT?

DOJ had used Section 2 to force some states to maximize the number of heavily minority districts. In *Johnson v. DeGrandy*, the Supreme Court rejected a lower court decision that called on Florida to maximize the number of Hispanic districts in the state House.[35] Although, as noted earlier, Section 2 did not require jurisdictions to have a number of minority districts roughly proportional to the minority's share of the population, the Supreme Court relied heavily on proportionality in supporting the plan from the state legislature rather than that of minority plaintiffs. Even though plaintiffs' alternative plans would have created an additional predominately Hispanic district, the court ruled that unnecessary since both Latinos and blacks dominated a number of districts roughly proportional to their share of the Dade County population. Justice Souter's opinion observed that "One may suspect vote dilution from political famine, but one is not entitled to suspect (much less infer) dilution from mere failure to guarantee a political feast."

In *DeGrandy*, the court also had to wrestle with the problem of two sizable minorities. One way in which to create an additional Latino district would have divided an African American concentration. The court found the state's plan that did not subdivide blacks acceptable.

## Gingles's First Prong

The discussion thus far of Section 2 has involved efforts to link geographically disparate concentrations of a single minority. Underlying the *Shaw*-type challenges was the first prong of *Gingles*, which requires that the minority group be sufficiently *compact* and numerous to form the majority in a district. With the *Shaw* cases restricting state efforts to combine geographically dispersed concentrations of a single minority, a question that has arisen is whether geographically proximate populations of *differing* ethnic groups can form the basis for a Section 2 suit challenging a districting plan. For example, assume that neither African Americans nor Latinos are sufficiently numerous to constitute a majority within a district, but if united the combined population of the two minorities would be a majority. Would a jurisdiction be obligated to draw a district in which the combined minority groups constituted a majority?

Courts will not assume that diverse minority groups share common interests; plaintiffs must prove that they do. For plaintiffs to prevail they must demonstrate that the two, or more, minorities do indeed share political preferences in elections.[36] Proof of shared candidate preferences is easier in general elections than in primaries or nonpartisan contests. With the major exception of Cuban-Americans in south Florida, most Latinos join African Americans and Asian Americans in supporting Democratic candidates in general elections. However, in primaries and non-partisan elections such as are often used in municipalities, Hispanic voters may support an Anglo who is running against an African American.[37] This phenomenon appeared repeatedly during the 2008 Democratic presidential primaries where Hillary Clinton typically attracted heavy support from Latinos in her unsuccessful contest against Barack Obama.

José Garza, an attorney with the Mexican-American Legal Defense and Education Fund, noted the differences between blacks and Latinos, warning, "I think public-interest applicants have to be cognizant of the fact that our goals will not always be in lock step."[38] A number of factors influence the degree to which African American and Latino voters join forces.[39] Inter-ethnic conflicts become particularly fierce when two groups share living space, especially if the population will sustain the creation of a district dominated by one group or the other but not two districts in which each ethnic group could dominate one. The example of Houston's 29th Congressional District as drawn in the early 1990s demonstrates the difficulty of separating Latino and black residents even when the population is sufficiently large. The

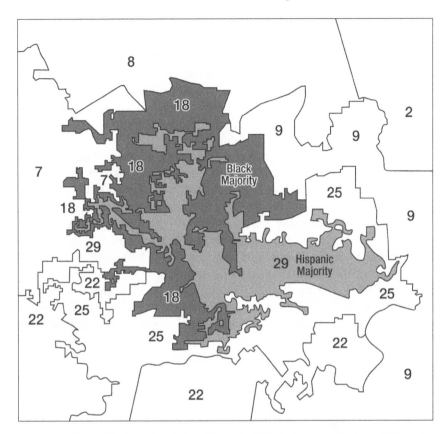

**Figure 3.3   Texas Districts 18 and 29 as Drawn in 1992 to Separate Blacks and Hispanics.**
*Source*: *Congressional Districts in the 1990s: A Portrait of America* (Washington, DC: CQ Press, 1993), 715. Reprinted with the permission of CQ Press Inc.

plan created a 60 percent Hispanic origin population 29th District along with an 18th District in which blacks constituted a slight majority. As shown in figure 3.3, the black district wrapped around much of the 29th District and neither district had readily identifiable boundaries.[40]

## SECTION 5 REVISITED

The evidence that reducing minority concentrations in congressional districts did not defeat minority incumbents encouraged some rethinking of how heavily minority district populations need to be. In the 1970s, many believed that for African Americans to control an election outcome their share of the population needed to be around 65 percent.[41] The rationale for this belief was that the minority population tended to be younger than the white population, that minority adults registered to vote at lower rates than whites, and that among registrants minorities turned out at lower rates than whites. By the early 1990s, DOJ no longer pushed to have minorities constitute approximately two-thirds of a district's population but instead required that minorities make up a majority of the voting age population in order to satisfy *Gingles*'s first prong. In 2001, DOJ sought unsuccessfully to force Georgia to beef up the minority percentage in three Senate districts.[42]

In 2009, the Supreme Court had to deal with a different aspect of the numerosity standard. The North Carolina constitution forbids the splitting of a county. When this "whole county provision" was applied to District 18, it resulted in a district 35.33 percent black in its voting age population (VAP). Prior to the 2001 redistricting, the district had a black majority but population shifts made it impossible to avoid lowering the black percentage. Plaintiffs wanted a 39.36 percent black VAP but that would have necessitated splitting a county. The plaintiffs argued that Section 2 of the Voting Rights Act took precedence over the "whole county provision." The state split Pender County to create the blacker district and that led to the challenge heard by the Supreme Court. The trial court considered District 18 at 39 percent black to be a de facto majority-black district since enough whites would support the candidate preferred by African Americans to elect that individual. While the Supreme Court acknowledged that states could create districts in which a coalition of blacks and whites would elect the black-preferred candidate, it refused to find that Section 2 *required* the creation of such districts.[43] The Court observed: "Section 2 does not impose on those who draw election districts a duty to give minority voters the most potential or the best potential to elect a candidate by attracting crossover voters."

## BOX 3.2   J. GERALD HEBERT

Gerald Hebert may have been involved in more voting rights cases than any attorney in the country. For twenty-one years, he served in the Civil Rights Division of the U.S. Department of Justice, ultimately becoming the acting chief. While there he concentrated his efforts in the Voting Rights Section, although early in his career he worked on some school desegregation cases. Hebert joined DOJ the same year that the Supreme Court ruled that redistricting plans must secure preclearance. Among his responsibilities were evaluating redistricting plans submitted to DOJ seeking preclearance. He was also at DOJ when the amendment of Section 2 of the Voting Rights Act greatly expanded the scope of DOJ responsibilities. After 1982, DOJ attorneys used Section 2 to challenge at-large election formats in hundreds of local governments across the nation. In numerous instances in which at-large elections were found to limit minorities' ability to elect their candidates of choice, the most common remedy instituted single-member districts. While at DOJ, Hebert was lead attorney in more than 100 cases, several of which reached the U.S. Supreme Court.

Since leaving DOJ in 1994, Hebert has shared his expertise as an adjunct professor of law at Georgetown, American University, and the University of Virginia. He has also continued to represent clients seeking to replace local at-large systems with single-member districts and plaintiffs displeased with redistricting plans. Congressional Democrats recruited Hebert, who served as general counsel for IMPAC 2000, their effort to influence redistricting following the 2000 census. In 2004, he joined the Campaign Legal Center as its senior director for Voting Rights and Redistricting, a job that keeps him in courtrooms across the nation litigating redistricting cases.

## WHEN PARTY TRUMPS RACE

Following the 1990 census, many minority group leaders had as their top priority maximizing the number of districts in which their preferences had a high probability of winning. Both the career civil servants and the political appointees at DOJ supported those ambitions.[44] The careerists in DOJ's Voting Rights Section charged with conducting Section 5 reviews wanted to see minorities elected and eagerly enforced calls for higher minority concentrations in preclearance jurisdictions as described earlier. Bush administration political appointees had a different motivation. They recognized that creating additional majority-minority districts could promote Republican ambitions and the top Republican appointee admitted that some of his decisions were politically motivated. John Dunne, Assistant Attorney General for Civil Rights, acknowledged:

> You know, I can't tell you that I was sort of like a monk hidden away in a monastery with only the most pure of intentions. I am a Republican. I was part of a Republican administration. And to tell you that that at no moment during the course of my, the discharge of my responsibilities was I totally immune or insensitive to political consideration, I don't think would justify anybody's belief.[45]

To design heavily minority districts necessitated aggregating minorities from surrounding districts and, especially in the South, as districts adjacent to new black ones became whiter they also became more Republican.[46] In southern legislatures, Republicans frequently joined African American members to push plans maximizing the number of majority black seats. For this reason Louisiana's Zorro District shown in figure 3.1 was characterized as "the illegitimate child of an illicit political love affair between blacks and Republicans."[47]

As already shown, African Americans increased their share of congressional and state legislative seats in the South following the 1990 round of redistricting. Their partners in pushing for plans that maximized the number of districts having black majorities also benefited. Most estimates place the number of congressional seats gained by Republicans because of the racial gerrymandering between nine and seventeen. Both minorities and Republicans gained from the race-based new plans while white Democrats lost seats.[48] By 1995, all five southern congressional districts represented by Democrats in 1991 that lost 10 percent or more of their black population had elected a Republican.[49] David Lublin goes so far as to say, "The most telling criticism of racial redistricting may be that it undermines the representation of minority interests even as it assures the election of more racial minorities to the U.S. House of Representatives."[50] The conservative Republicans who replaced moderate white Democrats rarely supported items of the African American political agenda.

The impact of bleaching surrounding districts in order to concentrate African Americans in districts in which they would constitute a majority transformed the partisan makeup of Georgia's congressional delegation. Before the 1992 redistricting, Georgia had eight white Democrats, one black Democrat, and a single Republican. After gaining a seat and going through the redistricting process that required three submissions before the Department of Justice gave its approval, Georgia had three majority-black districts and in 1992 each of these elected an African American. The 1992 election also saw Republicans gain three seats. As table 3.4 shows, Republicans picked up the 1st District where the black population dropped from 32 percent to 23 percent. They also won District 3 where the black population fell by 17 percentage points and in District 4 where it was cut in half down to 12 percent. The 1994 election, which produced the first Republican majority in the House since 1954, saw Republicans win the 8th District, where the black population had been reduced by 15 percentage points, and the 10th District, where it had been cut by five points. Republicans also defeated the Democratic incumbent in the 7th District, although not because of racial change since the black population inched up from 9 to 13 percent.

Political scientists John Petrocik and Scott Desposato offer a different explanation for why racial gerrymandering hurt Democrats.[51] They explain that white Democratic members of Congress became vulnerable as a result of the new plans swapping out large numbers of their constituents. The negative evaluations of the Democratic Party in 1992 and 1994 coupled with

**Table 3.4  Changes in the Racial Makeup of Georgia Congressional Districts Following the 1992 Redistricting**

| District | 1991 | | 1993–1995 | |
| --- | --- | --- | --- | --- |
| | % Black | Incumbent | % Black | Incumbent |
| 1 | 32 | White Democrat | 23 | Republican |
| 2 | 37 | White Democrat | 57 | Black Democrat |
| 3 | 35 | White Democrat | 18 | Republican |
| 4 | 25 | White Democrat | 12 | Republican |
| 5 | 67 | Black Democrat | 62 | Black Democrat |
| 6 | 20 | Republican | 6 | Republican |
| 7 | 9 | White Democrat | 13 | Republican* |
| 8 | 36 | White Democrat | 21 | Republican* |
| 9 | 5 | White Democrat | 4 | Republican** |
| 10 | 23 | White Democrat | 18 | Republican* |
| 11 | New District | | 64 | Black Democrat |

*Source*: Prepared by author.
* Changed from Democrat to Republican in 1994.
** Incumbent elected as a Democrat but changed parties in 1995.

many voters lacking familiarity with their Democratic incumbents wiped out a number of these Democrats that redistricting had made marginal. The Petrocik–Desposato explanation concurs with research showing that incumbents usually do less well with voters newly added to their districts than with those whom they have previously represented and with whom they have cultivated a personal attachment.[52]

The loss of support whether from white or black Democratic voters proved especially devastating to their party in the Deep South. In the late 1990s, the five Deep South states had only four white Democrats in Congress. At the beginning of that decade, these states sent twenty-four white Democrats to Congress.

Creation of additional minority districts had less impact outside the South. David Lublin attributes the difference to the presence of liberal whites available to replace blacks removed from a district so that bleached districts in the North continue to elect Democrats.[53] Liberals were in too short a supply to be substituted for blacks in the South. White Democrats suffered additional losses so that after the 2011 round of redistricting, John Barrow (GA-10) was the last white Democrat representing the Deep South. After his defeat in 2014, no white Democrats represented the subregion until Charleston, South Carolina, elected Joe Cunningham in 2018.

Racial redistricting exacted a cost on southern Democratic state legislators. Lublin estimates that of 105 seats lost by Democrats between 1990 and 1994, 45 could be attributed to redistricting.[54] These losses cost Democrats control of some southern legislative chambers that had been majority Democratic for generations. Lublin and Voss estimate that redistricting cost Democrats the control of both the South Carolina and Virginia Houses and enabled

Republicans to hold on to their majority in the North Carolina House longer.[55] In some other states redistricting kept Democrats from making gains in 1992. Another consequence of the racial gerrymandering which resulted in more Republicans winning state legislative seats was to help the GOP develop a farm team of experienced officeholders who, in time, successfully competed for higher offices.[56]

### Not All Bleaching Helped Republicans

Texas provides an exception to the general proposition that newly bleached districts elected Republicans. In the Lone Star State, Representative Martin Frost (D) designed a plan that extracted blacks from Republican districts rather than Democratic districts and Democrats maintained control of the delegation throughout the decade.[57] Of eight Republican districts, all but one saw its black percentage decline, while in District 21, the black percentage remained constant at 3 percent. In District 8 the black percentage dropped by fifteen points, while District 2 experienced a nine-point decline in its black population. Of thirteen districts with white Democrats, six saw their black percentage *increase* while two held constant. Only four of the districts with white incumbents experienced a loss in black percentages. While the increases tended to be very small, the fact that most white Democrats found themselves no worse off in terms of their percentage of black constituents contrasts sharply with the experiences in Alabama and Georgia.

A major factor in Frost's ability to protect most of his fellow white Democrats was the presence of a number of Republican districts from which blacks could be removed.[58] Recall that Georgia had only one district with a Republican in 1991 and, while the black percentage there dropped from 20 to 6 percent, that could not possibly meet DOJ's demands for the creation of two new majority-black districts. Similarly, in Alabama while both districts represented by Republicans gave up some black voters, that alone would not have sufficed to create the new majority-black 7th District. Frost drew his plan with such skill and foresight that even though by the end of the decade Republicans filled every statewide elected office, Democrats held seventeen of the thirty seats, a majority that persisted until the Tom DeLay–inspired mid-decade redistricting of 2003.

## CHANGING RACIAL COMPOSITION
## AND ROLL CALL VOTING

Not only did the affirmative action gerrymanders imposed by DOJ in the early 1990s change the composition of legislative chambers; they may have affected the voting choices made by sitting legislators. While bleaching districts in order to create new majority-minority ones wiped out some white Democrats, others survived. With fewer black constituents, these white Democrats confronted a more conservative constituency and may have shifted to the right to better represent the median voter in their new district. If white Democrats who lost some of their black constituents became less responsive to African American policy concerns, that plus the new Republicans could result in a loss in substantive representation that could offset gains in descriptive representation attributable to the creation of majority-minority districts. Former Congressional Black Caucus member Craig Washington registered his concern about the potential trade off. "I would rather have three white representatives who vote with me and one who votes against me, than one black who votes with me and three whites who vote against me."[59]

Scholars have found evidence to bolster the concerns articulated by Washington. Overby and Cosgrove, who examined all members of Congress and not just southerners, report a strong relationship between changes in a district's racial composition and the roll call behavior of Democrats and rural legislators.[60] Sharpe and Garand find that white members of Congress who got much whiter districts following redistricting became significantly more conservative.[61] Modest changes in the racial makeup of a district did not trigger a change in legislator behavior. Southern members became significantly more liberal as the percent black in their districts increased. On the other hand, Bullock observed no change in the voting behavior of southern white members of Congress that could be linked to changes in the racial makeup of their districts.[62] Shotts contends that the presence of new minority legislators more than offset any shifts to the right by white members of Congress so that delegations transformed by affirmative action gerrymanders emerged as more liberal than before.[63]

## NEW DECADE, NEW APPROACH

By the beginning of the twenty-first century, minority priorities in some southern states had shifted. During the course of the 1990s, Democrats, who had controlled every southern legislature for decades, lost both chambers in Florida, South Carolina, and Virginia; the Texas Senate; and saw Republicans control the North Carolina House for two terms. Since, with rare exception, African American legislators belong to the Democratic Party, when Democrats lose control of a chamber, black legislators lose influence and their ability to achieve the policy preferences of their constituents suffers. In many chambers only members of the majority party chair committees. Even in chambers with a tradition of allowing minority party members to chair some committees, the majority party's leadership controls the agenda. Stark tradeoffs had accompanied the gains of the early 1990s in descriptive representation. "What after all, was the point of increasing black representation only to tip control of the legislature to an opposing party openly hostile to almost any remedy to past and present discrimination?"[64]

Shifts in political control to the GOP, loss of political influence by black legislators, and greater willingness among whites to vote for African Americans came together to alter black legislators' strategy following the 2000 census. Previously blacks had objected to seeing African American concentrations split to bolster the political fortunes of white Democrats.[65] Now black caucuses no longer sought to maximize the number of seats likely to elect African Americans. Even the inducement of a new district likely to elect an African American to Congress from Houston failed to win the support of most members of the Texas Legislative Black Caucus for the DeLay plan. In Texas and elsewhere the priorities became to (1) maintain African American incumbents and (2) redistribute excess black voters so as to bolster the political fortunes of white Democrats.

That African American legislators accepted smaller black concentrations in their districts may stem from experience and scholarly work showing that districts could be less heavily minority without endangering the ability of black voters to elect their preferences. The lower threshold for a secure black district varies. Representative Melvin Watt (D-NC) explained that he could win in a less heavily black district than would be needed by his colleague in North Carolina's other black district because whites in Watt's urban district were more likely to support an African American candidate than were the whites in the rural 1st District.[66]

David Epstein contributed to multiple publications which make the point that African Americans have a better than even chance of electing their choices in districts less than 50 percent black VAP. To have a better than even chance of electing a black to Congress from the South, districts need be only about 40 percent black adults.[67] To have at least a .5 probability of electing a black to the South Carolina Senate, the district needed to be only 47 percent black.[68] In the Georgia General Assembly, Epstein estimated that just over 44 percent black adults in a district sufficed for African Americans to have at least an even chance of winning open seats.[69] At 50 percent black VAP, the probability of African Americans electing a preferred candidate in Georgia rose to 75 percent.[70] The experiences following *Shaw v. Reno* reinforced Epstein's estimates. As reported in table 3.2, whiter districts continued sending African Americans to Congress.

African American legislators approved decreasing the black VAP in Georgia's twelve majority-black Senate districts by an average of 10 percentage points. DOJ objected to three 51 percent black VAP districts when Georgia sought a declaratory judgment for its 2001 redistricting plans.

When this case came before the Supreme Court in *Georgia v. Ashcroft*, the Court initiated a dramatic departure from the non-retrogression standard, and in so doing adopted the approach suggested by Bruce Cain, which indicated two acceptable ways for minority influence to come into a legislative chamber.[71] "Indeed, the state's choice ultimately may rest on a political choice of whether substantive or descriptive representation is preferable," wrote Justice O'Connor.[72] The Court ruled that jurisdictions could pursue either of two paths. One would be the traditional approach of maintaining or increasing racial concentrations. Alternatively, jurisdictions could have fewer districts that had overwhelming concentrations of minority populations in conjunction with a number of "influence" districts having minority populations between 25 and 50 percent. An influence district, while unlikely to elect a member of the minority group, nonetheless would have a sufficient minority population to determine the outcome of the election. Consequently the winner, probably a white Democrat, would be responsive to minority concerns. In support of the proposition that white Democratic legislators would support black policy goals, Carol Swain contends that after controlling for the percentage of blacks in a constituency, white and black Democrats had very similar votes on roll calls.[73]

*Ashcroft* had the potential to prevent the ratchet effect produced by *Beer*'s non-retrogression standard. If Section 5 was interpreted to mean that the minority percentage can never be reduced by a new plan, then at a minimum minority concentration would remain constant in each majority black or Latino district and, more likely, increase. Table 3.5 shows the ratchet effect as the percent African American often increased over time in southern congressional districts covered by Section 5 that elected black members of Congress. When Atlanta sent Andy Young to Congress in 1972, he prevailed in a 44 percent black district. DOJ demands boosted Georgia's 5th District to 65 percent black prior to the 1982 election. After decreasing black percentages in the 1990s and 2000s, it experienced a slight increase in 2013. During the 1980s, African Americans won seats in Louisiana and Mississippi. The Louisiana district was 45 percent black when it elected William Jefferson. The 2nd District of Mississippi was drawn to be 54 percent black at the beginning of the decade, but litigation prompted a remapping that boosted the black percentage to 58 percent, at which point Mike Espy, an African American, won the seat. Following the 1990 census both these districts became blacker and remained above 60 percent black. As shown in table 3.2, several of the majority-black districts created in the early 1990s were successfully challenged and redrawn and it is the figures for the redrawn districts that provide the baseline in table 3.5. All of the districts subject to a *Shaw* challenge became blacker over time, with the three that had a black minority ultimately becoming at least plurality black. The two unchallenged districts became less black following the 2000 census and remained about the same in the

Table 3.5    Ratchet Effect in Southern Section 5 Congressional Districts That Elected African Americans before 1992

| | Percent Black | | | | |
|---|---|---|---|---|---|
| | *1973* | *1983* | *1993* | *2003* | *2013* |
| GA-5 | 44 | 65 | 62 | 56 | 58 |
| LA-2 | | 45 | 61 | 64 | 63 |
| MS-2 | | 54* | 63 | 63 | 65 |
| AL-7 | | | 67 | 62 | 64 |
| GA-2 | | | 39** | 45 | 50 |
| GA-4 | | | 37** | 53 | 57 |
| NC-1 | | | 50** | 51 | 52 |
| NC-12 | | | 36** | 45 | 49 |
| SC-6 | | | 62 | 57 | 57 |
| VA-3 | | | 54** | 56 | 57 |
| GA-13 | | | | 41 | 54 |

*Source*: Black percentages for 1973, 1993, and 2003 from Michael Barone and Grant Ujifusa, *The Almanac of American Politics*, 1974, 1994, and 2004. The 1980s percentage is from Alan Ehrenhalt, ed., *Politics in America, 1984*, and *Politics in America, the 100th Congress*.
* 58% black by the time an African American won the seat.
** Figures are for the districts as redrawn following a *Shaw* challenge.

next decade. Georgia's 13th District, created in 2002, became thirteen points blacker in the next decade with a black majority.

In the challenge to the Texas plan drawn by Republicans in 2003, the plaintiffs who represented Democrats, African Americans, and Latinos sought to use the Supreme Court's positive statements about influence districts in *Ashcroft*. The plaintiffs contended unsuccessfully that districts in which either Latinos or blacks constituted a sizeable minority and in which Democrats won election should be protected against the Republican gerrymander that removed Democrats from these districts.[74] Had the plaintiffs' position prevailed, then it might have become impossible to reduce minority concentrations in any district represented by a Democrat in which the minority population exceeded 25 percent. Acceptance of the plaintiffs' position might have extended the non-retrogression approach to influence districts.

*Ashcroft* was not popular with Congress. When extending Section 5 of the VRA in 2006, Congress adopted language indicating that the Court's opinion was not in keeping with congressional intent.

Brunell's previously mentioned advocacy for one-party districts sees nothing wrong with ratcheting up minority concentrations. With African Americans giving 90 percent or more of their votes to Democratic candidates, the more heavily black the district, the larger the share of its residents who will be pleased with the election result. Brunell says of overwhelmingly black and overwhelmingly Democratic districts, "these districts are, in many ways, the districts that should be emulated around the country."[75] From this perspective the congressional plan used in Georgia in 1992 and 1994 with its three majority-black districts succeeded since those three districts housed almost 62 percent of the state's African Americans who sent three black members to Congress with overwhelming majorities. As noted above, by 2000 many black legislators would have opposed Brunell's proposal.[76]

## REVERSING THE RATCHET

As table 3.5 shows, ratcheting black populations continued into the 2010s. Most of the legislatures charged with redistricting southern states had Republican majorities. When in control, Republicans boosted black concentrations, explaining that the non-retrogression standard in Section 5 required that, at a minimum, they dare not reduce black percentages. As the decade wore on, lawsuits questioned the need to pack additional African Americans into districts that had elected blacks, sometimes for decades. The civil rights challenges of the 2010s revealed that Section 5 of the Voting Rights Act, which proved effective in preventing cracking in previous decades, was ill-designed to block packing, the issue of the new decade. All of the districts challenged for packing, that will now be discussed, had passed preclearance.

Plaintiffs in Alabama challenged the decision of the state's legislative leadership to maintain the black percentages in all of the state's majority-black districts. To keep the underpopulated Senate District 26 at 72.75 percent black, 15,749 African Americans and 36 whites had to be added in the new plan. The state maintained the same number of majority-black Senate districts as in the previous plan and added one majority-black House district, in keeping with its interpretation of the demands of Section 5 of the VRA. The net effect of maintaining the black percentages in the majority-black districts was, as Republicans recognized decades earlier, to create more districts that they were likely to win. The trial court accepted the state's explanation that this was done to avoid retrogression. The dissenting judge on the trial panel sounded a theme similar to that articulated in the *Shelby County* case that struck down the triggers in Section 4 of the Voting Rights Act. Judge Myron Thompson observed that "the State of Alabama was relying on racial quotas with absolutely no evidence that they had anything to do with current conditions."[77] The Supreme Court reversed, noting that Section 5 did not require maintenance of a specific percentage of minority residents, but instead it was only necessary that the minority concentration suffice to elect their preferred candidates. The Court also criticized the state for applying a single standard statewide rather than tailoring plans to the conditions in individual districts.[78] In an echo from an earlier generation, Alabama had run afoul of the *Miller v. Johnson* test that invalidates districts drawn predominantly on the basis of race.[79] In another case, Virginia's plan that had all of the black House of Delegates districts at least 55 percent black voting age population was thrown out for packing.[80]

Another suit challenged the black concentration in Virginia's 3rd Congressional District. Like in the Alabama case, the Virginia litigation involved a claim of packing, specifically that the 3rd Congressional District, represented since 1993 by Bobby Scott, had an unnecessarily high concentration of African Americans. The state defended the plan, arguing that the non-retrogression standard for Section 5 of the Voting Rights Act that was still in effect when the map was drawn precluded any reduction in the black percentage. The trial court found race to be the predominant factor in shaping Scott's district in which the black percentage had risen to 57.2 percent. The court ordered a new plan that reduced the black percentage from 57 to 45.5 percent and boosted the black percentage in the 4th District from 31.4 to 40.9 percent.[81] In evaluating the situation, the court relied on testimony that even in a plurality black district with 42 percent of the population white, African Americans, if united, could elect their preferred candidate. The court recognized the decisiveness of the Democratic primary and that black voters would dominate that sphere.

Critical in evaluating claims like those raised in Virginia is the willingness of whites to vote for an African American who won the Democratic nomination. The share of whites willing to vote for a Democrat varies from state to state and within states so that a black percentage in the forties sufficed in Virginia but would not be an environment in which African Americans could have success in a rural district in the Stagnant South. The Democratic attorney general of Virginia declined to appeal and the Supreme Court refused to hear an appeal filed by three GOP members of Congress. The congressional appellants claimed that the plan did not rely predominantly on race but was an incumbent-protection plan. The Supreme Court concluded that the members of Congress lacked standing, although they claimed they were hurt by the new judge-drawn map.[82]

The reasoning that in Tidewater Virginia African Americans could succeed in districts that lacked a black majority has received additional support. The state's 4th District, which retained a white plurality (48.8 percent) in the new plan, sent African American Donald McEachin to Congress in 2016 with 58 percent of the vote. In 2017 a decision that unpacked the black populations in a number of state House districts resulted in changes that contributed to the ability of Democrats to reclaim a majority in that chamber later that year, the first time for Democrats to lead the Virginia House of Delegates in twenty years.[83]

Elsewhere, the Supreme Court also demanded the unpacking of the two North Carolina congressional districts that had elected African Americans beginning with 1992 and twenty-eight state legislative districts.[84] The Court explained that the success of black congressional candidates over many years indicated that these districts did not need the concentrations of African Americans assigned in the post-2010 redistricting. In the plan implemented prior to the 2016 election, the much-litigated 12th District, the notorious I-85 District that originally stretched from Charlotte to Durham, achieved its most compact form as it was limited to Mecklenburg County (Charlotte). Although whites outnumbered blacks in the district 40–37 percent, it continued to elect Alma Adams, an African American, with landslide proportions (73 percent of the vote in 2018). The elongated 12th District that extended from Charlotte to Greenville had a 49 percent black population according to the 2010 census. The largely rural 1st District also became much more compact and its black population dropped from 52 to a plurality 44 percent. It, too, continued to reelect an African American.

Lest it appear that packing is currently the only concern, in 2019 a Mississippi suit called for an increase in the black concentration in a 51 percent black voting age population district that continued to elect a white senator. The opinion recognized that in the rural, impoverished Mississippi Delta, black turnout lagged white participation by 10 percentage points.[85] In 2019, with an increased black concentration, the district elected an African American.

Hamstringing of the preclearance provision of Section 5 as a result of the Shelby County case removes the non-retrogression justification that states used to maintain or pump up minority percentages in selected districts.[86] It remains to be seen whether the absence of preclearance will disadvantage minorities in the next round of redistricting. The challenges of the 2010s focused on issues of packing in districts that DOJ had precleared. Minority representatives will be on the lookout for instances of packing post-2020. Despite congressional opposition to the unpacking of districts in *Georgia v. Ashcroft*, recent Court opinions will probably lead to an increased number of districts in which blacks constitute no more than a bare minimum needed in the population while careful redistricting bodies will make district-by-district assessments.

If Democrats win the presidency, secure a majority in the Senate, and maintain their House majority in 2020, updating the VRA's Section 4 to address problems noted by the Supreme Court in *Shelby County* may have high priority. If a rewrite of the VRA included protections against packing, it could play a role in whatever jurisdictions were identified by new trigger mechanisms. Could Congress approve a rewrite that could survive judicial challenges in time for review of plans adopted in 2021 and 2022? Or would the situation resemble the 1982 reauthorization of the VRA that came too late to impact that decade's redistricting?

## CONTROVERSY

### Arguments For

Section 5 of the VRA was the most successful piece of civil rights legislation ever passed. It quickly eliminated barriers to black registration and voting[87] and has prevented cracking of minority concentrations in the course of redistricting. Drawing new districts that included concentrations of minorities was critical in diversifying the makeup of legislatures.

The 2021–2022 redistricting will be the first in half a century done without the protections afforded minorities by Section 5. While Section 5 was effective in preventing cracking, it failed to counter packing. The challenges to packing targeted districts approved by DOJ but found to violate the Equal Protection Clause since they sorted people by race.

Section 2 of the VRA in 1982 created the basis for requiring the replacement of multi-member and at-large electors with single-member districts. Single-member systems are not designed to achieve proportional representation. Therefore in order to include representatives from minority groups it became necessary to design districts likely to elect those kinds of legislators.

In addition to the symbolic significance of descriptive representation, representatives from minority groups change the legislature. Minorities raise issues that white legislators ignore, which changes the institution's agenda. Black members of Congress more often sponsor legislation and amendments with a racial emphasis than do whites who represent sizable minority populations. Black members also differ from whites with large black constituencies in devoting more attention to racial concerns, giving racial matters greater emphasis in their newsletters, and including more pictures of blacks in their newsletters.[88] African American members of Congress provide better service to their black constituents and secure more federal projects and funds for their districts than do white legislators.[89]

Writing before the decisions in the latter half of the 2010s that unpacked black districts, Christian Grose argued in favor of districts in which the African American population was low enough to make them electorally competitive. His research indicated that representatives from marginal districts scored best in terms of allocation and service responsiveness.[90]

Black legislators are also more likely to support civil rights initiatives than whites, even after controlling for the racial composition of the district and the partisanship of the legislator. Grose estimates that the difference attributable to the race of a Democratic legislator, controlling for other factors, is 5 percentage points, less than the impact of the district's racial makeup.[91]

Districts designed to elect minorities usually deliver. African Americans who live in districts that elect black legislators tend to be more politically aware than blacks in districts represented by whites. Blacks represented by an African American know more about their legislators' records and are more likely to recall the name of their legislator, to contact their representative, and to give the legislator high job approval.[92]

At times when most black voters cast ballots for candidates who lose the presidency and their state's senatorial and gubernatorial elections, U.S. House elections are the only high profile offices for which most African Americans back winners.[93] Federal pressures to create majority-black districts have increased the numbers of African Americans who have backed a winner, an experience that has positive consequences for the political system. Recent challenges to packing will increase the numbers of African Americans who benefit from having a black representative.

## Arguments Against

Section 5 of the VRA uniquely altered traditional federalism. The preclearance provision infringed on state sovereignty by requiring all or parts of sixteen states to obtain the approval of the national government before implementing new districting plans. At times DOJ forced states to take actions that the courts subsequently found to be unconstitutional.

Rewriting Section 2 of the Voting Rights Act to make it easier for minorities to achieve descriptive representation constituted a major shift from the traditional emphasis in American politics on individual rights to a notion of group rights. By replacing the need to prove an intent to discriminate with a results or effects test forces jurisdictions in which minorities do not have a share of seats proportionate to their share of the population to design majority-minority districts.[94] Expecting minorities to have a proportionate share of the seats is unrealistic since representatives in American collegial bodies compete in single-member districts and not in multi-member districts with electoral rules intended to produce proportional representation as are used throughout continental Europe.

The careful separation of white and minority voters in the course of implementing Section 2 in the early 1990s hastened the partisan transformation of the South, a criticism if you are a Democrat but a positive result for Republicans. Bleaching surrounding districts to create the new majority-minority districts opened the way for many new Republicans in southern congressional delegations and state legislatures.

Republicans elected from bleached districts have little incentive to support initiatives favored by African Americans since the Republicans' districts have few minority voters and those who live there infrequently vote for GOP candidates. Freshman Republicans elected from bleached districts had especially conservative voting records.[95] Consequently southern legislatures may have become more conservative as some minority legislators but even greater numbers of conservative Republicans replaced moderate Democrats.

Redistricting is the most political activity undertaken by a legislature. In addition to the partisan tensions that regularly accompany redistricting and the desperate struggles of some legislators to save their careers and the opportunistic efforts of others to secure more compatible districts, the early 1990s saw racial tensions fanned in the struggle to meet DOJ and/or to avoid litigation. Months of conflict during which blacks accused their white colleagues of racism while white Democrats grew increasingly frustrated with their minority colleagues for collaborating with Republicans left residues of racial distrust that persisted and infected debates on policy issues that in the past had not had racial overtones.

## Rebuttal

While a consensus exists that the racial gerrymanders cost Democrats congressional seats, dissenters claim that Republicans made no gains as a result of the new districts.[96] Kenneth Shotts rejects the claim that increasing the numbers of Republicans in southern congressional delegations created an environment more hostile to minority policy preferences.[97] His research shows delegations to be more liberal following the racial gerrymanders of the 1990s. Grose reports that following the affirmative action redistricting of the 1990s, southern delegations became more conservative, but much of that, he warns, may be due to regional realignment to the GOP—a change facilitated by the bleaching of surrounding districts to create the new majority-minority districts.[98]

## CONCLUSIONS

The Voting Rights Act and subsequent court decisions have made equitable treatment of minorities second only to equal population as a consideration in districting politics. Creating equal population districts opened the way for the first African Americans to win legislative seats in the modern South. The ranks of minorities expanded once most of the South had to obtain federal approval before implementing new districting plans. The authority conferred under Section 5 of the VRA enabled DOJ to prevent gerrymanders designed to minimize black representation. In time these protections got extended to states that had concentrated language minorities.

Amending Section 2 of the Voting Rights Act extended the reach of federal law nationwide and initially allowed minorities to challenge hundreds of local arrangements where at-large or multi-member districting thwarted minorities' political ambitions. DOJ used Section 2 to require that jurisdictions subject to Section 5 maximize the number of districts likely to elect minorities. Other states adopted similar approaches in order to head off litigation.

Ultimately the Supreme Court found that a number of the racially gerrymandered districts in the early 1990s violated the Equal Protection Clause since the major consideration in drawing these districts had been to separate blacks from whites. The districts drawn to replace those struck down by the courts had lesser concentrations of minorities yet, with one exception, continued to elect minority legislators.

The ability of minorities to win in districts, some of which were not majority-minority, emboldened black state legislators to support reductions in the black percentages in districts. Since 2000, many African Americas have supported plans that have lower concentrations, including some that lack a black majority. With black participation rates often equaling and sometimes exceeding those for whites, African American preferences can win Democratic nominations in what would once have been considered black-influence districts and then secure sufficient white support to win the general election. Reversing the ratchet can also increase the numbers of blacks in districts likely to elect white Democrats, thereby promoting prospects for Democratic legislative majorities which would advance black policy preferences.

*Chapter 4*

# The Populations Are Equal and Minorities Have Not Been Discriminated Against, Now What?

The two most important factors that must be considered when drawing districts are the attainment of population equality among districts and the equitable treatment of minorities. The need for population equality is based on the Equal Protection Clause of the Constitution's Fourteenth Amendment. Concern about the treatment of minorities grows out of the Voting Rights Acts. These are legally enforceable. This chapter examines elements secondary to the first two elements, although states frequently stipulate that some of these factors be considered when drawing new maps. These factors include contiguity, compactness, respect for political boundaries, maintenance of communities of interest, and the protection of incumbents.

While it has proven possible to achieve both equal populations among districts while simultaneously protecting the interests of minorities, as mapmakers consider additional factors it becomes impossible to achieve the whole range of ideals. As shown in some of the maps in the previous chapter, the effort to create minority districts frequently resulted in ungainly looking districts that violated any ideas of compactness. Districts that score poorly on measures of compactness have often split counties or other political units. Recall that, historically, counties had been the basis for districts and rarely did congressional plans divide counties except in the largest urban areas. In this chapter, we will frequently note how various standards come into conflict.

## CONTIGUITY

Contiguity is the idea that a person could go from one end of the district to the other without leaving the district. With a few exceptions, like the Upper Peninsula of Michigan and Virginia's Delmarva Peninsula, legislative districts have usually met the contiguity expectation. In 2019, thirty-three states specifically required that congressional districts be contiguous and all states specified it for their legislative districts.[1] Even when not set out as a consideration, other than instances where counties are divided by water, contiguity is generally honored. Louisiana's Saint Martin's Parish is the only major geographic unit of which we are aware that consists of two parts separated by another political unit (in this case Iberia Parish projects between the two parts of Saint Martin). The contiguity requirement makes it inappropriate to create a predominately black district by simply designating the heavily black areas in a series of cities as parts of a single district without linking them by a land corridor. To achieve at least a claim of contiguity, North Carolina's District 12 in 1993 extended across much of the Piedmont from Durham to Gastonia.

Districts such as North Carolina-12 stretched the concept of contiguity to the point that critics claim that it had been violated. North Carolina's 12th District, which appears in figure 3.2, seems to bisect the 6th District. Portions of the 6th District lie above and below the 12th with components of each district united through touch-point contiguity. That is, at places these districts achieve contiguity in the way that diagonal black squares on a checkerboard are contiguous at a single point. At that same point diagonally opposed red squares are also contiguous. Or in the four corners of the United States, New Mexico and Utah have touch-point contiguity as do Colorado and Arizona. Figure 4.1 shows two instances of point contiguity in North Carolina as Districts 6 and 12 crossed each other on diagonals.

A second practice that has led to questions about contiguity involves the use of water. Traditionally, water contiguity has been accepted as necessary to connect an island to the mainland or to link Michigan's Upper Peninsula

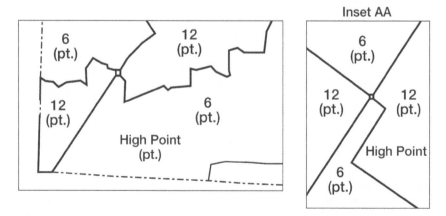

**Figure 4.1   Examples of Touch-Point Contiguity in a 1992 North Carolina Congressional Map.** *Source*: U.S. Bureau of the Census, 1993, GP-30.

to the rest of the state. Some recent plans use water to link parts of a district while avoiding including populations that differed from the majority of those within the district. For example, Virginia's 3rd District, which was drawn as a majority-black district in 1991, used the channel of the James River as a connector. In places the district was only as wide as the river and therefore avoided including anyone who lived on either bank as it linked heavily black neighborhoods in Norfolk and Newport News with the black portions of Richmond and some rural counties upstream. The river was not simply something that the district crossed; the district actually went down the waterway leading some to refer to this as duck contiguity. An example of duck contiguity where a district skipped along a chain of islands avoiding the nearby mainland in order to connect GOP voters appears in figure 6.3.

A less controversial aspect of contiguity ties parts of a district together by crossing unpopulated territory. A narrow neck may link two parts of a district by going across the runway of an airport, a park, or an unpopulated portion of a military base. On maps these show up as narrow necks that connect two population concentrations. At times these may be desirable because they bring together communities of interest that have sprung up on either side of uninhabitable property. At other times, a neck or duck contiguity may be used to pack political partisans into a single district, thereby reducing their influence.

## COMPACTNESS

The most compact geometric shape is a circle. But it would be impossible to have a state's legislative districts made up of a series of circles. A second best geometric shape for compactness would be a square or a rectangle.

According to the National Conference of State Legislatures, as of 2019, thirty states called for their congressional districts to be compact and forty states expected compact legislative districts. Many people believe that having compact districts is desirable because it facilitates campaigning. A compact district may make it easier for voters to know which district they live in and, related to that, who represents them. In the non-compact districts shown in chapters 3 and 6, one could readily understand how voters could be confused as to who represented them, as Edward Blum discovered in Houston. When a neighborhood is divided, voters may see signs for candidates along one side of the street on which they live and yet discover upon getting to the polls that they do not live in the district of the candidates whose advertising they have seen.

In *Shaw v. Reno*, Justice Sandra Day O'Connor emphasized her concern about the shape of North Carolina's 12th District. This long, skinny I-85 District, as shown in figure 3.2, stretched across 160 miles of the Carolina

Piedmont and seemed on its face to violate the notions of compactness. Justice O'Connor observed, "We believe that reapportionment is one area in which appearances *do* matter."

While a glance at North Carolina-12 gives a sense of a non-compact district, the assessment of compactness is not exclusively a matter of impression. Numerous measures of compactness exist.[2] From the multitude of measures of compactness, three became important considerations in the litigation that followed the *Shaw* case. On many measures a circular district would receive a score of one. As the value approaches zero, the less compact the district on any of the measures. Litigants often present multiple measures since they capture different aspects of non-compactness.

One of the measures of compactness, the Reock dispersion score, first calculates the area encompassed in the smallest circle that completely surrounds a district.[3] Then the area in the district is calculated and the dispersion score is the percent of the circle that is included in the district. A circular district would have the maximum score of one while a long narrow district would have a low score.

Other scores are based upon the perimeter of the district. The popular Polsby-Popper measure calculates the perimeter of the district and then a circle having the circumference equal to the perimeter of the district is drawn.[4] The Polsby-Popper score is the percentage of the area of the circle having the same perimeter as the district that is included in the district. Obviously, again, a circular district would have a score of one and the smaller the value, the more contorted the perimeter of the district with numerous indentations and extensions produces a circle with a larger perimeter.

A third measure, the convex hull, suggests putting a hypothetical rubber band around a district.[5] The score is the percentage of the area surrounded by the hypothetical rubber band that is in the district. The measure would yield a high score for regular geometric shapes such as a square, rectangle, pentagon, and so on. However, a district in which portions have been cut away in order to avoid including certain populations would have lower scores.

Each of the approaches used to assess geography can also measure compactness as applied to population. Compactness first became widely discussed in the context of the racial gerrymanders of the 1990s but is also appropriate for exploring whether mapmakers have manipulated lines to include or exclude members of a political party or a racial or ethnic group. Plans challenged in the 1990s frequently excluded white populations as they sought to capture geographically far-flung minority populations. Calculating the share of the population in a circle or convex hull that lives in a district could indicate the presence of a gerrymander.

Courts have not established thresholds for what constitutes extremely low compactness. Pildes and Niemi have suggested that scores below .15 on

Reock or .05 on Polsby-Popper indicate extremely non-compact districts.[6] Ansolabehere and Palmer use the "original gerrymander," the one from which the name is derived and depicted in figure 5.1, as a baseline.[7] Using the three measures of compactness in this chapter, they find that congressional districts less compact than the original gerrymander have become more common recently. According to their calculations, 28 percent of the congressional districts in place were less compact than the original gerrymander on at least one of the measures and, of the 109 least compact, 93 were drawn in the 1990s or later.

There is no prohibition on drawing districts that score poorly on one or more of the compactness measures. However in challenges from the 1990s that raised questions of the significance accorded race, courts might consider evidence that the district scored poorly on a compactness measure as indicative that traditional districting principles had been subordinated to considerations of race. Compactness scores have also been introduced in litigation in the new century, but by that time, legislatures had ceased referencing race as a motivation for the maps that they created. Recently, evidence of non-compact districts has been stressed in claims of partisan gerrymandering. A notable example was Pennyslvania-7, the ignominious Goofy kicking Donald Duck district as shown in figure 4.2, which at one point narrowed to the width of a restaurant.

As table 4.1 shows, the district at the heart of the *Shaw* decision was among the least compact in the nation. North Carolina-12 ranked 433rd in terms of the Reock score, 431st on the Polsby-Popper measure, and 429th on the population score. Texas-29, a district drawn to create a Hispanic majority in Houston and invalidated in *Bush v. Vera*, had the lowest Polsby-Popper score in the nation, while the heavily black 18th District which split the city of Houston with the 29th ranked 433rd. Texas-29 filled less than 1 percent of a circle having the circumference equal to the district's perimeter. All but two of the eleven districts with the lowest Polsby-Popper scores, none of which filled as much as 3 percent of the circle, faced legal challenges. Of the legal challenges only those to Illinois's "Earmuff District" and North Carolina-1 did not succeed, although the state redrew the latter to make it more compact. The other two districts among those with the worst perimeter scores, Texas-6 and -25, both abutted districts invalidated in *Bush v. Vera* and derived their strange shapes in large part because of the shapes given their majority-minority neighbors.

The Reock measure shows that six districts filled less than 10 percent of the encompassing circle. A predominately black district in south Florida scored as the least compact district of the 1990s using Reock. Although a suit challenged Florida-23, the court ruled that the litigation had come too late in the decade. Table 4.1 shows that challenges succeeded against four of the eleven

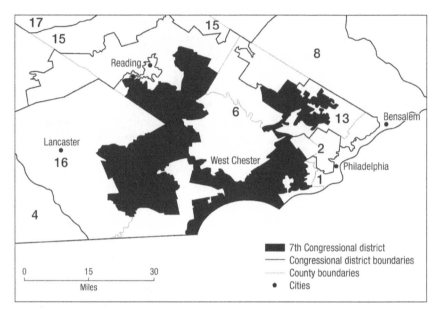

**Figure 4.2   The Goofy Kicking Donald Duck District.** *Source*: Pennsylvania Spatial Data Access, U.S. Census Bureau.

least compact Reock districts. The 2013 version of North Carolina-12 again made lists of the least compact and at least one observer judged it the least compact in the nation.[8]

The report assessing congressional districts for the 1990s prepared by the Congressional Research Service applied the convex hull to the population and not to area. The least compact district as calculated using convex hull for the population was Colorado-4. Neither this district nor the next five in terms of low population scores had to defend its plan in court. Only three districts with low scores on the population compactness measure drew a legal challenge. Of these three, Florida-23 escaped unscathed when the judge dismissed the suit.

On the population measure, five districts which ranked in the bottom eleven in the nation included a quarter of the population in the area that would be captured if a hypothetical rubber band were to be placed around the district. Texas-18 and -29, which had some of the poorest scores in the perimeter measure, nonetheless contained approximately 40 percent of the population in the immediate vicinity of the district. The compactness measures are far from identical although some districts like North Carolina-12 and Florida-3 scored poorly on all of them.

Table 4.2 reports a ranking of what Azavea considers to be the ten least compact districts in place in 2013. The ranking rests on the three measures. Interestingly, the two least compact districts are the descendants of the two districts that ranked among the least compact twenty years earlier, as reported

Table 4.1   The Least Compact Congressional Districts in 1993

| District | Rank | Score |
|---|---|---|
| A. Polsby-Popper Scores | | |
| *Texas – 29 | 435 | .008 |
| *Florida – 3 | 434 | .011 |
| *Texas – 18 | 433 | .011 |
| *Louisiana – 4 | 432 | .013 |
| *North Carolina – 12 | 431 | .014 |
| * Texas – 30 | 430 | .016 |
| Texas – 25 | 429 | .021 |
| *New York – 12 | 428 | .021 |
| Texas – 6 | 427 | .025 |
| **Illinois – 4 | 426 | .026 |
| **North Carolina – 1 | 425 | .028 |
| Most compact Wisconsin – 5 | | .718 |
| B. Reock Scores | | |
| **Florida – 23 | 435 | .033 |
| California – 36 | 434 | .043 |
| *North Carolina – 12 | 433 | .045 |
| Hawaii – 2 | 432 | .052 |
| New York – 8 | 431 | .065 |
| Florida – 17 | 430 | .082 |
| * Florida – 3 | 429 | .111 |
| New Jersey – 13 | 428 | .115 |
| * New York – 12 | 427 | .122 |
| Tennessee – 4 | 426 | .124 |
| *Louisiana – 4 | 425 | .125 |
| Most compact Kentucky – 6 | | .641 |
| C. Population Scores Based on Convex Hull | | |
| Colorado – 4 | 435 | .18 |
| Florida – 20 | 434 | .21 |
| Ohio – 13 | 433 | .21 |
| Texas – 4 | 432 | .23 |
| Arizona – 6 | 431 | .24 |
| Texas – 14 | 430 | .25 |
| ** Florida – 23 | 429 | .25 |
| *Florida – 3 | 428 | .26 |
| *North Carolina – 12 | 427 | .27 |
| Texas – 21 | 426 | .27 |
| Most Compact Nebraska – 2 | | .99 |

*Source*: Created by the author using figures in David C. Huckabee, *Congressional Districts: Objectively Evaluating Shapes*, CRS, Report for Congress 94-449 GOV, May 24, 1994.
* Successfully sued for being drawn predominately on the basis of race.
** Unsuccessfully sued. The suit against Florida-23 was dismissed because it was filed so late in the decade. The court found for the state (defendant) in Illinois-4.

in table 4.1. North Carolina-12 in 2013 continued to twist its way along I-85 northwest to Greensboro while Florida-5 took much the shape of Florida-3 in the 1990s as it linked black communities in Jacksonville and Orlando. These two districts plus Louisiana-2 are majority-minority. A generation earlier, all but two of the least compact on Polsby-Popper were minority districts. The

Table 4.2   The Least Compact Congressional Districts as of 2013

| District | Reock | Polsby-Popper | Convex Hull |
|---|---|---|---|
| NC – 12 | 2 | 2 | 1 |
| FL – 5 | 3 | 4 | 2 |
| MD – 3 | 27 | 1 | 3 |
| OH – 9 | 1 | 14 | 4 |
| TX – 35 | 5 | 12 | 5 |
| NC – 4 | 13 | 10 | 6 |
| LA – 2 | 28 | 11 | 7 |
| FL – 22 | 6 | 23 | 18 |
| MD – 6 | 9 | 31 | 8 |
| NY – 10 | 42 | 42 | 16 |

Entries show the ranking of the district on the measure.
Source: Redrawing the Map on Redistricting, 2012 (Philadelphia, PA: Azavea, 2012).

number of 2013 least compact districts that were majority-minority was also less than the eight on the Reock measure in 1993.

Christopher Ingraham also developed a list of the ten least compact districts.[9] His choices for ignominy include six of the Azavea districts and has the same worst three, although Ingraham reverses the order of Maryland-3 and Florida-5. He also has two of the most widely criticized (and spoofed) districts which did not make the Azavea list, Pennsylvania-7 (Goofy kicking Donald Duck) and Illinois-4 (Earmuff District). Ingraham's selections are more heavily weighted toward majority-minority districts with four being longstanding black districts while three others are majority Hispanic.

Table 4.3 ranks the ten states with the least compact districts as of 2013. Topping the list are Maryland and North Carolina, the states involved in the litigation in which the U.S. Supreme Court washed its hands of claims of partisan gerrymandering, as will be discussed in chapter 5. Maryland's districts, portions

Table 4.3   States Having the Lowest Average Compactness Scores as of 2013

| State | Reock | Polsby-Popper | Convex Hull |
|---|---|---|---|
| Maryland | 2 | 1 | 1 |
| North Carolina | 5 | 4 | 4 |
| Louisiana | 7 | 3 | 3 |
| West Virginia | 8 | 5 | 2 |
| Virginia | 4 | 7 | 13 |
| Hawaii | 18 | 2 | 25 |
| New Hampshire | 1 | 8 | 12 |
| Illinois | 6 | 9 | 5 |
| Pennsylvania | 11 | 10 | 6 |
| Rhode Island | 3 | 18 | 10 |

Entries show the ranking of the state on the measure.
Source: Redrawing the Map on Redistricting, 2012 (Philadelphia, PA: Azavea, 2012).

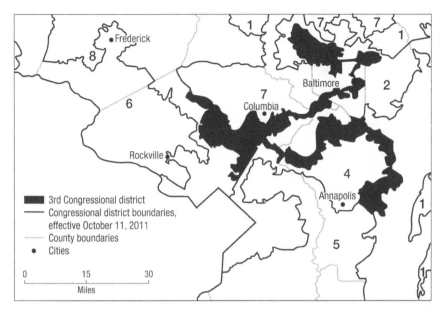

**Figure 4.3    Maryland Congressional Districts Implemented in 2013.** *Source*: Maryland Mapping & GIS Data Portal.

of which appear in figure 4.3, were less compact, especially on the convex hull measure, in 2013 than a decade earlier.[10] Figure 4.3 features District 3, the only one of Maryland's eight districts to make the "Worst 10" lists. Districts 2, 4, and 7 also have narrow necks and tight twists and turns. A slim, contorted finger of District 2 traces the two northern blobs of District 3. Except for the 6th District, which will be discussed in the next chapter, partisan machinations did not dictate the shape of these districts. Race did play a role as the plan designed by Democratic governor Martin O'Malley carefully allocated Democratic voters so as to maintain the 4th and 7th as majority-black districts. Chapter 5 also addresses the Pennsylvania plan invalidated by the state Supreme Court, while part of the Virginia map was found to pack African Americans, a topic considered in chapter 3. Contributing to the low compactness scores for several states, such as Rhode Island and Hawaii, are their ragged shorelines. Indiana and Nevada had the most compact statewide plans for the 2010s.

Much of the criticism concerning partisan gerrymandering during the 2010s focused on GOP-drawn districts in states like North Carolina, Pennsylvania, and Michigan, as discussed in the next chapter. However, when all states with more than one district are considered, comparison of the average district compactness concludes that Democrats ignored this traditional districting principle more than did Republicans.[11] On each of the three measures considered here, Democratic districts scored less well than those fashioned by the GOP. Legislatively drawn plans in states not controlled by one party were more compact than those drawn by Republicans or Democrats on the convex hull measure, but on the other two measures they scored between the two parties' plans. In keeping with the suspicions of reformers, partisan plans tended to have less compact districts than plans drawn by other entities. Districts in plans prepared by independent commissions scored slightly better on Reock but were a little less compact than districts prepared by courts on Polsby-Popper and convex hull. In two of the nation's most populous states, restricting the influence of the legislature coincided with more compact districts in 2013 than in 2003. In California, authority to redistrict was shifted from the legislature to an independent commission, while in Florida the legislature retained the authority to draw new districts but a constitutional amendment banned efforts to advance the interests of a party or incumbent.

Although not scoring as exceptionally non-compact, districts in south Texas shown in figure 4.4 exemplify a bacon-strip approach. Moving from east to west, Districts 27, 34, 15, and 28 begin on the Rio Grande River and extend northward in search of necessary population. It would have been possible to design more compact districts but the design selected facilitated greater representation of Hispanic interests.

## RESPECT FOR POLITICAL BOUNDARIES

The National Conference of State Legislatures reports that twenty-nine states call for preserving political subdivisions when drawing congressional districts. Forty-three states include similar expectations for their legislative districts.[12]

When I have attended hearings conducted by legislative redistricting committees prior to the preparation of a new map, rural residents frequently asked that their county not be split between districts. These witnesses did not care too much about whether their county went into a predominately Democratic or a heavily Republican district so long as it remained united. Three-quarters of the local officials surveyed by the Rose Institute preferred to see their communities kept intact.[13] The county high school serves as a unifying institution in many rural communities. Rural voters identify with the county high school's athletic teams or band and rally behind it as they compete against the high schools of other counties. People throughout the county go to the county seat not only for legal matters but also for shopping, and all read the weekly county newspaper. With these shared experiences, they do not want to see their county divided between congressional, Senate, or state House districts. Smaller cities and counties when split worry that no legislator will find them

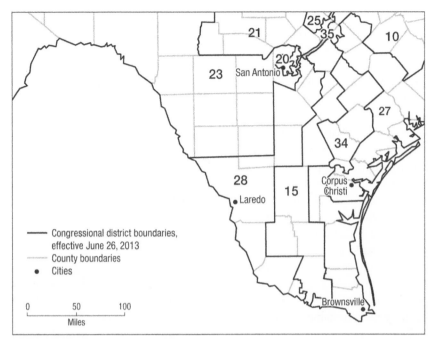

**Figure 4.4  Bacon Strip Districts in South Texas.** *Source*: Texas Department of Transportation Open Data Portal.

a sufficiently significant portion of the district to command the legislator's attention.[14]

Rural residents' preference for maintaining the integrity of their county goes back to the use of counties as the traditional basis for legislative representation. Prior to *Baker v. Carr*, except in the Northeast and the largest urban areas, most state legislators represented single counties. Frequently counties that got one or more legislative seats filled them in countywide elections. In the upper chamber of a legislature, the county boundaries were also important with senatorial districts composed of multiple counties in rural areas. Until *Wesberry v. Sanders*, few congressional districts outside of America's largest cities split county boundaries.

In many states in the first rounds of redistricting following the *Baker* and *Reynolds* decisions, efforts were made not to split counties. To avoid dividing counties, multiple legislators might be elected at-large from a county or from a district made up of multiple counties. Ultimately the demands for less and less population deviation among districts forced states to divide counties. States that needed to secure DOJ approval of their redistricting plans had to switch to single-member districts if a multi-member district would submerge a minority concentration that could dominate a single-member district. Challenges brought pursuant to Section 2 of the Voting Rights Act, as described in the previous chapter, forced states and many local governments to subdivide multi-member or at-large districts in order to create single-member districts in which the majority of the population belongs to a minority group.

Dividing counties in urban areas has now become widely accepted and is usually non-controversial since urban voters identify less with their county than do rural voters. Urban areas may actually enhance their position in the legislature by having multiple representatives. Cain notes that different legislators may represent different interests within the community.[15] A clear example would be the representatives of minority communities within a larger urban area.

Even with the demands for tiny population deviations, states with numerous counties can often draw congressional districts using counties as their primary building blocks. Iowa's constitution prohibits splitting counties between congressional districts. In 2003 the difference between the most and least populous districts was 134 individuals. Some jurisdictions, for example North Carolina, place avoidance of splitting counties right below population equality and equitable treatment of minorities in terms of priority.

The pressures in the 1990s to craft predominately minority districts which could be achieved only by aggregating minority residents in distant communities resulted in more violations of county boundaries than at any time in the past. Table 4.4 shows the extent to which majority-black districts split counties in southern states subject to Section 5. In every instance, the frequency with which counties were split in order to form a majority-minority district exceeded the incidence of split counties in the remainder of the state. Moreover the numbers of counties divided in order to create the majority-minority districts far exceeded the number of splits in the entire state in the previous decade. In Alabama, the newly designed, 67 percent black 7th District had fourteen counties, of which five were only partially in the district. Of Alabama's remaining fifty-three counties, only two were split between districts. The plan drawn for the 1980s split a total of just two counties. Thus to create the heavily black new district, five more counties were split than in the entire previous plan. None of Florida's three majority black districts contained all of a single county. Creation of the 3rd and 23rd Districts necessitated putting together black concentrations in multiple counties. The twenty-one counties split to create these three districts exceeded the fifteen splits in the 1980 plan. In the most extreme example, Louisiana's 4th District, known as the Zorro District because it looked something like a Z, contained parts of twenty-eight of the state's sixty-four parishes. District 4 included only four entire parishes.

Before minimizing population differences became common, most states could largely avoid splitting counties. The narrowing of the population deviations demanded by courts has necessitated more county splits. Splitting counties reached new heights in the 1990s when jurisdictions believed that

Table 4.4  Counties Split for New Majority-Black Congressional Districts and Elsewhere in Southern Districts Drawn in the Early 1990s

| State | District No. | Splits in Black District(s) | Splits in Other Districts* | 1980 Splits |
|---|---|---|---|---|
| Alabama | 7 | 5/14** | 2/53*** | 2/67 |
| Florida | 3 | 14/14 | 8/46 | 15/67 |
| | 17 | 1/1 | | |
| | 23 | 7/7 | | |
| Georgia | 2 | 12/35 | 6/102 | 3/159 |
| | 11 | 8/22 | | |
| Louisiana | 4 | 24/28 | 4/36 | 7/64 |
| North Carolina | 1 | 19/28 | 15/62 | 4/100 |
| | 12 | 10/10 | | |
| South Carolina | 6 | 11/16 | 2/30 | 1/46 |
| Virginia**** | 3 | 11/18 | 11/123 | 6/141 |

*Source*: Charles S. Bullock III and Richard E. Dunn, "The Demise of Racial Districting and the Future of Black Representation," *Emory Law Journal* 48 (Fall 1999), 1218.
*Counties split because they are shared with a majority black district and a predominately white district are not included in this column.
**Number of counties split/total number of counties in district.
***Number of counties split/total number of counties in state not included in majority-black districts.
****Includes independent cities and counties.

they had an obligation to maximize the number of minority districts. Today, legislatures often violate county lines in order to pack members of a single party into a district. Some majority-minority districts continued to split counties as the versions of Florida-5 and North Carolina-1 and -12 put into effect in 2013, with the Florida district and North Carolina-12 being elongated, narrow strips that did not contain any entire county.

Daniel Bowen has developed a measure for respect for political boundaries. He calls his measure coterminosity calculated as the share of a district's boundary that also serves as a state, county, or municipal boundary. He reports that congressional districts that score high on coterminosity have constituents more likely to contact their representative, have more positive contacts, and to be aware of projects the legislator secured for the district (allocation responsiveness).[16]

## MAINTENANCE OF COMMUNITIES OF INTEREST

As one of their principles for congressional districting, twenty-one states call for maintenance of communities of interest. Preserving communities of interest is a goal in twenty-four states when redistricting the legislature. While redistricting committees are often encouraged to avoid splitting communities of interest, rarely are workable definitions provided to define what constitutes a community of interest. As we saw in chapter 3, if the community of interest is defined in racial or ethnic terms, then the Voting Rights Act provided the basis for a challenge. One major case dealt with alternative communities of interest. Hasidic Jews in New York City went to court when the legislature split the one district from which they had been able to elect their preference in order to create a majority-black district.[17] The Supreme Court upheld the decision by the New York legislature to draw a heavily African American district even though that eliminated the prospects for the Hasidic Jewish community. The Court reasoned that the legislature appropriately gave precedence to black concerns since the Voting Rights Act specifically addressed the interests of that community.

The challenges to the elongated, race-based districts of the 1990s raised questions about what constitutes a community of interests. Defendants in these cases argued that shared racial characteristics might suffice to define a community of interest even if the district stretched over hundreds of miles. Attorneys defending these districts pointed to shared socioeconomic characteristics, noting that the residents of these majority-minority districts tended to be less well educated and less affluent than the average for their state. These arguments proved unsuccessful when the record showed that the legislature had been primarily concerned with drawing a district in which a minority group would dominate. At the very end of the 1990s North Carolina successfully defended a district that plaintiffs had claimed was race based by claiming that the legislature had been motivated chiefly by partisan rather than racial concerns.[18]

Figure 4.6 shows how Illinois went about separating ethnic groups in an effort to provide representation for different communities of interest. In black is the "Earmuff District" first devised in 1992 and maintained ever since as a majority Hispanic district. It encircles three sides of the 55 percent African American 7th, a district that relies on a thin tendril to connect its southeastern portion. District 3, whose northeast corner utilizes a narrow neck that squeezes between District 4 and 7, was almost 80 percent white in 2010. The 1st District extends a finger into what with a more compact design would be the 7th District in order to include Barack Obama's home.

The Florida congressional map implemented in 2013 but subsequently changed also provided examples of communities of interest. The 1st District represented the western Panhandle. District 22, shown in figure 4.5, linked affluent communities along the Gold Coast from West Palm Beach through Boca Raton and down to Fort Lauderdale. Just to the west, District 21 contained newer developments and a relatively large Jewish population.

Brunell points out that maintenance of communities of interest and respect for county lines will conflict to the extent that communities of interest spread across county boundaries.[19] This may be the case for a minority population while, in contrast, an area of a state, like Florida's Panhandle may largely track with counties.

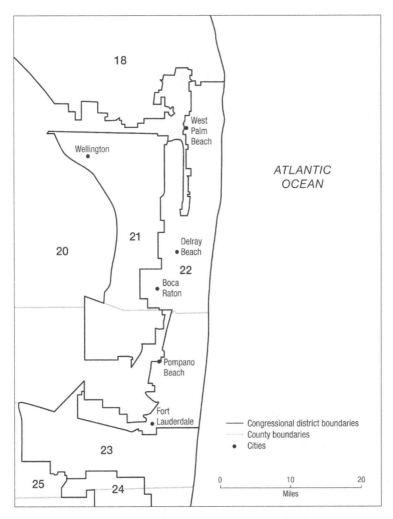

ATLANTIC OCEAN

**Figure 4.5   South Florida Congressional Districts.** *Source*: Florida Legislature, Florida Geographic Data Library.

## PROTECTING INCUMBENTS

Especially when it comes to drawing the lines for state legislative districts and local legislative bodies, protecting incumbents often gets high priority because it is incumbents who create the new districts. Bruce Cain articulates the case for including the location of incumbents among the factors considered by a legislature. "It is hardly consistent with democratic theory to argue that a government whose legitimacy depends on duly elected representatives should permit their unnecessary and arbitrary removal."[20] Not pairing

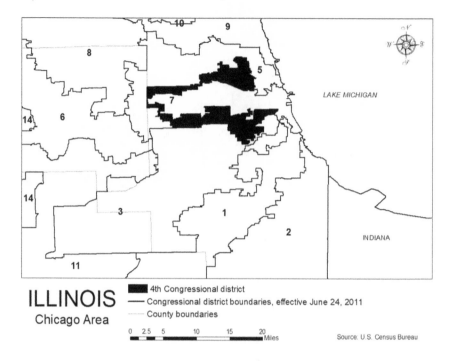

**Figure 4.6    Illinois's "Earmuff District."** *Source*: U.S. Census Bureau.

incumbents is included in the guidelines of eight states when drawing congressional districts and in eleven states when drawing legislative maps. Even when there is no obligation to protect incumbents, some jurisdictions try not to imperil incumbents or to make their districts more competitive. Protecting incumbents cannot justify deviations from the equal population standards nor would it withstand a challenge under the Voting Rights Act. One scholar estimates that the congressional plans drawn following the 2000 census sought to protect 231 of the House incumbents.[21]

Plans prepared by legislatures in states where each party controls one chamber or where the governor does not belong to the same party as a majority of the legislators often produce plans that protect both parties' incumbents. On the other hand, when a single party controls the legislative process, it will likely protect its own incumbents but may seek to defeat opposing incumbents. For example, when Texas Republicans redrew their congressional map in 2003, they separated eleven of the seventeen Democratic incumbents from the bulk of their constituents and this resulted in the defeat of four of these incumbents, the retirement of a fifth, and a sixth incumbent changed parties and became a Republican.[22]

A 2004 Georgia case further defined the appropriate weight to be given incumbency. In remapping the state legislative districts, Georgia

Democrats protected their own incumbents while going out of their way to pair Republican incumbents. Even though prior to redistricting Democrats' districts tended to be underpopulated while Republicans' districts were frequently overpopulated, only one Democratic incumbent failed to have a district in which to run under the new plan and she retired. On the other hand, eight of twenty-two incumbent Republican senators and thirty-six of seventy-three Republican representatives found themselves paired with another legislator.[23] Nine House districts forced two Republicans to compete for a single seat while four multi-member districts forced three Republicans to compete for two seats. The Republican senators who left the legislature because of the pairings took with them fifty-one years of seniority. The extent to which Democrats went to put multiple Republicans in the same district was shown in figure 1.3, which depicts House District 137 that wandered across parts of five southwest Georgia counties in order to put the only two Republicans in that corner of the state into a single district.

When the Democrats' plans came under review by a federal court, the unequal treatment of Democratic and Republican incumbents figured into the decision that invalidated the plans. The court rejected one of the Democrats' justifications for the plan, which was incumbency protection.[24] As the court noted, it protected only Democratic incumbents and a plan that treated incumbents so differently depending on their partisanship did not provide an adequate justification for the population deviations in the plan.

As an aside, efforts to defeat Republican incumbents had major negative consequences for the Democratic Party. Democrats singled out Sonny Perdue for punishment because while he had been the Democratic president pro tempore of the Senate—the highest office in that chamber—he switched allegiance and became a Republican. Irate Democrats immediately punished Perdue by taking away his office in the Capitol and relegating him to the back of the Legislative Office Building across the street. He also paid a price in terms of his committee assignments as he lost seats on powerful committees and ended up on a set of distinctly second-rate ones. When it came time for redistricting, Democrats continued their revenge by transforming his district. Perdue, rather than seeking reelection in his drastically changed district, ran for governor and defeated the incumbent Democrat in 2002. A Republican member of Congress saw his district disappear when Democrats extended Jack Kingston's (R) 1st Congressional District more than halfway across the state and sent a finger into Colquitt County just far enough to pick up Saxby Chambliss's (R) home. Rather than face his fellow Republican, Chambliss ran for the U.S. Senate and defeated the incumbent Democrat Max Cleland.

While incumbency is almost always a factor in plans drawn by legislatures, it may be less significant when commissions carry out the task. In the states that have redistricting commissions and in Iowa, the entity responsible for drawing the districts may not consider where incumbents live. Five states that allow the legislature to redistrict prohibit it from considering where congressional incumbents live. In Iowa, almost half of the state legislators ended up paired with other legislators in the 2001 plan.[25]

Even in efforts to protect incumbents, it is unlikely that all can be given districts in which they feel comfortable. In both 1972 and 1982, the number of districts in which no incumbent competed increased substantially over the number in the previous election.[26] Undoubtedly some of these incumbents who retired could have won additional terms but the uncertainty introduced by having to run in newly configured districts raised the costs of running to an unacceptable level.

Incumbents can become especially vulnerable when the legislature fails to complete its obligation to produce a new map. In some instances judges direct the expert tapped to fashion a map not to consider where incumbents live. Fourteen states prohibit consideration of where incumbents live when drawing congressional districts and fifteen states include the same prohibition when fashioning new legislative maps. Not surprisingly, maps drawn with no consideration of incumbency invariably pair current members. In some instances the court has allowed adjustments to unpair incumbents when that can be done by making minor changes in the map.[27]

## CORE PRESERVATION

Related to the success of an incumbent following redistricting is whether the core constituency of the incumbent has been maintained intact in the incumbent's district. Removing core supporters from an incumbent's district may well condemn that legislator to defeat, as may a districting plan that divides the incumbent's strong supporters among multiple districts, forcing the incumbent to choose one district in which to run. As of 2019 eight states included in their principles to guide redistricting a statement calling for maintenance of district cores in congressional plans. Maintenance of a district's core is called for in nine states when redrawing legislative maps.

Of course instances in which incumbents get paired almost by definition assure that at least one incumbent has been divorced from the core of the district she represented. When an area is losing population, this may be unavoidable. However when a party sets out to disadvantage the opposition, separating an incumbent from the core of the district is an effective technique. When Texas carried out the mid-decade redistricting in 2003, one of the Republicans' chief objectives was the defeat of Martin Frost (D). In their successful attack on Frost, Republicans placed parts of his district in five new districts. Another target, Charles C. Stenholm (D), got paired with a Republican incumbent, Randy Neugebauer, with the new district consisting of 58 percent of Neugerbauer's old district and 31 percent of Stenholm's old district. The Republican, having the core of his old district in the new one, easily defeated Stenholm 58–40 percent.[28] Democrats have also divorced opposing party incumbents from key portions of their constituencies. In order to eliminate Roscoe Bartlett (R), Maryland Democrats substituted Washington suburbanites for his rural Republicans along the Pennsylvania border.

## AVOID PAIRING INCUMBENTS

As noted in chapter 1, a basic gerrymandering trick pairs the incumbents of the party not involved with crafting new districts. Eight states ban unnecessary incumbent pairing for their congressional plans, a ban included by eleven states for their legislative chambers. The attempt to protect incumbents has a strong southern flavor, with five states in the Old Confederacy throwing a lifeline to state incumbents while four seek to protect their members of Congress. Another three Sun Belt states seek to protect incumbents at both the state and congressional levels. The southern and Border states with their traditions of one-party politics may have wanted to protect incumbents, recognizing that with seniority in Congress came more federal dollars.

## OTHER CONSIDERATIONS

In addition to the factors discussed above, idiosyncratic considerations may prove extremely important to individual incumbents. Legislators may seek to block plans that remove from their districts the homes of relatives or, even more importantly, generous contributors. Access to potential contributors may also prompt incumbents to oppose removing facilities such as airports from their districts. Representatives John Lewis (D-GA) and Eddie Bernice Johnson (D-TX) have fought to retain international airports in their districts. The airlines, their suppliers, and those who have contracts to operate businesses in the airport provide campaign dollars.

## CONTROVERSY

### Arguments For

Counties provided the primary building blocks for legislative districts for most of the nation's history and in less populated areas people still identify with counties, so to the extent possible counties should be kept whole in districting plans. Even when the need to minimize population deviations makes it impossible to avoid splitting counties, mapmakers should strive to avoid districts that connect far-flung pieces of geography by means of touch points, waterways, or narrow necks since those designs make it difficult for voters to know what district they live in. In more compact districts, voters are more likely to know the name of their legislator. Moreover, campaigning is easier in compact districts while in needlessly far-flung districts, incumbents may rarely visit the more distant parts. Splitting small counties makes it less likely that either legislator who represents the area will be responsive to that community's needs.

Districts should retain the core populations of incumbents since they have established relationships with their constituents. Moreover, the incumbents' experience benefits both their constituents and the legislature. The replacement of incumbents should come about as a result of voter dissatisfaction and not because of mapmakers' decisions.

## Arguments Against

The factors in this chapter cannot all simultaneously be achieved. Not only do they often conflict with one another; they are often at odds with the primary demands for population equality among districts and the avoidance of discriminatory practices. These secondary items are not legally enforceable and, to the extent that mapmakers try to honor them, it makes their jobs more difficult.

Communities of interest, especially in urban areas, do not coincide with county or city boundaries, so that giving precedence to traditional political boundaries may split communities of interest. Moreover, to unite communities that share interests may require drawing strange-looking districts in order to bring together people with shared values while avoiding those who lack the relevant characteristic and remain within the narrow population parameters permitted by courts.

Dividing a city or large county between districts may enhance the influence of that entity. There will be two legislators to lobby on behalf of the community with each representing a different component, perhaps with one coming from a minority population. Having representatives from both political parties will ensure a seat at the table who can articulate the community's concerns regardless of which party has a majority in the legislature.

The primary way to get major policy change requires replacing incumbents. Protecting incumbents denies the legislature the new blood of policy innovations. Displacing incumbents by combining their districts or removing their cores is a standard part of redistricting where the majority takes advantage of the minority. It has been this way for hundreds of years and will probably continue to be practiced in single-member district political systems.

## CONCLUSIONS

The factors reviewed in this chapter have been lumped together as traditional districting principles. Thirty-two states included one or more of these in their guidelines for remapping congressional districts as of 2019; every state requires that its legislative districts be contiguous and all but two include at least one of the other considerations.[29] Only New Mexico and Oklahoma include all six of the elements considered in this chapter for their congressional districts. These two states plus Arkansas and South Carolina consider all six factors when redistricting the state legislature.

A state's guidelines for redistricting can become important if the plan is subsequently challenged in court. The degree to which the jurisdiction honored the criteria it articulated can help in the state's defense and may become a factor in the court's decision. A state may be able to justify minor population deviations by noting that it adhered to traditional districting principles established prior to the session. On the other hand, if a jurisdiction fails to honor the principles laid out prior to the redistricting session that may provide a basis for a court throwing out the plan.

To some extent the factors reviewed in this chapter are a "wish list" in the sense that it would be very difficult if not impossible to achieve all of these objectives simultaneously while also minimizing population differences and protecting the political interests of minorities. The greatest difficulty usually involves efforts to create majority-minority districts. Attaining that objective may prevent creation of more compact districts, result in disregarding political boundaries, and separate some incumbents from the core of their former districts. In the early 1990s, the concept of contiguity got stretched in the creation of some majority-minority districts, although it might have been possible to have created the desired districts without resorting to touch-point or water contiguity. Of the ten least compact districts drawn in place in 2013, several have been majority-minority for decades.

Respect for political boundaries must also give way to requirements that districts have equal populations. While Iowa has succeeded in maintaining whole counties when designing congressional districts, many states would find it impossible to avoid splitting counties when drawing congressional districts. No state could draw districts for its own legislature without dividing counties and probably no state could apportion seats in its legislature without crossing some county lines. The requirements for equalizing populations among districts and not disadvantaging minorities by stacking them in multi-member districts dictate the drawing of many single-member districts. If the minority population spreads across county lines, it may be necessary to ignore those lines when creating majority-minority districts.

Protecting incumbents becomes impossible when states lose congressional districts. It may also be impossible to maintain each incumbent's district even when the number of seats remains constant in areas of a state that have experienced substantial population loss or have failed to grow at anything approaching the rate of the rest of the state.

## Chapter 5

# Partisan Gerrymandering

## *All's Fair in Love, War, and Redistricting, Saith the U.S. Supreme Court, But Others Beg to Differ*

The gerrymander overcometh all. What demographics give, legislators can take away in the dead of the night.[1]

Even the most egregious partisan gerrymanders do not "lock-in" one party's control over the state.[2]

Partisan redistricting plans are not as successful as those who generate them expect, in part because the results are influenced by national political swings.[3]

So trying to say that a certain degree of political gerrymandering or partisan gerrymandering is too much is trying to figure out, like, how much gambling in a casino is too much.[4]

We conclude that partisan gerrymandering claims present political questions beyond the reach of the federal courts. Federal judges have no license to reallocate political power between the two major political parties, with no plausible grant of authority in the Constitution, and no legal standards to limit and direct their decisions. . . . What the appellees and dissent seek is an unprecedented expansion of judicial power.[5]

[I]n the blood sport of redistricting, the most cravenly political results are won with calculating prudence.[6]

But for the federal judiciary to be ignorant of politics is dangerous. By failing to understand the way congressional elections work, or by choosing not to think much about it, federal judges have already created chaos over the difficult issue of how districts should be drawn.[7]

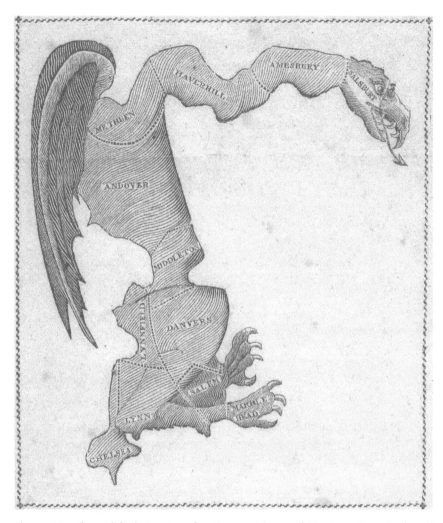

**Figure 5.1  The Original Gerrymander.** *Source*: Library of Congress, Rare Book and Special Collections Division.

Partisan mischief dates back to the earliest congressional election when Patrick Henry sought to design a congressional district that would defeat James Madison's bid for a seat. Also, during the early days of the Republic, Massachusetts governor Elbridge Gerry's effort to promote the fortunes of his party at the expense of the Federalists added "gerrymander" to the lexicon. The governor would no doubt be pleased to see that his actions earned him a place in every introductory course in American politics. That the practice continues would not surprise him and he might be impressed by the sophistication with which today's politicians carry out the activity for which he provided a name.

Single-member districts are particularly well suited to partisan gerrymandering, although multi-member districts with few seats as used in Ireland and Japan can also be manipulated to advance partisan fortunes.[8] The necessity of adjusting district boundaries in the United States after each census has created unprecedented opportunities to practice the art. While the decades during which districts were infrequently redrawn caused many problems as noted in chapter 2, inaction did prevent the current practice of a party that controls the redistricting process seeking to advance its goals at the expense of its opponents. The impetus to eliminate multi-member districts—which were the most common format for choosing state legislators sixty years ago—generated by the Voting Rights Act extended the need to adjust district boundaries to many cities and counties that had previously chosen all of their commissioners or councilors at-large. These obligations, coupled with sophisticated software, mean that the opportunities to gerrymander have never been greater than today.[9]

## SUCCESSFUL PARTISAN GERRYMANDERS

Partisans devote so much attention to drawing districts that will benefit their party because they hope their handiwork will last for a decade. Usually districts get drawn only once a decade, so that the individuals who get to craft the new map soon after the release of census figures can try to determine the partisan makeup of a legislative chamber for as many as five elections. As we will see later in this chapter, these efforts may prevail even in the face of substantial changes in partisan preferences in the electorate. Not surprisingly, however, there are other instances in which the clever machinations of a mapmaker come undone and can even backfire.

Because districting plans usually remain in place for a decade, parties invest resources in preparing for the process.[10] In states where legislators draw the maps, the surest way to be positioned to carry out a redistricting is to control all the relevant power positions immediately after the census. Party leaders recognize that if they can score a trifecta by simultaneously controlling the governorship and both chambers of the legislature, their plan will at a minimum not hurt them and, more likely, provide advantages.[11] Partisan gerrymanders of congressional districts are especially likely when the size of a state's delegation changes and the parties are competitive.[12] When states lose seats, the party in control can assess that loss against its opposition. If the state gains seats, the party in control strives to design a plan that will give it a better than even chance of winning the new seat or seats. In an extreme example, Texas Republicans produced a plan likely to give them three of the four new seats allocated to the Lone Star State by the 2010 census, even though the vast bulk of the new residents responsible for the state gaining seats were Hispanics who tend to vote for Democrats.[13] When the delegation size does not change, the majority party may nonetheless gain a seat or two by redrawing the districts. The sizes of state legislatures rarely change, so parties try to control the process in order to devise a more helpful plan.

A party that has little prospect of a trifecta may seek to win the governorship or a majority in one chamber in the election immediately preceding redistricting. That kind of success will enable the minority party to block the most partisan ideas from the opposition and may force a compromise plan. If compromise proves impossible, a party that controls only one of the units involved with redistricting can veto the effort, which will necessitate a court-drawn plan. Courts try to avoid taking sides in partisan conflicts and therefore plans designed by judges are fairer to both parties than plans drawn when one party has total control.[14]

## RESPONSIVENESS AND BIAS IN THE LEGISLATURE

The opportunity to reconfigure the political map of a jurisdiction has promoted widespread suspicions about the fairness of the outcome. Responsiveness and bias are two bases on which plans are judged.

### Responsiveness

Responsiveness, also referred to as the swing ratio, measures the degree to which the makeup of a legislative chamber will change when voter preferences change. Responsiveness and a higher swing ratio occur when a legislature has numerous competitive seats. Since the swing ratio is calculated as the percentage gain in seats by a party divided by its percentage gain in votes, a high swing ratio indicates that a relatively small improvement in a party's share of the votes statewide translates into a larger pick up in seats. For example, an election in which Democrats increased their share of the vote statewide by 2 percentage points while adding 5 percentage points to their share of the legislative seats has a swing ratio of 2.5.

An extensive analysis of redistricting of state legislatures between 1968 and 1988 shows that in the first elections held under both partisan and bipartisan redistricting plans the swing ratios exceed those for elections not preceded by a new set of districts.[15] Disrupting relationships between legislators and constituents produces heightened competitiveness, at least in the short term, in part fueled by increased numbers of open seats.

Most political scientists see advantages in designing competitive districts. Two arguments have been offered in favor of promoting partisan competition. First, districts with some prospect for partisan change will make a legislative body more responsive to shifting public preferences. Since legislators tend not to undergo dramatic changes in their preferences, achieving substantial new policy directions requires the replacement of one partisan majority with a majority from the opposing party.

Second, some have contended that competitive districts produce moderate legislators. The evidence for this second point is mixed. Indeed, the two reasons for having competitive districts are inconsistent. If competitive districts are desirable because they promote alteration in partisan control of the legislature and that in turn leads to different policy outputs, then it follows that when partisan control changes, newly elected legislators will have policy preferences quite different than those of their predecessors. Research finds that a change in partisanship results in the new legislator representing a different set of values and preferences within the district.[16] This is because legislators from opposing parties represent different reelection constituencies, to use Richard Fenno's terminology.[17] While swing districts may produce legislators more likely to engage in bipartisan efforts to resolve issues confronting the legislature, the overall record of legislators from marginal districts is quite similar to that of their fellow partisans and unlike the record of most members of the opposition party. The *National Journal* ranks members of Congress from the most liberal to the most conservative. Recently, it has been rare for any Democrat to be more conservative than the most liberal Republican. It was not always this way. During the 1940s, 1950s, or 1960s a number of southern Democrats had more conservative voting records than the moderate Republicans who came from the Northeast and the West Coast.

If legislators use redistricting to eliminate competition, then a new plan may be less responsive to shifts in voter preferences. Legislators who win by comfortable margins have little reason to fear retribution at the polls. They have greater latitude to vote as party leaders or interest groups request even if that means voting against constituency preferences. A more positive view of freedom from constituent demands holds that electorally secure members can behave as trustees and vote what they believe to be in the best interests of the nation or state. Yet a third perspective is that one-party district incumbents' only electoral fear is a primary challenge. With the only threat to reelection lurking in the primary, where the bulk of the voters will be strong partisans, the incumbent may take more extreme positions in order to head off a challenge from the party's radical fringe. For example, in 2020, the only threat to an incumbent in a solidly red district would come should the legislator not give full-throated support to President Trump. Fear is not misplaced since more extreme candidates have toppled leaders in both parties, as when Dave Brat knocked off Eric Cantor (R-VA) in 2014, while more recently Alexandria Ocasio-Cortez (D-NY) retired House Democratic caucus chair Joseph Crowley.[18]

David Cottrell compared the competitiveness of simulated plans with the actual plans for the 113rd Congress. He found that the plans adopted resulted in districts about 3 percentage points safer than did the simulations that relied on algorithms that consider equalizing populations, contiguity, and compactness but not partisanship or incumbency.[19] Partisans drew a few more safe districts for their members with both Republicans, but also Democrats, producing fewer competitive Democratic districts than came out of the simulations. A study of redistricting plans from the early 1990s and 2000s concluded that plans fashioned by a court or a commission produced a larger share of competitive districts than when a legislature designed them.[20]

## Bias

A second measure used to assess the fairness of districting plans compares the degree to which a plan advantages one party over the other. The calculation of bias recognizes that single-member districts are not intended to and rarely do result in parties having shares of seats in the legislature equal to their share of the votes. While all electoral systems pay a bonus to the largest party, the dividends are especially great in single-member election systems.[21] Calculating bias tests the assumption that a fair system pays the same size dividend to Democrats when they win a given share of the vote as would go to Republicans if they polled that percentage of the vote. Thus, if Democrats get 56 percent of the seats when winning 52 percent of the vote, then in a bias-free plan Republicans would also get 56 percent of the seats when winning 52 percent of the vote. Bias is measured as the deviation from the expectation that a plan will give each party the same seat bonus should it win a given majority of the vote.

Popular expectations consider bias more likely to be pronounced in a partisan plan than in a bipartisan plan. As examples of bias, the Brennan Center estimated that Ohio Democrats would need 54.7 percent of the vote to gain a fifth seat. Democrats got 47.6 percent statewide in 2018 but remained with only four of sixteen seats.

Gelman and King's study of twenty years of redistricting of state legislatures finds that "the difference in seats between a Democratic- and Republican-controlled redistricting plan is, on average, a substantial 4 percent of seats."[22] A surprising finding coming out of this study is that while partisan plans favor their creators, partisan as well as bipartisan plans result in *fairer*, that is, less biased, arrangements than if redistricting had not occurred. To explain this unexpected result the authors note that "the largest effects of redistricting change an existing huge bias in favor of one party to small bias in favor of the other."[23]

In the past even partisan plans rarely attempted to maximize a party's advantage. Factors other than maximizing partisan advantage, like equalizing populations and not discriminating against minorities, impose restraints on those who craft partisan plans.[24] In addition to the redistricting considerations introduced in previous chapters, party leaders may confront opposition within their own ranks. To maximize the number of seats that a party could hope to win will necessitate spreading the party's supporters strategically across districts. Incumbents who coast to victory would have to give up their excess supporters in order to convert districts that the party loses narrowly into districts that it can win. Often incumbents who objectively appear unbeatable feel threatened and fight to maintain their comfortable margins, thereby reducing the time spent campaigning. Even incumbents willing to compete in less secure districts for the good of the party may veto proposals that would deprive them of specific areas.

A complaint of those concerned about partisan gerrymandering has been that the plans drawn following the 2010 census were more extreme than those of earlier decades. North Carolina offers an example of a plan that pushed the upper limits. In explaining why he supported a congressional plan that provided Republicans with a 10–3 advantage, a Republican legislative leader explained that he pushed this plan because it was impossible to design an alternative that would give Republicans eleven seats. The demise of the requirement that selected states secure approval of plans from federal authorities may encourage adoption of extreme plans. With change in partisan control of the U.S. House on the line in each election, state legislators are more likely to push the envelope.

With more detailed data, the constraints on a party seeking to maximize its winnings under a new plan may have become weaker. Republicans won 13 of 18 Pennsylvania seats in three consecutive elections (2012–2016) despite often failing to poll a majority of the statewide vote. North Carolina is another example of a competitive state where the GOP dominated the House delegation during the 2010s.

## RESPONSIVENESS OF ANOTHER TYPE

Responsiveness can take a meaning other than the degree to which changes in the electorate translate into shifts in the partisan control of seats. Those who study the consequences of redistricting have also explored whether legislators change their behavior following significant reconfigurations of their districts. If given a substantially different constituency, does the legislator vote differently on roll calls in order to represent the preferences of the median voter in the new district? Do legislators given electorally safe districts become less attentive to the concerns of their constituents?

An incumbent who loses in the "redistricting lottery" and gets a much less hospitable district confronts several options. Retirement may be especially attractive to older incumbents who do not want to expend the energy and raise the funds needed to introduce themselves to their new constituents.[25] A second option is to remain true to your principles and prepare to lose gracefully. A third possibility is to shift toward the position of the median voter in the new district. Research shows that incumbents who manage to win reelection in their altered districts bring their roll call voting in line with their new constituents.[26]

Legislators who win reelection with little if any opposition may devote less energy to district concerns and may ignore constituent policy preferences. Among the least partisanly competitive districts are many of those represented by African Americans. Swain speculates that the electoral security of these districts may result in incumbents being less responsive to their constituents.[27] However, Claudine Gay shows that California legislators representing majority-minority districts where serious partisan challenges rarely occurred were as responsive to their constituents' preferences as representatives of majority-white districts and reacted to changes in public opinion.[28]

## PARTISAN GERRYMANDERS AND
## THE COURTS, PART I

That a party would take advantage of its opponent in the course of redistricting seemed so obvious that it contributed to the Supreme Court's refusal to consider a 1940s challenge to the malapportioned Illinois congressional delegation. Justice Felix Frankfurter dissuaded the court from entering the "political thicket" because he saw redistricting as an entirely political issue.[29] When the Court finally acknowledged the justiciability of challenges to unequal apportionment plans, it based its opinion on unequal treatment of different parts of the state. The court did not object to plans that had equally populated districts but which discriminated against one of the political parties. Justice Sandra Day O'Connor, the only recent member of the Supreme Court to have served as a state legislator, consistently refused to overturn partisan gerrymanders. When politicians draw new district lines, partisanship will almost always be a factor. It may be muted under some circumstances but for political actors partisan considerations are never totally obliterated. As Justice Byron White acknowledged, "District lines are rarely neutral phenomena."[30]

In most states the legislature redraws congressional and state legislative districts. A norm in many states allows each chamber a largely unfettered hand in designing its own districts which the opposite chamber then rubber stamps.[31] When one party controls a state's redistricting process, it can take advantage of the opposition and draw lines that enhance the majority's position.[32] On the other hand, if parties share control of the redistricting process, then while partisanship will no doubt influence the placement of some district lines, the ultimate plan will more likely provide a balance. Indeed, when each party controls part of the process, the resulting plan may seek to protect both parties' incumbents. Parties do not always exploit their upper hand, as demonstrated in California where in 2002 the Democrats who controlled the process nonetheless opted to protect incumbents of both parties with the exception of one Democrat. The result was a bipartisan gerrymander so effective that in the course of 265 elections held during the decade only once did a district experience a change in partisan control.

Despite a tendency for legislatures when redrawing districts to make them secure for one party, or the other, some states have acted to rein in partisanship. The Arizona constitution and the redistricting standards adopted in Washington call for the creation of partisanly competitive districts.[33] The initiative process amended the Florida constitution which now bans plans that advantage a party or incumbent.

While courts have rarely required that parties treat one another fairly, if a plan seeks fairness as its objective, courts in the past tolerated greater deviation from the one person, one vote standard. When Connecticut devised a plan designed to produce a legislature in which the partisan makeup would reflect partisan distribution in the electorate, the Supreme Court rejected a challenge that questioned the population deviations.[34]

## California 1980s

Although long dead (Nancy Pelosi holds Burton's seat), former Representative Philip Burton (D-CA) continues to be recognized as one of the most astute wielders of the redistricting pen. Burton took the lead in drawing the congressional plan for California following the 1980 census. His plan, one of ten partisan gerrymanders that decade[35] and widely criticized for the way in which it separated Democrats and Republicans with the advantage going to his fellow Democrats, performed as its creator had anticipated. The last election under the previous plan sent 22 Democrats and 21 Republicans to Congress. This balance in the congressional delegation paralleled the Senate representation which had a Democrat and a Republican. Against this background of an evenly divided state, Burton's plan rewarded Democrats with 29 of the 45 seats the new census gave California. At the end of the decade, the state still had a divided Senate delegation and a Republican governor in place of the Democrat who approved Burton's plan. George Bush won the state's electors with 51 percent of the vote in 1988. Nonetheless, the Burton gerrymander largely held with Democrats retaining a 26–19 advantage at the end of the decade.

## Texas

A second example of the longevity of an effective gerrymander comes from Texas where another member of Congress, in this case Martin Frost (D), performed much as Burton had in California. Frost turned his attention to redistricting the Lone Star State following the 1990 census which gave Texas three new congressional seats. Republicans already controlled one Senate seat and easily carried the state in the three presidential elections of the 1980s. Even in 1988 when Democrats nominated the state's senior senator Lloyd Bentsen for vice president, Democrats managed only 43 percent of the vote in the presidential election against another Texan, George Bush. With Republican fortunes rising in Texas the GOP hoped to expand on its eight congressional seats. Frost drove a stake through the heart of that ambition.

Frost's audacious plan sought to increase the minority presence in the delegation while simultaneously protecting the seats of his fellow Anglo Democrats. His plan rewarded Mexican Americans and African Americans, two increasingly critical components of the Democratic coalition. He created a district in Dallas likely to elect an African American and anchored another district in the Rio Grande Valley which would almost certainly send a Hispanic to Congress. The third district, which appears in figure 3.3, became part of one of the most convoluted line drawing exercises anywhere in the nation, as it separated Houston-area Latinos from blacks so as to maintain the 18th District as one likely to elect an African American while creating a heavily Hispanic district just to the east. The growing Republican electorate got packed into a few districts where the GOP piled up overwhelming majorities.

The effectiveness of the Frost gerrymander got an immediate test. In 1992, the total vote received by Democratic congressional candidates came to just over 2.8 million while Republicans attracted 2.6 million voters for their congressional candidates statewide. While the Democratic congressional vote in Texas only narrowly exceeded that for Republicans, Democrats extended their control over the delegation by winning twenty-one of thirty seats. The performance of Republican congressional candidates paled against their state legislative candidates, who won 42 percent of the state Senate seats and 39 percent of the House seats in 1992 compared with 30 percent of the congressional delegation.

Two years later, Republicans running for Congress did even better, taking 57 percent of the vote statewide.[36] In this year when Republicans captured a majority of the U.S. House for the first time in forty years, they experienced only modest gains in the Texas delegation, increasing their numbers from nine to eleven. Despite having won a majority of the votes, Republicans received fewer than 40 percent of the seats, being underrepresented by 20 percentage points. Frost had so successfully gerrymandered that winning 8.5 percentage points more of the vote netted Republicans 6.7 percentage points more seats for a swing ratio of 0.79. In 1996, as table 5.1 shows, the Republican vote share came in at 54 percent and they held 20 of the 29 partisan offices in Texas elected statewide. Yet they came nowhere close to that share of the congressional seats as they held only 43 percent of the Texas seats in Congress. For the remainder of the decade, Democrats frequently had a share of the seats 10 percentage points greater than their share of the statewide vote for Congress. As an indication of the pro-Democratic bias in Frost's plan, in 1992, 51.6 percent of the vote won Democrats 70 percent of the seats. In 2000, the GOP almost matched the 1992 Democratic vote share, yet Republican's 50.8 percent of the vote got them just 43.3 percent of the seats. These figures demonstrate a clear failure of the plan to perform as one would if it lacked bias, as defined earlier in this chapter.

While the Frost plan played a major role in allowing Democrats to thwart the will of the majority of the statewide electorate, two other factors contributed. One is the well-known ability of incumbents to retain their positions even as the partisan preferences of the electorate change. And the other relates to the cheap seats argument discussed in chapter 2. The heavily black and Latino districts rarely involved competitive elections and many of the residents in these districts had relatively less education and lower incomes. These conditions contributed to lower rates of turnout than in the more affluent districts that elected Republicans.

When it came time to redistrict following the 2000 census, Texas failed to adopt a new plan. Republicans controlled the governorship and had a narrow

**Table 5.1  Democratic Vote Share and Share of the Congressional Seats in Texas**

| Year | Vote Share | Share of Seats |
|------|-----------|----------------|
| 1992 | 51.6% | 70.0% |
| 1994 | 43.1% | 63.3% |
| 1996 | 45.8% | 56.7% |
| 1998 | 46.1% | 56.7% |
| 2000 | 49.2% | 56.7% |
| 2002 | 45.1% | 53.1% |
| 2004 | 41.4% | 34.4% |

*Source*: Author.

majority in the Senate. But the 78–72 Democratic House majority refused to accept plans offered by Republicans. Ultimately a three-judge federal panel devised the new plan for the state's thirty-two districts. The presiding judge explained precisely how the court went about crafting the map. The court first placed the existing seven Hispanic and two black districts on the map. Next the judges drew in the two new districts gained through reapportionment and placed them in areas that had experienced the most rapid growth. "We then drew in the remaining districts throughout the state, emphasizing compactness, while observing the contiguity requirement. We struggled to follow local political boundaries that have historically defined communities—county and city lines."[37] The resulting map avoided pairing any incumbents as it relied heavily on the preexisting map so that 78 percent of all Texans had the same member of Congress in the new districts as in the old ones. The court opinion concluded that "the plan is likely to produce a congressional delegation roughly proportional to the party voting breakdown across the state."[38] In the new plan, 21 of 32 districts voted for George Bush in the 2000 election. In 19 of these districts Bush polled more than 60 percent of the vote, compared with the 59 percent he received statewide.

While the court expected its plan to reflect partisan voting preferences in the state, the power of incumbency overcame these efforts. In 2002, Democrats retained seventeen seats, the same number they had under the previous plan, while the Republicans added the two new seats to the thirteen they had previously held. Republicans won only 47 percent of the seats even though they took 55 percent of the statewide congressional vote. Even though Republicans controlled all twenty-nine of the state's partisan positions elected statewide, they could not yet win control the congressional delegation. Gains registered for other offices led Republicans to expect far more than a gain of two seats. "A gain of five is our worst-case scenario," Representative Joe Barton (R) had predicted. "We could get to plus-ten but we would need to be creative."[39]

The unwillingness of the Democratically controlled state House to go along with the Republican plan did not help the Democrats when it came to the state legislature. Under Texas law, if the legislature fails to adopt a districting plan, then the Legislative Redistricting Board (LRB), which consists of the lieutenant governor, House Speaker, attorney general, comptroller, and land commissioner, will draw districts for the state House and Senate. In 2002, the LRB had only one Democrat, House Speaker Pete Laney, which allowed Republicans to shape the state legislative chambers. The 2002 elections produced a House with an 88–62 Republican majority. In the Senate, Republicans emerged with nineteen of the thirty-one seats.

While states have usually drawn new districts only once in a decade unless ordered to make changes as a result of losing lawsuits, Texas Republicans saw a chance to right what they perceived to be a long festering wrong. U.S. House Majority Leader Tom DeLay (R) hoped that redrawing Texas would give Republicans in the U.S. House more breathing room since, after the 2002 election, they had only a 229–205 margin. Steve Bickerstaff provides a detailed account of the political machinations that went into the adoption of a new Texas congressional plan.[40]

The DeLay plan sought to put in play each of the seats filled by Anglo Democrats while protecting Republican, Latino, and African American incumbents. The plan enhanced the black concentration in a Houston district which facilitated the election of a second African American from that city. It also drew a district rooted in the Rio Grande Valley that extended to Austin that had the potential to send another Latino to Congress. Martin Frost, whose handiwork allowed Democrats to control the Texas delegation during the 1990s and traces of which persisted through the 2002 election, attracted special attention from the Republican mapmakers eager to retire him. They dismantled his district and spread its parts among five districts in the Dallas–Fort Worth Metroplex with 26.5 percent of the old district's population being the largest piece kept intact.

The new plan achieved much of what Republicans had hoped for. Frost lost reelection 54–44 percent. Four other Anglo Democrats also either lost election or retired while Ralph Hall, the most senior and conservative of the Democrats, successfully sought reelection as a Republican. Freshman Anglo Democrat Chris Bell lost the primary to an African American who became Texas's third black member of Congress. Of the four who lost general elections, three had to compete against a Republican incumbent in a district that favored the GOP.

In 2004, for the first time, Republicans secured a larger share of the delegation seats (66 percent) than of the vote (59 percent). The swing ratio in 2004 was just over five. While it is common for the party that receives most of the votes in a single-member district system to obtain a seat bonus, the payoff for Texas Republicans, even in 2004, remained smaller than Democrats had enjoyed for decades. Seabrook concludes that the 2003 GOP plan was fairer than the Democratic gerrymander of the previous decade.[41]

## The 2010 Round of Redistricting

Republicans stole a march on Democrats when it came to preparing for redistricting after the 2010 census. The GOP, aided by the Tea Party Movement, the usual mid-term push back against the president's party, but also careful planning and a generous budget, did exceptionally well in 2010 state legislative elections. In addition to reclaiming a majority in the U.S. House, Republicans gained almost 700 state legislative seats and displaced

Democratic majorities in twenty-one state legislative chambers. Republicans, who in previous decades had often looked on as Democrats drew new maps—if they were allowed in the committee rooms when plans were perfected—had served their apprenticeship and in 2011–2012 demonstrated their mastery. Now it was Democrats' turn to scream "Unfair!" Their success positioned the GOP to redraw seventeen states that contained 40 percent of the U.S. House seats compared to five states with 10 percent of the seats where Democrats controlled the legislative process and the governorship. Independent commissions, courts, or bipartisan efforts redrew the other half of the seats.

Caught up in the firestorm of partisan politics, parties exploited their positions when they had a trifecta. McGann and his co-authors demonstrate that parties having a trifecta carried out partisan gerrymanders in electorally competitive states but not where they had a commanding position.[42] Following the 2011 round of redistricting, bias favoring the GOP increased in twenty-two states including four in which a prior Democratic bias was eliminated. In contrast, the only two states in which conditions for Democrats improved came in states strongly slanted toward the GOP. The nationwide bias was over 9 percent, about three times as great as a decade earlier. The national figure meant that if the GOP secured half the vote, it would get 55 percent of the seats. McGann and colleagues projected that Democrats would need 54 percent of the vote nationwide to win a majority in the House. In 2018, Democrats won 54 percent of the two-party congressional vote nationwide and won 54 percent of the seats.[43]

Table 5.2 shows the linkage between the share of the votes won and the share of congressional seats won under differing conditions of partisan influence in 2012. In the states in which one party drew the new districts, it won more than 70 percent of the seats when taking about 55 percent of the vote. In states where neither party controlled redistricting, Republicans' share of seats was 2 percentage points less than their vote share. Democrats got "slightly more than half the vote and 56 percent of the seats."[44] With Republicans controlling so many more seats, even though Democrats increased their nationwide share of the vote in 2012 by 4.1 percentage points over 2010 and

**Table 5.2  Shares of the Popular Vote and Congressional Seats Won in 2012 under Differing Partisan Configurations**

| Control of Redistricting | % of the Votes Won | % of Seats Won |
|---|---|---|
| Republicans | 53 | 72 |
| Democrats | 56 | 71 |
| Courts, Commissions, or Divided Government | | |
| Republicans | 46 | 44 |
| Democrats | 50+ | 56 |

*Source*: Created using information in Griff Palmer and Michael Cooper, "How Maps Helped Republicans Keep an Edge in the House," *New York Times* (December 14, 2012).

outpolled Republicans by 1.1 million votes, Republicans emerged with thirty-three more seats than the Democrats won.

## North Carolina

For decades North Carolina's congressional maps have been ground zero for gerrymandering lawsuits. Challenges to the I-85 District, created by Democrats in 1992, that extended from Charlotte to Durham at some points no wider than two lanes on the Interstate, made it to the Supreme Court four times. In the next decade, Obama carried North Carolina in 2008 when Democrats won the governorship and unseated a GOP senator. Even after the 2010 GOP wave, Democrats had a 7–6 edge in the congressional delegation despite winning just 46 percent of the vote—evidence of a Democratic gerrymander. While the 2010 wave could not dislodge the Democratic congressional majority, it cut a wide swath through the state legislature, giving Republicans majorities in both chambers for the first time.

The Tar Heel State's congressional plans designed by Republicans in 2011 became the poster child for a partisan gerrymander as becomes obvious when inspecting table 5.3. The first election in the new districts saw Republicans narrowly lose the congressional vote statewide yet win nine of the thirteen districts. Across the next three elections, Republicans held ten seats despite managing only narrow majorities in the electorate. Even a new map, drawn after the decade's initial map was thrown out as a racial gerrymander, failed to dislodge any of the ten Republicans. In 2018, the Republican majority of the vote resulted from the late Walter Jones having no opposition. Democrats won a majority of the vote in the twelve districts they contested. A more equitable distribution through the 2010s would have seen Republicans with seven seats. As shown in table 5.4, in the presidential elections on either side of the 2010 census, parties evenly split the Tar Heel vote and following the 2010 election the congressional delegation divided as evenly as possible with seven Democrats and six Republicans. When challenged in court, plaintiffs' experts testified that the plan's results could not have occurred by chance.

**Table 5.3   Republican Vote Share and Share of the Congressional Seats in North Carolina, 2012–2018**

| Year | Vote Share | Share of Seats |
|------|-----------|----------------|
| 2012 | 49.1% | 69.2% |
| 2014 | 55.7% | 76.9% |
| 2016 | 53.4% | 76.9% |
| 2018 | 51.0% | 76.9% |

*Source*: Author.

**Table 5.4   Examples of One-Party Congressional Redistricting Plans from the 2010s That Benefited the Party Drawing the Districts**

|  | Delegation 2010 | 2008 Presidential Vote | Delegation 2012 | 2012 Presidential Vote |
|---|---|---|---|---|
| *Republican Plans* | | | | |
| North Carolina | 6R-7D | 49%R-50%D | 9R-4D | 50%R-49%D |
| Pennsylvania | 12R-7D | 44%R-54%D | 13R-5D | 47%R-52%D |
| *Democratic Plans* | | | | |
| Illinois | 8D-11R | 62%D-37%R | 12D-6R | 58%D-41%R |
| Maryland | 6D-2R | 62%D-36%R | 7D-1R | 62%D-36%R |

*Source*: Author.

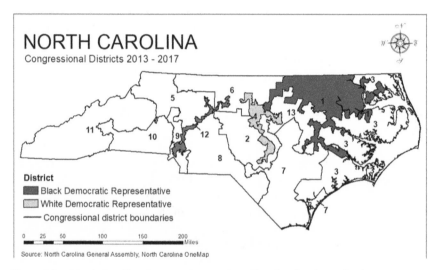

**Figure 5.2   North Carolina Congress, 2013–2017, Showing the Three Electing Democrats in 2014.** *Source*: North Carolina General Assembly, North Carolina One Map.

Figure 5.2 shows the North Carolina congressional districts drawn based on the 2010 census and from which three Democrats were elected in 2014. The design supports the conclusion of Azavea, as reported in table 4.3, that the Tar Heel State map was the second least compact. The 1st and 12th Districts that have elected African Americans since 1992 continue to retain shapes much like those of twenty years earlier in order to maximize black percentages with the former at 52.1 percent black and the latter 49 percent black.[45] The 4th District, which elected the third Democrat, was drawn at a third black. The average black percentage in the ten Republican districts was just under 15 percent. The three Democratic districts give further evidence of packing as Barack Obama polled more than 70 percent in each of them in 2012. In the GOP districts, Obama averaged 41 percent with a range of 38 to 43 percent. The Republican districts were safe for the party but had far smaller shares of wasted votes than the Democratic districts. Note also, how at several points District 3 exemplifies duck contiguity and the hook on the east side of District 2 that wraps around the 4th District.

## Pennsylvania

Pennsylvania, which joined North Carolina as one of the maps most often condemned as a partisan gerrymander during the 2010s, voted for President Obama twice giving him a ten-point edge in 2008 and half that margin four years later, as shown in table 5.4. At the time of the redistricting the state had a Republican and a Democratic senator and a Republican governor. The 2010 GOP wave reversed the congressional delegation from twelve Democrats and seven Republicans to a 12–7 Republican majority. The GOP-controlled legislature that redrew the state had to eliminate a district and in doing so it set out to consolidate the gains made in 2010. The new plan assessed the lost seat against the Democrats but also managed to create a thirteenth GOP district leaving Democrats with only five seats. The Brennan Center for Justice estimated that the plan netted the GOP four more seats than a more equitable design would have produced.[46] Chen and Cottrell's simulations using the 2008 presidential vote agree that the Pennsylvania plan favored Republicans but they believe that the advantage amounted to less than a seat.[47]

## Illinois

While more Republican than Democratic maps generated controversy during the 2010s, Democrats also practiced redistricting magic although they controlled the process in fewer states. Table 5.4 includes information for the two states in which Democratic handiwork most often drew criticism. Like in Pennsylvania, the 2010 red wave cost Democrats control of the Illinois delegation as it went from a 12–7 Democratic advantage to an 11–8 Republican majority. But Democrats who controlled the state legislature used redistricting to restore the status quo ante. Illinois lost a seat and that came out of the GOP holdings. Democrats achieved much more as they reclaimed four seats for a dozen while the GOP slumped to six wins. While Illinois regularly made the list of 2011 gerrymanders, those who have studied the impact of the plan conclude that because of the disproportionate share of the Democratic support concentrated in Chicago, Democrats had to pull out all the stops to secure a share of seats in line with their share of the votes.

## Maryland

Maryland, with the highest black percentage of any non-southern state, is reliably blue. Nonetheless the opposite sides of the state—the Eastern Shore and the strip that extends west to West Virginia—consistently sent Republicans to Congress. Maryland voters gave President Obama 62 percent of the vote in each election yet held 75 percent of the congressional districts. Notwithstanding that advantage, following the 2010 census, Democrats designed a plan to eliminate the western Republican. The 6th District had reached almost the entire length of the Mason-Dixon Line until it abutted the Republican 1st District. The new Democratic plan pitched the 6th south to Bethesda in the Washington suburbs. The old 6th District came close to the ideal population for the state, that is, the population of the state divided by the number of districts, which could have been achieved by removing 17,249 people. However rather than making the tweaks needed to bring the district's population in line, Democrats replaced 66,000 Republicans with Democrats.[48] The old district had a Cook Partisan Voting Index of R+13. The new district had a Cook Index of D+4. Roscoe Bartlett's (R) ten-term career ended in 2012 as he lost by 21 percentage points. Two years earlier, Barrett won by twenty-eight points. The Maryland plan joined one from North Carolina in the 2019 Supreme Court decision about the justiciability of partisan gerrymandering claims.

## UNSUCCESSFUL PARTISAN GERRYMANDERS

Phil Burton, Martin Frost, Tom DeLay, and less visible partisans in 2011 all succeeded in crafting plans that paid handsome dividends to their parties. However, as the poet Robert Burns observed, "The best laid schemes o' mice and men gang aft a-gley." And so can redistricting plans in what have been labeled "dummymanders."[49] The term dummymander suggests that the creators misread the electoral tea leaves when drawing the district. In some instances, the districts may have accurately reflected partisan strength when drawn but the creators failed in their objectives because they did not anticipate demographic trends. Suburbanization, the in-migration of a new ethnic group, or mobilization of a group, like suburban women who turned against Republicans in 2018, can transform a district that initially supported one party into one that elects candidates of the other party. An examination of seven partisan gerrymanders done in the 1970s concluded that only one succeeded.[50] With better and more comprehensive data and less split-ticket voting, gerrymandering of today may prove more reliable than in earlier times.

Table 5.5   The Republican Gerrymander in Indiana That Did Not Succeed

| Year | Vote Share | Share of Seats |
|------|-----------|----------------|
| 1982 | 50.8% | 50% |
| 1984 | 52.9% | 50% |
| 1986 | 49.0% | 40% |
| 1988 | 48.3% | 30% |
| 1990 | 45.1% | 20% |
| 1982–1990 | 49.2% | 38% |

## Indiana 1980s

Indiana lost its eleventh congressional seat following the 1980 census. The Republican-dominated legislature and governor devised what was considered at that time to be the most pro-Republican gerrymander in the nation.[51] Republicans who had held five of the eleven seats hoped to improve their standing with the new plan. The first test of the plan yielded inauspicious results as Republicans won a slight majority of the statewide congressional vote and, as table 5.5 shows, split the delegation holding on to their five seats. The GOP gerrymanderers had hoped for more than a fair plan; they hoped that they could translate a majority of the vote into more than a majority of the seats.

In 1984, with Ronald Reagan amassing 62 percent of Indiana's vote, the GOP share of the state's congressional vote rose to 53 percent. Despite the increase, Republicans failed to make headway. Indiana's Republican secretary of state certified fellow partisan Richard McIntyre as the winner of the 8th District by a margin of 34 votes. The Democratic candidate, Francis McClosky, appealed that decision. The Constitution makes each chamber of Congress the final arbiter of contested elections. The Democratic majority awarded McClosky the seat, finding that he had managed a four-vote majority. (As a sidenote, the seating of McClosky is the triggering event for the radicalization of Newt Gingrich and his followers which, a decade later, culminated in Republicans taking control of the House.)

In 1986, the Republican vote share slipped to 49 percent but their share of House seats declined to four. They were lucky to hold on to that since John Hiler won reelection by only 47 votes. In 1988, Republicans lost another seat reducing them to three and the final election held under the plan they had gerrymandered saw their numbers fall to only two of ten districts despite still winning almost half the vote statewide. The gerrymander failed to perform for Republicans because they had created too many marginal seats, seats that gradually moved toward the Democrats. Unlike in North Carolina, Pennsylvania, or Illinois in the 2010s, Republican greed in Indiana not only failed to give them a bonus of a sixth or even seventh seat but also made it

Table 5.6    Republican Vote Share and Share of the Congressional Seats in Pennsylvania*

| Year | Vote Share | Share of Seats |
|------|-----------|----------------|
| 2000 | 50.04% | 52.3% |
| 2002 | 60.3% | 63.2% |
| 2004 | 55.5% | 63.2% |
| 2006 | 45.3% | 42.1% |
| 2008 | 44.0 % | 36.8% |

\* Pennsylvania does not report results for candidates who have no opponent. In 2000, one Republican had
  no opponent and therefore the Republican vote share is reduced. In the other three election years, the
  total Democratic vote is reduced because of the absence of any challenger to the Democrat. In 2002,
  one Democrat had no opponent; in 2004 two Democrats had no opposition. In 2006, one Democrat
  drew no opponent.
*Source*: Author.

impossible for them to retain a share of seats roughly approximating their support in the electorate.

## Pennsylvania 2000s

A second story of redistricting gone bad again involves Republicans, this time in Pennsylvania. The Pennsylvania congressional delegation in 2001 had eleven Republicans and ten Democrats and, as table 5.6 shows, the parties evenly divided the popular vote. Reapportionment cost the Keystone State seats as it has after every census beginning with 1930. The new allotment gave the state nineteen seats. The Republican legislature set out to capitalize on the opportunity to draw the new districts and crafted a plan to boost their share of the seats to thirteen or even fourteen.[52] Although the plan did not deliver as Republicans hoped, it elected a dozen Republicans and only seven Democrats when the GOP took 60.3 percent of the statewide congressional vote in 2002.

Two years later, Republicans got a substantial bonus in seats when they retained twelve seats even as their vote share slipped to 55.5 percent. In 2006, Democrats made major gains in Pennsylvania as they took control of the U.S. House. Democrats picked up four Pennsylvania seats so that the GOP share fell to 42.1 percent with a swing ratio of about two. This closely approximated the GOP component of the popular vote which dropped 10 percentage points from 2004. The GOP's decline continued in 2008 as they lost another seat so that their 44 percent of the vote yielded only 36.8 percent of the seats.[53] The Republican gerrymander did not give them substantially more seats than their vote share except in 2004. Their efforts failed to sustain them when Democrats surged in 2006.

Although Republicans designed the Pennsylvania plan to favor their party, the elections in this decade suggest that the plan had little bias. In 2004 when Republicans got 55.5 percent of the vote it translated into 63.2 percent of the seats. Four years later, Democrats took about the same share of the vote and they got 63.2 percent of the seats.

## BIPARTISAN GERRYMANDERS

An alternative, often favored by incumbents of both parties, produces districts that are secure for one party or the other and discourage competition between the parties. The same techniques used to gerrymander a state to favor one party can also craft districts in which the minority party in a district has virtually no chance of success. Bipartisan gerrymanders are likely when neither party has complete control over the redistricting process. In a state in which the congressional delegation size remains unchanged, a new plan may simply bolster the prospects for incumbents of both parties. Incumbents happily swap out supporters of the opposition to a neighboring district in return for an increase in their own supporters coming from a district that elects a member of the opposite party. Most congressional districts (233) drawn to adjust for the 2000 census were in bipartisan plans, up from 147 a decade earlier.[54] In 2011, bipartisan plans designed only eleven districts.

California accounted for more than a fifth of the districts in bipartisan plans in 2002.[55] As one might anticipate with a bipartisan plan, members of both parties fared well. In 2002, thirty members of the California delegation won with two-thirds of the vote. Another nineteen members received 60–67 percent of the vote. Only four members, all of whom were Democrats, took less than 55 percent of the vote. All twenty Republicans had more than 60 percent of the vote although this plan was crafted by a legislature dominated by Democrats. Table 5.7 compares the heavy distribution of very safe seats in 2002 with the two previous elections. Whether the comparison is with the 2000 presidential election or the previous mid-term election, the numbers of seats won with more than 60 percent of the vote increased while the numbers won with less than 55 percent of the vote dropped. Little partisan change occurred in California during the decade at the end of which Democrats

Table 5.7 Competitiveness in California Congressional Districts, 1998–2002

| Winner's Vote | 1998 | 2000 | 2002 |
|---|---|---|---|
| Less than 50% | 2 | 3 | 0 |
| 50–54% | 5 | 6 | 1 |
| 55–59% | 7 | 5 | 3 |
| 60–66% | 12 | 15 | 19 |
| More than 67% | 26 | 23 | 30 |

*Source*: Author based on results published in issues of *The Almanac of American Politics*.

held a 34–19 advantage, a gain of one seat. The bipartisan gerrymander withstood the 2006 Democratic surge, the 2010 GOP wave, and the growing Democratic strength in the state's presidential returns where Barack Obama took 61 percent of the vote in 2008 up from Al Gore's 53 percent eight years earlier.

Gerrymandering has generally been used in this volume and elsewhere to indicate one group taking unfair advantage of a weaker group. How can it be, then, that a bipartisan or sweetheart compromise meets the conditions so as to bear the label of gerrymander? Who is being disadvantaged if both parties join hands in support of a plan?

Some would argue that the public gets shortchanged when the parties conspire to create uncompetitive districts. Nicholas Seabrook goes so far as to warn, "The biggest threat to democracy, in the form of the subversion of electoral competition, is not partisan gerrymandering but bipartisan ger-rymandering."[56] At the heart of a bipartisan gerrymander, each party comes away with a set of districts in which it is almost guaranteed a victory. The minority party's voters in a district get consigned to perpetual defeat, deny-ing them influence on the outcome, which is the same claim made during the 2010s by plaintiffs attacking partisan gerrymanders like the just-discussed North Carolina congressional plan. These voters may become discouraged and cease participating although that seems unlikely since their votes, while having no impact on the outcome of the congressional contests, may still be important for statewide or local offices. Alternatively, Ronald Weber warns that the absence of competition in a congressional district may discourage participation by individuals of *both* parties and these individuals' votes could determine the outcome of statewide offices.[57]

Another possible disadvantage to designing uncompetitive districts is that incumbents, recognizing that they are invulnerable, become unresponsive to their constituents' desires. This seems unlikely on issues about which the constituents have serious concerns. While the incumbent may be safe from challenges from the opposite party, there remains the possibility of a primary challenge, a hard lesson learned by senior Democrats Joe Crowley (NY) and Michael Capuano (MA) in 2018 and Daniel Lipinski (IL) in 2020 and Majority Leader Eric Cantor (R-VA).[58] Moreover, in a district made up disproportionately of members of one party, there may be little disagreement on policy preferences so that unless the incumbent has personal reasons for opposing the constituency, why not vote with the constituency and satisfy its expectations.[59] Inattention to constituency relations seems a more common affliction that defeated these members in safe districts, although Lipinski being out of step on abortion was a factor in his defeat.

District competitiveness may influence the distribution of federal fund-ing for projects. With electoral security comes seniority and with seniority comes greater influence often in the guise of committee or subcommittee leadership so that a legislator from an uncompetitive district, all other things being equal, may be especially effective in securing pork barrel projects.[60] The politically powerful who often come from secure districts and, in the past when earmarks were allowed, they could insert for projects and contracts. An alternative perspective, however, suggests that it is only the most electorally insecure incumbents who will go to the additional trouble of winning new projects for their districts.[61]

Many decades ago Anthony Downs argued that in competitive districts, each party has an incentive to move toward the ideological center in order to appeal to the decisive swing voters or Independents.[62] Each party's nominees might assume that they can count on the support from their fellow partisans and thus move toward the center so that the choices confronting the electorate in the general election differ relatively little. While that view still has adherents,[63] most research concludes that while representatives from competitive districts are more moderate than their fellow partisans from more secure districts, Republicans are always to the right of Democrats.[64] Moreover, when party control of a competitive district changes, the positions taken by the new member of Congress differ vastly from those of the predecessor.[65]

If a bipartisan gerrymander results in few competitive districts, a legislature is less likely to respond to changes in the electorate's preferences. As previously discussed, since changing legislative outputs usually requires changing the personnel, if few constituencies change partisan hands, then only if the legislature is almost evenly divided between the parties is there much prospect that an election will inject enough new blood to alter government policy. In a legislature having a high swing ratio, a small shift in the public's partisan preferences can substantially change party control of seats and usher in a cluster of new policies, but bipartisan gerrymanders dampen that prospect.

## COMPETITIVENESS

During the late 1950s and first half of the next decade, approximately 60 percent of the House incumbents won reelection with more than 60 percent of the vote.[66] Since then the number of competitive districts has declined. Beginning with 1966, more than 60 percent of incumbents have won reelection with at least 60 percent of the vote and frequently the figure exceeded 70 percent. In 2004, more than 85 percent of the House incumbents polled at least 60 percent of the vote.[67] The leading scholars of candidate recruitment stated, "Competition in congressional elections—has all but disappeared."[68]

Sam Hirsch, who litigated numerous voting rights cases, concluded that the redistricting conducted after the 2000 census "was the most incumbent-friendly in modern American history."[69] Bolstering that assertion, Hirsch pointed out that the forty-three incumbents who won reelection with less than 60 percent of the vote in 2002 was half the average number who had been in similarly competitive contests in the *immediate aftermath* of the three previous post-redistricting elections. An editorial writer reviewing the weak 2002 challengers sneered, "The magnitude of incumbency's triumph in last week's elections for the House of Representatives was so dramatic that the term 'election'—with its implications of voter choice and real competition—seems almost too generous to describe what happened on Tuesday."[70] The fifty-four incumbents who lost in 2010 would surely disagree.

Despite the widespread agreement that the incidence of marginal districts has declined, not all formats for redistricting are equally likely to reduce competitiveness. After analyzing two decades of data, Seabrook concludes that plans drawn by a party with a trifecta actually result in greater competitiveness than those designed by bipartisan agreement.[71] He reports that states with bipartisan-drawn plans intended to protect the holdings of both parties, not surprisingly, had the least competitive districts while those drawn by Republicans had the most competitive districts. Plans prepared by Republicans were also the ones least likely to perform for a decade as the creators intended while districts in bipartisan-drawn plans tended to remain in the hands of the same party as in California during the 2000s. Plans prepared by partisans, both Republicans and Democrats, are more likely to have competitive elections and to experience changes in partisan control because as partisans try to maximize their number of seats, they produce more districts with narrow margins (the phenomenon at the center of the efficiency gap) and, over the course of a decade, the opposition flips some of these districts. Partisan plans emphasize expanding the holdings of the party drawing the plan while bipartisan plans prioritize protecting incumbents.

While redistricting, particularly bipartisan gerrymandering, seems to offer an explanation for the greater security enjoyed by incumbents beginning in the mid-1960s, political scientists writing in the 1970s who explored the impact of redistricting concluded that heightened incumbent security could not be attributed to the drawing of less competitive districts.[72] However, one study uncovered little evidence of partisan redistricting in the 1970s.[73]

While scholars writing in the 1970s found little evidence that redistricting produced greater electoral security, politicians overwhelmingly believe that the drawing of district lines has significant consequences. By large margins the potential candidates interviewed by Sandy Maisel and his collaborators saw district drawing as impacting partisan prospects.[74] And it is not just prospective candidates who judge redistricting to be consequential. The efforts

Table 5.8   Defeats and Retirements of U.S. House Incumbents by Decade

|  | Incumbent Defeats | | Retirements | |
|---|---|---|---|---|
|  | No. | Per Election | No. | Per Election |
| 1944–50 | 152 | 38.0 | 117 | 29.3 |
| 1954–60 | 100 | 25.0 | 121 | 30.3 |
| 1964–70 | 107 | 26.8 | 122 | 30.5 |
| 1974–80 | 103 | 25.8 | 185 | 46.3 |
| 1984–90 | 43 | 10.8 | 120 | 30.0 |
| 1994–2000 | 68 | 17 | 164 | 41.0 |
| 2004–2010 | 102 | 25.5 | 134 | 33.5 |
| 2014–2018 | 51 | 17 | 145 | 48.3 |

Source: *Vital Statistics on Congress: Data on the U.S. Congress,* updated March 2019 (Washington, DC: Brookings Institute, 2019), accessed December 14, 2019.

made by each party to influence the drawing of district lines, support litigation to challenge what they perceive to be unfavorable lines, and recruit candidates in anticipation of redistricting sessions all indicate that they see the placement of district lines as having a great and lingering impact.

At first blush, it appears that partisan gerrymanders may have contributed to a substantial reduction in competitive districts and thus fewer incumbent defeats. Table 5.8 charts the decline in the number of incumbent defeats over time. The table excludes years ending in "2" immediately following redistricting when the newly configured districts may account for a number of defeats sometimes because two incumbents must face one another. The remaining four elections that are included for each decade present figures for periods when little if any redistricting took place. A dramatic drop has occurred since the 1940s when 152 incumbents lost in the last four election years of that decade. During the next three decades, incumbent defeats stabilize at about 100 before plummeting to only 43 defeats in the 1980s. The 1990s show an increase largely attributable to the defeat of 34 Democrats in 1994 when Republicans claimed their first House majority in forty years. Had the incidence of defeats in 1994 been no greater than for the other three elections of the decade, then only 44 or 45 defeats would have occurred.

Early assessments of the post-2000 redistricting judged it to have reduced the numbers of competitive congressional districts to an all-time low.[75]

In 2002, political mapmakers, with few exceptions, went for maximum incumbent protection plans. Take Iowa [which is discussed later in this chapter], for example, where an independent redistricting commission drew the state's five districts county by county without taking politics into consideration. That process netted more competitive seats in Iowa than in California, Texas, and Illinois combined.[76]

In the first three election cycles in that decade, the electorate rejected forty-eight incumbents. However the 2010 wave election wreaked the most damage to the ranks of incumbents since 1948 as fifty-four Democratic legislators lost. The 2010 tsunami raised incumbent defeats for the decade to the level observed during the 1950s, 1960s, and 1970s. The 2010 results underscore how conditions can change during the course of a decade so that districts thought to be secure for one party become untenable due to changes in the population or shifts in partisan preferences among long-term residents. It is not surprising that the greatest incumbent vulnerability came at the end of the decade, the point farthest removed from the data on which the mapmakers relied.

The first three elections of the 2010s, like the first three during the 2000s, have seen about fifty incumbents defeated. If 2020 defeats are in line with those from 2014 to 2018, then the total for the decade will be close to the figure for the 1990s. However, if 2020 is more like 2010, the total for the decade will be near 100. Even if 2020 is more like 2018 when thirty incumbents did not survive, the total for the decade will exceed eighty. The claims that shrewd technicians have utilized mountains of data to manipulate maps so as to prevent voters from ridding themselves of incumbents, while accurate early in a decade, may be overstated when a full decade is considered. However, note that the bulk of the defeats in the 1990s and 2000s came in a single wave election. Redistricting appears to make districts generally safe except for extraordinary circumstances, much like a levee or seawall may protect a community except when a hundred-year flood occurs.

Another perspective on the relationship between redistricting and incumbency advantage comes from Cox and Katz, who show that an altered district can prompt a weak incumbent to retire.[77] The need to reestablish population equality among districts culls those who have lost touch with their constituents. When one considers that the incidence of retirements was greater beginning with 2014 than in the past, the rate of defeats among those standing for reelection during the current decade is in line with the 1990s but higher than the 1980s. As this is being written, the total number of House members not seeking reelection in 2020 is not known, but in light of announcements thus far, the total retirements for the 2010s will pass 180. To the extent that incumbents retire when defeat appears imminent, the gerrymandering of the 2010s may prove little more successful in inoculating incumbents from threats than the handiwork of earlier decades. The average number of departures via retirement and general election defeat for the 2010s ranks fourth among the eight decades in table 5.8. The small number of defeats in the 1980s, combined with the infrequency of retirements, suggests that the plans of that decade were the most hospitable to incumbents.

The electoral success of House incumbents is not guaranteed. Incumbents spend extensive resources and much of their own time trying to persuade voters to return them to office. In these efforts incumbents have numerous advantages. David Mayhew observed many years ago, "If a group of planners sat down and tried to design a pair of American national assemblies with the goal of serving members' electoral needs year in and year out, they would be hard pressed to improve on what exists."[78] Members of Congress frequently return to their districts at taxpayer expense, make hundreds of personal presentations, use the frank to fill constituent's mail boxes with newsletters, spend hours every week on the telephone soliciting campaign funds, assign staff to process casework, and issue press releases claiming credit for anything good that happens in the district through email, Twitter, and blogs.

Bipartisan gerrymanders can make all or most incumbents more secure but new maps designed to dislodge incumbents have also succeeded. And while partisan change in congressional seat control disproportionately comes in contests without an incumbent, some incumbents lose.[79] Key to defeating incumbents is to separate them from constituents they have represented.[80] New voters added to a district have no relationship with the incumbent and so for them the situation is like an open seat contest. A party in charge of redistricting that seeks to defeat an opposition incumbent can substitute voters who do not identify with the incumbent's party for the legislator's supporters as Texas Republicans did in 2004. The incumbent may not have time before the next election to cultivate support by traveling in the district, processing casework, securing projects and, consequently, be less well known among the district's new voters.[81] Lacking time to make connections in the new part of the district denies the incumbent a personal vote (voters committed to him or her) and therefore must rely more heavily on votes generated through party loyalty.

The bleaching of districts surrounding the majority-black districts created in the early 1990s contributed to the election of Republicans from the whiter districts as discussed in chapter 3. In addition, redistricting, by disrupting the relationships southern Democratic incumbents had with their Republican-leaning constituents, opened the way for Republican gains in districts that did not become substantially whiter. Seth McKee showed that in 1992 and 1994 and then a decade later following the Tom DeLay Texas gerrymander, voters added to districts of Democratic incumbents supported these legislators at substantially lower rates than did voters who had lived in the districts prior to the new maps.[82]

Disrupting existing relationships between incumbents and voters, especially in a district that gives evidence from presidential or other statewide elections of tilting toward the opposition party, may enable the out party to recruit a stronger challenger to the incumbent. For example, the two Texas Democratic incumbents defeated in 2004 faced challengers with at least ten years' experience as elected judges.[83] In 2000 and 2002, the incumbent Democrats had disposed of challengers who lacked office-holding experience.

Having an established calendar for redistricting also influences the behavior of the most promising potential candidates of the opposing party who can wait to seek a congressional seat when it is most likely to be open or has an incumbent weakened as a result of having supporters removed from the district.

In contrast with those who urge using redistricting to promote competitiveness, Thomas Brunell disagrees with those concerns and, instead, argues the virtues of uncompetitive districts. As mentioned in chapter 1, Brunell justifies packing on the basis that more people would be satisfied with Congress, its policies, and their legislators if most voters lived in districts in which their party constituted an overwhelming majority.[84] High concentrations of supporters of one party also make the task of the representative easier since cues from the constituency will overwhelmingly point in one direction.

## PARTISAN GERRYMANDERS AND COURTS, PART II

Until 1962, the Supreme Court considered the whole issue of redistricting off limits as a political question. During the 1960s and 1970s federal courts regularly responded to claims that plans failed to equalize populations or discriminated against minorities. But the concern dating back to the original gerrymander in 1812 had focused on alleged mistreatment of a political party. While the loss of a district due to cracking via clever line drawing is galling, an even broader concern arises when a party's share of legislative seats falls well below its share of the statewide vote. The American electoral system, unlike proportional representation widely used in Europe, makes no pretense of having the share of seats approximate the share of the vote. Nonetheless, situations in which a party that receives a majority of the statewide vote yet gets a minority of the seats strikes many—especially those in the disadvantaged party—as unacceptable. In 1986, the Supreme Court held that issues involving partisan gerrymanders were justiciable. The same Indiana Republicans who produced the congressional plan described earlier in this chapter set out to enhance their position within the state legislature and those efforts ultimately came before the high court.

Prior to 1986, a political party unfairly treated in the course of redistricting had no prospect of relief from the courts. In *Davis v. Bandemer*, the Supreme Court held out hope to disadvantaged political parties when it ruled that a party could use the Equal Protection Clause to challenge a plan.[85] The Indiana Democrats who sued in *Bandemer* did not get the new plan they sought, but the Court indicated what would be necessary for success. To win, a disadvantaged political party must prove both an intent to discriminate against it as well as an actual discriminatory effect. However, a party's showing that its share of the seats in the legislature came up far short of its percentage of the popular vote would not suffice. Justice Byron White, writing for the Court, observed that

> An individual or a group of individuals who votes for a losing candidate is usually deemed to be adequately represented by the winning candidate and to have as much opportunity to influence that candidate as other voters in the district. We cannot presume in such a situation, without actual proof to the contrary, that the candidate elected will entirely ignore the interests of those voters. . . . To prevail, a party must demonstrate that it is unable to influence the political process which would include both evidence of continued frustration of the will of a majority of the voters or effective denial to a minority of voters of a fair chance to influence the political process.

Interestingly, the one member of the Court who had served in a state legislature, Sandra Day O'Connor, sided with the minority who continued to believe that courts should not hear challenges to partisan gerrymanders.

Three years after *Bandemer*, California Republicans challenged the Burton Plan referenced earlier. The Republicans pointed out that in 1984 they had polled a majority of the popular vote but won only 40 percent of the seats. In the next election they again got a smaller share of the seats than the votes. They contended—as proved to be correct—that the Burton Plan had consigned them to minority status in the congressional delegation for the remainder of the decade. The trial court found that the plaintiffs had failed to meet the second part, the effects test, of the *Bandemer* decision because they failed to show that they had been shut out of the political process. The court noted that while Republicans won a smaller share of the congressional seats than of the vote, nothing prevented them from registering voters, organizing, voting, and campaigning.[86] As further evidence that Republicans had not been excluded from California's political process, Republicans had elected the governor and one of the senators in addition to having 40 percent of the state's congressional seats.

In 2004, the Supreme Court encountered the question of partisan redistricting again. The case involved the Pennsylvania congressional redistricting described earlier in this chapter. As in every case since *Bandemer*, the Court did not find the minority party sufficiently disadvantaged to warrant judicial intervention. The plurality opinion of the Court in *Vieth v. Jubelirer* subscribed to by four justices recommended reversal of *Bandemer* since no consensus had emerged as to what plaintiffs must prove to prevail.[87] The Court's four liberal justices believed that the plaintiffs had provided sufficient evidence to win but these four justices suggested three different standards to support their conclusion. The swing justice, Anthony Kennedy, did not find the evidence sufficient to throw out the Pennsylvania plan as an unconstitutional partisan gerrymander. However, he separated himself from the conservative quartet on the issue of reversing *Bandemer*. While Kennedy agreed that a standard did not exist, he held out hope that in the future a standard would be devised and therefore voted to continue considering the issue of a partisan gerrymander to be justiciable.

Justice Antonin Scalia, writing for the plurality, rejected the Fourteenth Amendment as a basis for finding for plaintiffs, noting that the Equal Protection Clause "guarantees equal protection of the law to persons, not equal representation in government to equivalently sized groups." The plurality opinion cited one of the leading casebooks on voting rights for the proposition that, throughout its subsequent history, "*Bandemer* has served almost exclusively as an invitation to litigation without much prospect of redress."[88] Justice Scalia pointed out that those who had sought relief under *Bandemer* had achieved nothing except to rack up substantial legal fees.

The hesitancy of the Supreme Court majority to find the Pennsylvania gerrymander so extreme as to deny political influence to the Democrats proved accurate. As noted earlier, the 2006 elections showed the responsiveness of the plan as Democrats gained four seats to achieve majority status. The Democratic share of the seats won in 2006 slightly exceeded their share of the vote. The plan did reasonably well in terms of bias. In 2004, Republicans won a dozen seats with 55.5 percent of the statewide two-party vote. Four years later Democrats got 56 percent of the votes and a dozen seats.[89]

The court's *Vieth* minority did not give up easily. When the *Larios* case from Georgia came before the high court, it affirmed the district court opinion that the legislature had violated the Equal Protection Clause in favoring south Georgia and Atlanta at the expense of north Georgia and the suburbs. However, two justices signed an opinion stating that they believed that the techniques used by Democrats in drawing the Georgia districts met the *Bandemer* thresholds.[90]


## ATTEMPTS TO MEET THE KENNEDY CHALLENGE


While gerrymandering has been a feature of American politics from the dawn of the Constitution, many have contended that it has become more of a problem now that mapmakers can use computers to refine their art through repeated trial and error. By one estimate, following the 2018 election, more than one in six Americans lived in a state in which the party that controlled the legislature failed to win a majority of the statewide vote. The states involved, Pennsylvania, Michigan, North Carolina, Ohio, Virginia, and Wisconsin, have been ranked as having the six most unfair maps. Grofman considers the first four states the worst with the last two plus Florida, Georgia, and Indiana as additional bad examples.[91]

Given such a large target, opponents of partisan gerrymandering spent much of the 2010s developing measures that they hoped would satisfy the challenge thrown down by Justice Kennedy. Republicans who had ridden the 2010 red wave to control of an unprecedented number of legislatures, including Michigan and Pennsylvania, devised plans that Democrats believed to be extraordinarily brazen attempts to disadvantage the minority party, and that spawned multiple lawsuits. Although courts have made explicit that parties should not expect to get a share of seats proportional to their share of the votes, the disparity between vote shares and seats undergirded the challenges. The challenges evaluated the statewide results of the maps until late in the decade when the Supreme Court returned a case from Wisconsin in which the trial court had found illegal partisan gerrymandering. In sending the case back to the district court, the Supreme Court explained that the analysis should be at the district level.[92] In a second case, North Carolina Democrats took aim at the congressional plan, previously discussed, that limited them to three seats beginning in 2014. In a third high-profile case Democrats were the bad boys. The Maryland congressional plan described earlier, which included some of the most contorted districts in the nation, did in senior Republican Roscoe Bartlett, leaving the state with only one Republican member of Congress.

During the course of the decade, plaintiffs had success at trial as, for the first time, they managed to pick the lock that opened the protections offered by *Davis v. Bandemer*. Federal trial court judges ruled that the Wisconsin state House plan was an illegal partisan gerrymander.[93] Congressional plans in North Carolina and Ohio were disallowed as were plans for both state legislative chambers and Congress in Michigan.[94]

Academics working on behalf of one or more of the challenges offered multiple measures to support the claim that the plans under review were extreme gerrymanders.[95] One approach popularized by Gelman and King relied on the concept of bias as discussed earlier in this chapter.[96] A fair plan would result in a party that won 50 percent of the vote receiving half of the seats. Winning more than half the vote would, as described earlier, produce a bonus. For example, a party that won 52 percent of the vote might get 55 percent of the seats. Under the Gelman and King approach, the plan would be fair if that 3 percent bonus were received by either party if its candidates polled 52 percent of the vote statewide. An unfair plan would require that the disadvantaged party win more than half the votes before it could secure half the seats. Republicans who won 53 percent of the vote in North Carolina in 2016 won 77 percent of the congressional seat. An attorney challenging the plan estimated that for Democrats to win just seven of the thirteen seats, they would need 58 percent of the vote statewide.[97] In Michigan, Republicans

**Table 5.9   Methods Suggested for Assessing Alleged Partisan Gerrymandering**

| Approach | Creators | Method |
|----------|----------|--------|
| Bias | Gelman and King | Is the bonus in seats the same for both parties if they receive a given majority, e.g., 52%, of the vote? |
| Simulations | Chen | What is the probability of observing bias this extreme relative to the bias in 100s or 1,000s of computer-drawn simulations? |
| Efficiency Gap | Stephanopoulous and McGhee | How similar are the numbers of Democratic and Republican wasted votes? |
| Mean-Median | McDonald and Best | How similar are a party's mean and median votes in a jurisdiction's districts? |
| Majority Rule | McGann et al. | The party that wins a majority of the votes should get a majority of the seats. |

*Source*: Author.

who drew the congressional maps held nine of fourteen seats from 2012 to 2016 but never secured more than 50.5 percent of the statewide vote.[98] When Democrats won 56 percent of the statewide vote in 2018 that translated into only half the seats.

The McGann team concluded that bias was more pervasive in the 2012 plans than those drawn a decade earlier with bias reaching extreme levels in nine states.[99] Multiple examples appear in this chapter and the next of situations in which the party winning the bulk of the votes remained the minority in the legislature. For example, Democrats challenged the GOP plan for the Wisconsin House after Republicans won less than half the vote statewide but won 60 percent of the seats. However, depending on the geographical distribution of Democrats and Republicans in a state, a biased outcome may not signal a biased gerrymander but what has been called a natural gerrymander. Republican bias may stem from a heavy concentration of Democrats in urban areas. Focusing on partisan symmetry will struggle to distinguish between a partisan gerrymander and a natural gerrymander.[100]

Jowei Chen offered an alternative, as shown in table 5.9, designed to distinguish between a natural and a partisan gerrymander.[101] He simulates the natural result using a computer-automated algorithm that includes "good" redistricting practices such as contiguity, compactness, equal population, and honoring local political boundaries. Chen's simulation factors in the geographic distribution of one party's supporters. The number of districts likely to elect a Democrat and the number that favor Republicans in each simulation is determined based on past election results. The probability of a plan having the partisan distribution of the plan being litigated is then determined. For example, in 46 percent of the simulated North Carolina congressional plans, Democrats won seven districts while in 32 percent of the plans, Republicans won seven districts. Only 0.7 percent of 24,000 plans showed Republicans winning ten seats, which was their take in 2018.[102]

A third approach calculated the number of wasted votes for each party. A party's wasted votes consisted of anything more than needed to win a district plus all of the votes it received in districts it lost. This measure, called the efficiency gap, calculates whether the minority party has far more wasted votes than the dominant party.[103] If the wasted votes are about the same for the two parties, the efficiency gap is small but if one party has far more wasted votes than its opposition, then the efficiency gap is large. If the minority party wins a few districts into which its supporters are packed while narrowly losing numerous other districts, the classic gerrymander, its number of wasted votes will far exceed the number for the opposition. Evidence presented in the challenge to Wisconsin's state House districts asserted that the Wisconsin plan was one of the least equitably drawn in any state in since 1972. Since states with few districts can easily result in large values, the efficiency gap is more appropriate in states with more districts.[104] Chen and Rodden's analysis showing that Democratic voters are "inefficiently" distributed, being heavily concentrated in urban areas which they win with overwhelming majorities while narrowly losing a number of rural and suburban districts, poses questions about the ability of wasted votes to identify intentional efforts to discriminate against a party.[105] In recognition of the potential impact of the distribution of partisans, plaintiffs suggested that an efficiency gap of 7 percent creates a rebuttable presumption of an illegal gerrymander.

A fourth compares the statewide mean and the median district vote. In a fair plan the two values will be very similar although probably not identical. The greater the disparity between the two values, the stronger the evidence of a partisan gerrymander.[106] If the median for the districts of one party tends to be substantially higher than its statewide mean, it suggests that its supporters have been packed thus raising questions about the fairness of the plan. Of the 2012 plans, Pennsylvania had the largest mean-median difference, 7.6 percent, with North Carolina close behind at 7.3 percent.[107]

McGann and his colleagues suggest a simpler test, the majority rule standard. They contend that at a minimum a majority of the electorate should be able to elect a majority of the legislature. "Stated intuitively, if we treat everyone equally, then in a two-party system, the results must respect the *majority rule* standard—if a party wins a majority of the vote, it must get at least 50% of the seats."[108] In 2012, the party that won a majority of the vote did not get a majority of the seats in Arizona, Michigan, North Carolina, Pennsylvania, or Wisconsin.[109]

A simpler approach is to simply examine the designs of the districts. As Justice O'Connor observed in *Shaw v. Reno*, when it comes to redistricting, looks matter. This approach is especially appropriate in states in which one party has a substantial advantage, for example, the challenge to Maryland's decision to eliminate one of its two Republican districts as challenged in *Lamone v. Benisek*.[110] The approach may also be more reliable than some that rely on statistical analyses when there are few districts. Wang and his colleagues suggest this approach for states with two to six districts.[111] However, some partisan gerrymanders do not have extraordinary-looking districts and some strange shapes result from concerns about something other than party, such as in Maryland where figure 4.3 shows how lines were drawn to maintain two majority-black districts.

While most of the efforts of the 2010s focused on disparities between vote and seat shares,[112] a different tactic turned to the Constitution's First Amendment guarantees of freedom to assemble and freedom of expression. Plaintiffs in *Rucho* contended that the plan being challenged impeded their "ability to mobilize their party's base, persuade independent voters to participate, attract volunteers, raise money and recruit candidates."[113] The freedom of association claim asserts that members of the minority party are discriminated against because of their partisanship since they have no hope of electing their preference in the challenged district.

Undergirding the various approaches outlined here is evidence of an intent to disadvantage of the opposition. North Carolina's Representative Lewis had no hesitation in owning up to a partisan gerrymander. "I acknowledge freely that this would be a political gerrymander. . . . I'm making clear that our intent is to use—is to use the political data we have to our partisan advantage."[114] In the absence of someone as forthcoming as Lewis, evidence might come from emails exchanged among those in the majority party or between redistricting committee members and staffers or comments made to the press. For this reason, the wizard of Republican gerrymandering cautioned his clients, "emails are the tool of the devil."[115] A California staffer warned legislators, "Never say anything AT ALL about redistricting—no speculation, no predictions, NOTHING. Anything can come back to haunt you."[116]

Scholars who have wrestled with the issue of what must be proven to win a partisan gerrymandering case have looked over the range of possible measures and concluded that the best approach documents unacceptability on multiple dimensions. Wang and his colleagues use the analogy of a toolbox to justify a multi-pronged approach since one size may not fit all fact situations. "In jurisprudence, as with home repair, it can be handy to have a kit containing more than one tool."[117] Different tools may be required depending on the number of districts in a jurisdiction, the level of partisan competition, geography, and so forth. Michael D. McDonald and colleagues offer a five-part test for assessing a statewide plan, along with a four-part test for a district-level assessment. Statewide, their approach includes the mean-median comparison while for districts they highlight cracking and the prospects for the minority party.[118] Wang suggests application of three tests.[119]

Plaintiffs in federal district courts had success as their experts offered analyses based on one or more of the approaches outlined above. In Wisconsin, a federal judge found the Republican legislature had carried out an unconstitutional gerrymander when reconfiguring the lower chamber. The GOP plan gave them a 60–39 advantage even though Democratic House candidates received 174,000 more votes.[120] Similar conclusions were reached by federal judges in Michigan and Ohio. At the congressional level federal courts called for redrawing the Maryland and North Carolina maps.

These decisions moving in the direction of fairer districts foundered on the U.S. Supreme Court's 5–4 conservative bloc. Chief Justice John Roberts wrote an opinion that reversed the *Bandemer* decision of thirty-three years earlier. In the North Carolina and Maryland appeals, the majority concluded that partisan gerrymandering was a political question and therefore federal courts could provide no relief.[121] While the Roberts opinion closed off the federal courts as a source of relief, he pointed to initiatives taken by states to rein in rampant partisanship.

## STATE COURTS

One of the sources of state relief suggested by Chief Justice Roberts is the courts. Within weeks after the U.S. Supreme Court refused to rule on North Carolina's congressional plan, a state court strode boldly into the political thicket and held the plans for the state legislature unconstitutional under the North Carolina constitution.[122] In 2018, Republicans maintained their control of both chambers, winning 29 of 50 Senate seats and 65 of 120 House seats despite securing less than half the vote statewide. Plaintiffs challenged the plans on multiple grounds and the state court found all of their arguments compelling. The plans for seventy-seven districts were found to violate the state Equal Protection Clause which the court explained was broader than the federal version. The plans also conflicted with the state constitution's Fair Election Clause since the plans denied any prospect of a Democratic victory in most districts thereby predetermining the outcomes. The court also ruled that packing Democrats into a few districts violated their right to free association and free speech. The plan violated the free association protection since it penalized the Democratic Party, impairing its ability to recruit candidates and raise funds. Voting, the judges held, constitutes a form of expression and the plans rendered Democrats' expression less effective than that of Republicans. The court opinion referenced as evidence of partisan intent the recently discovered files of the late Thomas

Hofeller, the longtime Republican mapmaking genius, who massaged massive data sets to optimize GOP prospects. "The evidence establishes that Dr. Hofeller drew the 2017 plans very precisely to create as many 'safe' Republican districts as possible, so that Republicans would maintain their super majorities, or at least majorities even in a strong election year for Democrats."

## BOX 5.1   THOMAS HOFELLER

The late Tom Hofeller is widely recognized as a redistricting genius. The adjective applied varies by party with Republicans opting for "brilliant" while Democrats choose "evil." Hofeller spent decades drawing maps. Once geographic information systems came available he collected extensive and varied data that he used to advantage his Republican clients with pinpoint accuracy. At times he worked for the Republican Party and at other times he functioned as a consultant.

Hofeller, the holder of a PhD in political science, began designing maps to help California Republicans in the early 1970s. When he died in 2018, he was still drawing GOP-friendly maps that ended up at the heart of judicial challenges in North Carolina. Along the way, Hofeller's work influenced numerous court decisions including some landmark rulings from the U.S. Supreme Court.

He was among the first to grasp the double-edged nature of the 1982 rewrite of Section 2 of the Voting Rights Act. He worked with the black plaintiffs in their successful challenge to at-large districts in the North Carolina legislature. Breaking these up and creating majority-black single-member districts, Hofeller recognized, simultaneously produced much whiter adjacent districts likely to elect Republicans.[1] The ruling in *Thornburg v. Gingles* primed the Bush Justice Department for the Section 5 oversight that restricted white Democrats who controlled southern legislatures from using black voters to bolster white Democrats and sowed dissention that began to unravel Democrats' biracial coalition. Mark Braden, who has frequently represented Republicans in redistricting litigation, sees historical significance in Hofeller's work. "Tom played a key role across the South in the destruction of the traditional Democratic Party."[2]

Following the 2010 wave election that gave Republicans control of an unprecedented number of state legislatures, Hofeller's skills were in high demand. His plans for North Carolina, Pennsylvania, and Texas were at the center of litigation during the decade. Hofeller's work sparked claims that partisanship had run amok and therefore courts should intercede. Ironically, decades earlier, he had helped with *Davis v. Bandemer*, the suit in which the Supreme Court had ruled claims of partisan gerrymandering to be justiciable.

In his later years, Hofeller was instrumental in pushing to use citizen adult population rather than the total population when drawing districts. He promoted the controversial idea of having the 2020 census ask about respondents' citizenship.

While Hofeller was very well known in redistricting circles, his visibility to the public came posthumously. His daughter, from whom he was estranged, came across 70,000 computer files when going through her father's belongings. She turned these over to Common Cause which was challenging North Carolina districts designed by her father. The discovery of Hofeller's handiwork, the precision with which he separated Republicans from Democrats and questions about whether he relied on race data—which would probably be unconstitutional—or partisan data as he claimed generated extensive media coverage.

[1]In part this draws on Michael Wines, "Thomas Hofeller, 75, Gerrymander Genius," *New York Times* (August 22, 2018).
[2]Ibid.

North Carolina was not the first state in which the state constitution was the battering ram used to knock down a partisan gerrymander. The Pennsylvania Supreme Court invalidated that state's congressional plan prior to the 2018 election. Following the 2010 election, Republicans had a 12–7 advantage in the congressional delegation. But even as the state gave Barack Obama a 300,000-vote win in 2012 and reelected Democratic Senator Robert Casey by more than half a million votes, Republicans won thirteen seats in the congressional delegation now shrunken to eighteen. The GOP gerrymander worked even though Democrats outpolled the GOP candidates by 83,000 votes statewide.[123] In 2018 the Pennsylvania Supreme Court invalidated the plan as violative of the state constitution. Specifically, the court found that by artificially reducing Democratic presence in the delegation the plan ran afoul of the guarantee for free and equal elections. The advantage conferred on the GOP and the strange shapes of some districts indicated that traditional redistricting principles had been ignored.[124] After the state court ordered new districts—a decision that the U.S. Supreme Court opted not to review—Democrats gained four seats in 2018 to equal Republicans' nine seats in the delegation. The new plan also complied with at least two traditional redistricting principles in that it had a higher compactness score and it split fewer than half as many counties as the GOP gerrymander.[125]

Undoubtedly plaintiffs will launch partisan gerrymandering claims in state courts in the 2020s. In all likelihood, some challenges will succeed while elsewhere state courts may see nothing wrong with the legislature's designs or not perceive a component of the state constitution or statutes that justify actions such as those taken in Pennsylvania and North Carolina. It should be noted that justices on both the North Carolina and the Pennsylvania Supreme Courts are elected and at the time they undid the GOP handiwork, Democrats had the advantage. Twelve states have provisions like the Free and Equal Elections Clause in Pennsylvania's Constitution, while other states have requirements that courts might seize on to strike down overly aggressive gerrymanders.[126] The Pennsylvania court asserted that the Free and Equal Elections Clause has a broader scope than the federal Constitution's Equal Protection Clause and, the Keystone judges noted with pride, predates the federal provision. But other courts may interpret those provisions differently than in Pennsylvania.

To the extent that state judges consider challenges to partisan gerrymandering, the task may be easier than the unsuccessful efforts in federal courts. To succeed at the federal level, a test would have to be applicable nationwide. In challenging a state plan, plaintiffs need only demonstrate that their test works in that jurisdiction. Also, some state courts might accept analyses that attack the plan statewide, an approach rejected by the U.S. Supreme Court that called for a district-level focus.[127]

Another consideration may be the permanence of the disadvantage built into the plan. In the Pennsylvania and North Carolina cases, multiple elections had been conducted using the plan and the results had changed little. However it is not necessary that a plaintiff wait until one or more elections have taken place using the plan since it is possible to estimate the number of seats each party will likely win through simulation.

It is likely that challenges in state courts will rely on more than one of the measures discussed above. In the Pennsylvania case, Jowei Chen presented simulations on the likely partisan splits in plans produced using traditional concerns and on the differences between the mean and median vote shares. Christopher Warshaw testified about wasted votes.

## ATTACKING PARTISAN GERRYMANDERS
## THROUGH DIFFERENT MEANS

With federal courts unwilling to overturn partisan gerrymanders, political parties that have lost in the legislature have sought to eliminate plans that disadvantaged them by raising other issues. In *Larios*, Georgia Republicans succeeded in their challenge to what all sides acknowledged to be a partisan gerrymander by attacking it for regional population deviations.

A second ploy by the party that loses in the legislature challenges the plan's racial equity. Both parties have used minorities as a stalking horse. In several lawsuits challenging the racial gerrymanders of the 1990s, such as the plans that advantaged Democrats in Texas, Republican activists were among the plaintiffs. Texas Republicans had initially attacked the congressional plan as a partisan gerrymander and, when that failed, launched a second attack raising equal protection issues but in the context of having separated minority and white voters on the basis of race, a claim that succeeded. In the next decade, Democrats challenged the DeLay Plan citing as one of their allegations that it eliminated minority influence districts. Following the 2010 round of redistricting, Illinois Republicans challenged Democratic-drawn maps on the grounds that GOP alternatives held out the prospect for a second Hispanic congressional district in Chicago. In the past, Democrats frequently argued for an alternative that they claimed more fairly represented minorities.

## REACTION GERRYMANDERING

The twenty-first century has witnessed a phenomenon in which states gerrymandered their congressional districts in an attempt to offset gerrymandering by the opposition party in another state. As recounted in the next chapter, Georgia Democrats manipulated the boundaries of their congressional districts in 2001 in an effort to pick up four seats. This triggered a reaction in Pennsylvania where, as noted earlier in this chapter, Republicans sought to offset the anticipated Democratic gains in Georgia. Michigan Republicans also drew new congressional districts which they justified as countering what Democrats had done in Georgia.[128] There have been suggestions that the Democratic work in Illinois in 2011 was in part an effort to offset, in a small way, Republican maps in other states like Pennsylvania, North Carolina, and Texas.

## REDUCING PARTISAN INFLUENCE IN DISTRICTING

When one party controls the redistricting process, it tends to enhance its position. As illustrated at the outset of this volume and in this chapter, the redistricting party may devise maps that enable it to win the vast majority of the seats even when it fails to get a majority of the vote. Republicans who, thanks to the 2010 wave election that secured majorities in many state legislatures, drew more districts in 2011 than ever before. While Democrats had exploited similar opportunities in the past (and did so when redrawing Maryland's congressional districts in 2011), they were outraged when Republicans turned the tables on them.[129] Arguably with more precise data, Republicans played the gerrymandering game better than Democrats had in previous decades. The effectiveness of the GOP plans set off new calls for depoliticizing redistricting by taking it out of the hands of legislators. Growing ranks of reformers called for the creation of independent commissions such as are used in Arizona, California, the United Kingdom, and many other countries. The desire to remove legislators from redistricting is caught up in the frequent criticism that currently legislators get to choose their constituents, a far cry from the tradition where constituents selected their representatives. A 2013 poll found that more than 70 percent of the respondents opposed letting legislators draw the districts in which they would run.[130] There was almost no difference between Democrats and Republicans on this issue. Despite heavily funded opposition by Democrats, more than 60 percent of Californians voted to create an independent commission.

Several approaches have been adopted in attempts to depoliticize redistricting. A growing number of states have tried, with varying degrees of success, to remove or at least temper the influence of politics in this most political activity. In some states a commission has sole responsibility while in other states the commission becomes active only if the legislature fails to devise a plan. While members of the commission may have less direct interest in the outcome than do legislators, not all commissions are buffered from partisan concerns and in some states active political players serve as commissioners. Generally, however, Chen and Cottrell found less bias in plans prepared by commissions than when a party with a trifecta had control.[131]

The Florida legislature continues to do redistricting but amendments to the state constitution ratified in 2010 reduce the weight that legislators can give to partisanship and incumbency. The courts enforced these requirements when Democrats challenged the plans for the state Senate and Congress. A new congressional plan implemented in 2016 led to Democrats picking up three congressional seats. Going into the 2020 election, Republicans had only a 14–13 advantage, down from their seventeen seats under the 2012 plan.

As explained earlier in this chapter, a non-legislative body which nonetheless consists of partisan officeholders assumes the responsibility for drawing Texas state legislative districts when the legislature fails to act. In New Jersey, an outsider chairs the Apportionment Commission which consists of five Democrats and five Republicans. Invariably Democrats and Republicans have competing plans. The nonpartisan chair can try to work out a compromise. If attempts at compromise fail, the chair endorsed one of the plans giving it the necessary sixth vote.[132]

The Iowa approach is frequently pointed to as desirable because it limits partisan influence; however, the plan does not come from a commission. Instead, the Legislative Services Agency draws the congressional map. In going about its task, the Agency faces constraints not imposed in most states. It cannot divide counties nor can it consider where the incumbents live, or the voting history of the counties. The Agency simply tries to minimize the population variations among districts and since Iowa has many counties with relatively small populations it has been possible to design congressional districts with relatively little population variation while meeting the other constraints. The legislature cannot change a plan submitted by the Legislative Services Agency but it can reject it as the Senate did in 2001. The Legislative Services Agency then submits a second and even a third plan if necessary for legislative consideration. The legislature cannot modify the first two plans but, should they both be rejected, legislators can amend the third plan.

Iowa's 2002 plan showed that the agency had honored the requirements of ignoring the homes of incumbents. The plan paired Republican incumbents Jim Leach and Jim Nussle in the same district. Both survived the 2002 elections, however, when Leach ran in the 2nd District, much of which had been in the 1st District that he had previously represented. Leach continued to represent five of the eight counties he had represented in the past, which included Cedar Rapids and Iowa City. Nussle ran in the new 1st District which contained nine of the counties from his old 2nd District and included Dubuque, Cedar Falls, and Waterloo. While the four incumbents who sought reelection succeeded, each of them had to introduce himself to a new set of constituents.

Table 5.10 shows that three of Iowa's four reelected incumbents saw their victory margins drop by 10 percentage points from 2000 to 2002. The reduced support for both Leach and Democrat Leonard Boswell put them in the marginal category. Incumbents who draw less than 55 percent of the vote often become targets in the next election as eager challengers and national party

Table 5.10   The Impact of the 2002 Redistricting on Iowa Congressional Incumbents

| | Vote Percentages | | | | | | |
|---|---|---|---|---|---|---|---|
| Incumbent | 2000 | 2002 | 2004 | 2006 | 2008 | 2010 | 2012 |
| Jim Nussle (R) | 55 | 57 | 55 | 55* | 65 | 50 | 57 |
| Jim Leach (R) | 62 | 52 | 59 | 51* | 57 | 51 | 56 |
| Leonard Boswell (D) | 63 | 53 | 55 | 52 | 56 | 51 | ** |
| Tom Latham (R) | 69 | 55 | 61 | 57 | 61 | 66 | 52 |
| Steven King (R)*** | 61 | 62 | 62 | 59 | 60 | 66 | 52 |

*Source*: Michael Barone and Richard E. Cohen, *The Almanac of American Politics, 2004* (Washington, DC: National Journal, 2003), and subsequent issues.
* Change in party control
** Boswell lost to Latham
*** King newly elected in 2002

organizations mark these incumbents as vulnerable. Even Tom Latham who had no opposition in 1998 fell to 55 percent of the vote in 2002. Only Nussle did better in 2002 than the previous election as his 57 percent of the vote marked his strongest performance ever. The new plan from the Legislative Services Agency did shake things up in Iowa even if all the incumbents survived. Heightened competitiveness in most of the incumbents' districts did not happen in other states. Iowa's congressional districts remained competitive through 2010. The winners in seventeen of the twenty-five elections held between 2002 and 2010 received less than 60 percent of the vote. In 2006 no Iowa candidate got as much as 60 percent of the vote as Leach and Nussle fell to Democratic challengers. The GOP wave of 2010 saw three Democrats reelected with 51 percent or less of the vote.

The Iowa delegation shrank to four members following the 2010 census but competitiveness remained the norm. In 2012, the maximum achieved by any candidate in the new districts was 57 percent and even Steve King (R), who had the safest district in the previous decade, managed just 52 percent. From 2012 to 2018, only two of the sixteen contests saw a candidate get more than 60 percent of the vote. In 2018, three members won with 49 to 51 percent of the vote, with the biggest winner taking 55 percent. This type of competitiveness persisting for years is extraordinary and is what many reformers would like to see.

Taking redistricting out of the hands of legislators does not ensure the level of competitiveness observed in Iowa. Arizona's Independent Redistricting Commission, which unlike most commissions consists of citizens rather than politicians, has two members of each party and they choose an Independent as the fifth member. The Commission's plan for the 2010s resulted in less competitive districts than in the previous decade when from 2004 to 2008, party control changed in three districts, and in 2008 three winners got less than 55 percent of the vote and another two were held to less than 60 percent. From 2012 through 2018, two districts were always won with at least two-thirds of the vote. Only the 2nd District experienced a change in party control. The plan smacked of a bipartisan gerrymander, generating little competition even as the delegation remained divided with neither party securing more than five of the nine seats through the 2018 election.

While independent commissions are lauded for removing politics, some doubt that politics can be eradicated from a process so freighted with political implications. Among the critics is one of the Republicans on the Arizona commission in 2011. He believes that Democrats stacked the deck to ensure that a Democrat would be selected chair, and with three votes Democrats packed GOP districts so that Republicans won only four of nine seats despite their candidates having 180,000 more votes than the Democrats received.[133] There have also been claims that Democrats managed to secure an advantage on California's independent commission. In the 2012 election, Democrats gained four congressional seats. Chen and Cottrell find that the Democratic gain in California is the most extreme for any state when compared against expectations based on simulations.[134]

In California while the parties are represented, it is not by legislators or other officeholders. The Citizens Redistricting Commission consists of five Democrats, five Republicans, and four Independents. Anyone can apply and 36,000 did by submitting four essays. The sixty finalists undergo a ninety-minute interview. The commission, banned from looking at where incumbents live, paired twenty-seven of them in 2011, which encouraged eleven members to retire while another seven ran and lost.[135]

Republicans who efficiently campaigned to elect state legislators who could protect the party's interests where redistricting was done by the legislature apparently believed that the California commission would indeed be independent and paid a price for that misplaced trust. Two ProPublica reporters document how Democrats recruited individuals to testify in favor of plans helpful to Democrats, moves that the GOP did not counter.[136] The overworked commissioners did not discover that some of the testifying individuals who purported to be interested citizens were Democratic operatives. And since the commission decided not to consider political data such as party registration or election returns, it had no idea as to the consequences of the plans it adopted. Democrats succeeded in expanding their ranks by four in contrast to outside observers who expected the GOP to make gains.

Even if independent commissions are not always truly independent of political influence, an advantage they provide is transparency. The hearings and proceedings are open to the public. Some courts have also required transparency when remedial plans are prepared. In contrast, when one party controls the process, the opposition is often little more than an observer, and in Wisconsin in 2011 map-making was conducted behind closed doors with Democrats and the public excluded.[137]

One explanation for the difficulty Democrats have in converting votes into seats springs from the concentration of Democrats in urban areas. Chen and Rodden simulate scores of plans to demonstrate that when applying traditional districting principles of equal population, contiguity, and compactness, the share of the districts won by Democrats consistently falls well below their share of the vote, even in states like Florida where in 2000 the presidential vote was dead even.[138] They attribute this "unintentional gerrymandering" to the heavy concentration of Democrats in urban areas where they win seats with large margins. Outside the major cities, Democrats dominate urban precincts but are out-voted when those precincts are combined with suburban and rural Republicans. While Republicans always win more seats than Democrats in the simulations, the simulations have the GOP getting fewer seats than the actual plan provided.[139] To the extent that there are demands to create heavily minority districts, the task of more efficiently distributing Democratic votes becomes more difficult.[140]

McGann and his co-authors challenge explanations pointing to unintentional gerrymanders. After a review of alternative maps, these scholars find no merit in either the urban concentration or the minority district explanation.[141] However they acknowledge that the concentration of Illinois Democrats in Chicago and the presence of one Hispanic district and three black districts made it difficult for Democrats to secure two-thirds of the state's seats. While bias increased from the 2002 to the 2012 maps, unintentional gerrymanders should have become less frequent since urban concentrations of Democrats decreased across the decades. To avoid an unintentional gerrymander in states marked by Democratic, urban concentrations, much less compact districts may be necessary. The McGann group also points out that the creation of additional minority districts in 2012 does not account for the increase in partisan bias.

## POLICY CONSEQUENCES OF GERRYMANDERING

One of the most troubling consequences of gerrymandering allows a party to secure most of the seats in a chamber although it fails to muster majority support in the electorate. In some instances, as in Georgia and Texas in the late 1990s and continuing until mid-decade redistricting in the next decade, the situation persists while elsewhere it may happen for a single election. When the minority party controls the legislature and the governorship, it can adopt policies that may not have majority support in state.[142] In the 2010s when this situation existed in Michigan and Wisconsin, these states took significant steps such as limiting collective bargaining which weakened labor unions, cutting spending on social programs, and altering revenue policies. Especially apropos this volume, when a party enjoys a manufactured majority at the time that new districts must be drawn, it may be able to extend its dominance into a new decade.

## CONTROVERSY

### Arguments For

With districting the most political activity, one must expect that a defenseless minority party will get the short end of the stick. Since members of both parties will exploit any advantage they have, to try to curb partisan gerrymanders is to swim against the tide. Partisan gerrymanders are indeed the political thicket that federal judges will avoid. Sandra Day O'Connor, the only recent judge to have served as a legislator, understood the inherently political nature of redistricting and refused to join her colleagues who wanted to undo plans that advantaged one party. Acknowledging that partisanship is endemic in the key partisan decisions surrounding new districts, how can a judge determine when there is too much partisanship?

Attempts to design plans that produce legislative bodies in which the parties have seat shares that approximate their percentage of the popular vote are unlikely to succeed over the course of a decade due to the absence of a proportional representation electoral system. Even efforts to treat both parties fairly can fail due to unforeseen circumstances such as shifts in voter loyalties and changing demographics. Inability to anticipate performance for a decade also means that often districts designed for the majority party flip to the opposition during the course of a decade.

Since citizens have much more positive attitudes about the government and their legislator when represented by the candidate whom they supported, Brunell urges legislators to prepare maps that minimize competition so that the winning party has an overwhelming majority. A set of one-party districts would maximize the share of the electorate that had the opportunity to see its preferred candidate in office.[143] Plans that dampen competition will promote long tenure by incumbents, and as legislators gain seniority they typically enhance their ability to shape policies preferred by their constituents and develop policy expertise that can be used to check excesses by the executive.

## Arguments Against

The majority party may come up with plans that succeed in keeping its opponents permanently consigned to minority status. In the worst-case scenario, a party that consistently attracts the bulk of the popular vote statewide cannot win a legislative majority because of the unfairness of the maps that pack its supporters into a few districts. Designing maps that produce an unresponsive legislature thwarts electoral majorities from achieving their policy preferences. If the districting arrangement consistently prevents a majority of the electorate from securing control of the legislature, public cynicism will grow and participation may decline.

Allowing mapmakers to arrange voters so as to minimize the number of competitive districts results in most legislators not having to appeal to swing voters. Legislators who need appeal only to their own partisans tend not to be politically moderate since the only threat will come in a primary from fellow partisans who take extreme positions. An absence of moderates may make compromises in the legislature difficult under circumstances of divided partisan control in the legislature or when the chief executive and the legislative majority belong to different parties.

Plans that take unfair advantage of the opposition are at the heart of the debate over gerrymandering, a debate that has raged for more than two centuries. The work of scholars during the 2010s has prepared multiple measures that can be used to determine when the typical advantage conferred by our single-member districts on the majority party have gone too far. State judges can now assess whether plans that would have occurred rarely by chance are so extreme that they may contravene state constitutional or statutory provisions.

## CONCLUSION

Efforts by one political party to take advantage of the other gave us the term gerrymander. Today, just as 200 years ago, redistricting involves raw politics. It is not surprising, therefore, that when a party has the power to do so, it takes advantage of the opposition. Under- or overpopulating districts, the distribution of minorities, and strange configurations have often had at base a desire to ensure one party a larger share of the seats than its proportion of the votes.

Clever politicians have managed to devise districting plans that helped their parties for at least a decade. In other instances, however, the intended beneficiary ends up losing seats as a result of trying to spread its supporters too thinly, reminiscent of the old saying that pigs get fat but hogs get slaughtered.

The losing party after a redistricting session will call the result a gerrymander and express righteous indignation at the failure of the majority to acknowledge basic fairness. Both parties use the same playbook. While the possibility has existed that the aggrieved party may be able to secure relief from the courts, for years that hope has proven as elusive as the pot of gold at the end of the rainbow. The 2019 term of the U.S. Supreme Court extinguished the hope that federal courts would intercede no matter how brazen the majority party had been. But even as the potential for federal intervention vanished, the possibility for relief granted by state tribunals emerged. The 2020s will reveal how willing state judges are to wade into the political thicket. In the near term, a party that loses the redistricting battle and who sues in federal court will continue to contend that the plan discriminates against racial or ethnic minorities or that it treats different geographical areas unequally—proven plays to dismantle a partisan gerrymander.

Plans not intended to disadvantage either party may come from independent commissions or legislatures when neither party has complete control. While these plans may be fairer from a partisan perspective, if they result in districts packed with one set of partisans, they will not promote competition. Moreover, simply taking redistricting out of the hands of legislators does not guarantee the elimination of partisan considerations.

*Chapter 6*

# Gerrymandering in Georgia
## *A Case Study*

The interesting case of Georgia particularly deserves a separate study in its own right, given the dramatic realized and potential Republican gains there as a result of racial redistricting.[1]

The state is not the same state it was. It's not the same state that it was in 1965 or in 1975, or even in 1980 or 1990. We have changed. We've come a great distance. I think in—it's not just in Georgia, but in the American South, I think people are preparing to lay down the burden of race.[2]

Over the past forty years the dominate forces behind Georgia redistricting have shifted from malapportionment and rural dominance in the 1960s and 1970s to fair racial representation in the 1980s and 1990s to most recently partisan gerrymandering.[3]

When it comes to reapportionment and redistricting, Georgia has traveled a long and difficult road. For fifty years, the Empire State of the South had to defend its maps repeatedly in federal courts. Until 2011, the Department of Justice found at least one of Georgia's plans lacking in racial fairness. Two factors accounted for Georgia's difficulties: malapportionment that advantaged rural communities and a history of racial discrimination.

## ONE PERSON, ONE VOTE IN GEORGIA

When the U.S. Supreme Court launched the Reapportionment Revolution in 1962, three practices made Georgia susceptible to judicial demands that districts have equal populations. As the measures of malapportionment in table 2.1 show, Georgia legislative districts had some of the nation's largest population deviations. Additionally, the county unit system gave rural voters an extraordinary influence in statewide elections.

## The End of the County Unit System

The 1917 Neill Primary Act used the Electoral College as a rough model for weighting votes in Democratic primaries for statewide and some congressional offices.[4] Candidates for governor and other offices subject to this legislation got unit votes for each county they carried. The eight most populous counties had six votes each, the next thirty largest got four votes each, and the remaining 121 received two votes each.[5] A statewide candidate could secure the Democratic nomination with as little as 12.5 percent of the popular vote by winning the 103 smallest counties with their total of 206 unit votes. The Talmadge machine relied on this malapportionment and in 1946 Gene Talmadge won the gubernatorial primary even though James Carmichael won a plurality of the popular vote.[6] During the life of the county unit system, Republicans were not a factor in statewide or congressional contests; the Democratic nominee invariably won the general election.

In the wake of the *Baker v. Carr* decision,[7] Fulton County resident James Sanders sued the state Democratic Party, arguing that the primary system which gave Fulton county 1.5 percent of the unit votes despite having almost 15 percent of the voters in the state violated one person, one vote. A three-judge federal panel found that the 6–4–2 scheme violated the new one person, one vote standard, but would have allowed the practice to continue if the disparity in the unit votes of counties did not exceed the difference in the weight of the votes of states in the Electoral College. The Supreme Court found the analogy to the Electoral College inappropriate and banned the county unit system.[8]

## State Senate

A separate suit challenging the apportionment of the state legislature produced a court order to distribute seats in one chamber on the basis of population.[9] The Senate consisted of fifty-four members, all but two of whom represented three-county districts. The counties took turns electing senators so that even the smallest county in the state got to elect a senator every third term. To insure that small counties had their turn to select a senator, only voters in the county in line to elect a senator got to vote in that election. This arrangement prevented senators from earning seniority, making that chamber much weaker than the House. For that reason and because redistricting the House would require changing the state constitution, Senate districts were redrawn prior to the 1962 elections. Atlanta's Fulton County went from one senator to seven while Savannah and Macon each got multiple senators. Where Senate districts previously had three counties, some grew substantially. The 14th District, which elected a peanut warehouser named Jimmy Carter, expanded from three counties to seven.[10]

## Congressional Districts

Having felled the county unit system and the malapportioned Senate, Atlanta-based plaintiffs turned their attention to the congressional districts. As discussed in chapter 2, District 5 had 823,680 people, more than twice the ideal district population for the state of 394,312. Seven of the ten districts were underpopulated by anywhere from -3.65 to -30.98 percent. The Supreme Court threw out the congressional district maps for violating the Equal Protection Clause.[11]

## State House

Beginning with the 1868 Constitution, the eight most populous counties had three members; the thirty next-most-populous counties received two representatives each; and the remaining 121 counties each had one representative. Because of population differences, one vote in tiny Echols County carried 133 times the weight of a Fulton County vote, and the representatives of about a quarter of the population could control the General Assembly as shown in table 2.1. Urban and high-growth counties were disadvantaged.[12] After the Supreme Court ruled in an Alabama case that both chambers of the state legislature must be based on population, Georgia held a special election in 1965 to fill the newly configured 205 House seats.

As occurred with the redrawing of the Senate three years earlier, the new House districts resulted in a more diverse legislature. Giving urban areas a share of seats proportional to their population opened the way for both African Americans and Republicans to crash a previously all-white, Democratic affair. The redistricted Senate welcomed its first black member in decades and three Republicans in 1963. In the House seven African Americans and twenty-three Republicans took the oath of office following the 1965 special election.

## One Person, One Vote in the Twenty-First Century

From the deluge of court challenges to districting plans evolved the notion that state legislative plans should limit population deviations to a range of 5 percent above or below the ideal. Many jurisdictions treated the +/-5 percent deviation as a safe harbor. These bounds held inequities in representation and voting to what seemed to be legally acceptable limits. A compelling state interest in having compact districts, following county and city boundaries, continuity of representation, or not splitting existing precincts can justify deviations in state legislative districts.

## THE DEPARTMENT OF JUSTICE, VOTING RIGHTS, AND REDISTRICTING

Because it used a literacy test and fewer than half of its adults voted in the 1964 presidential election, Georgia was one of the states with long traditions of discriminating against potential black voters made subject to Section 5 of the Voting Rights Act of 1965. Section 5 required that Georgia submit redistricting plans for federal approval prior to implementation. The state could either submit the plans to the U.S. attorney general or it could seek a declaratory judgment that a plan was not discriminatory from the district court in the District of Columbia.

The Department of Justice (DOJ) was slow in developing standards for implementing Section 5.[13] The expectations concerning redistricting became fleshed out as Georgia sought to comply when redrawing its districts. In 1970, Andy Young won the Democratic nomination in the 5th Congressional District which contained the City of Atlanta and some of its suburbs. Young managed 43 percent of the vote in his effort to unseat a two-term Republican. As the legislature went about reconfiguring the district to meet equal population requirements in 1971, it carefully excluded Young's home from the new 5th District. It also excluded the home of Atlanta Vice Mayor Maynard Jackson. Jackson, like Young an African American, might be a formidable candidate for the Democratic nomination. DOJ refused to accept this plan— the only congressional plan DOJ vetoed in the 1970s—until reconfigured to include the homes of these two possible candidates and the black percentage of the population increased from 38.3 to 44.2. In 1972 Young joined Houston's Barbara Jordan as the first southern black members of Congress in the twentieth century and Jackson became Atlanta's first African American mayor in 1973.

Georgia also had to redo its maps for the General Assembly and this necessitated a different map more favorable to African Americans put in place for the 1974 election. That year saw African Americans increase their seats in the House from fourteen to nineteen. The Senate continued to have two black members.

By 1980, the 5th District, which had been 44 percent black when it initially elected Young, had a 50.3 percent black majority. However, like

Table 6.1    Numbers of Majority-Black Districts and Black Legislators

|  | House | Senate | Congress |
|---|---|---|---|
| Plans Used, 1974–1980 | 24 | 2 | 0 |
| Blacks Elected, 1974 | 19 | 2 | 1 |
| Plans Used, 1982–1990 | 29 | 9 | 1 |
| Blacks Elected, 1990 | 27 | 8 | 1 |
| General Assembly Committee Plans, 1991 | 35 | 10 | 2 |
| LBC Task Force Plans, 1991 | 42 | 13 | 3 |
| Max Black Plans, 1991 | 51 | 15 | 3 |
| Plans used in 1992–1994 | 41 | 13 | 3 |
| Blacks Elected, 1992 | 31 | 9 | 3 |
| Plans Used, 1996–2000 | 37 | 11 | 1 |
| Plans used in 2002 | 38 | 13 | 2 |
| Blacks Elected, 2002 | 39 | 10 | 4 |
| Plans used in 2004–2012 | 41 | 13 | 2 |
| Blacks Elected, 2004 | 44 | 12 | 4 |
| Plan used in 2012–2021 | 49 | 15 | 4 |
| Blacks Elected, 2012 | 48 | 13 | 4 |
| Blacks Elected, 2018 | 51 | 15 | 5 |

*Sources*: Robert A. Holmes, "Reapportionment Strategies in the 1990s: A Case of Georgia," in *Race and Redistricting in the 1990s*, Bernard Grofman, ed. (New York: Agathon Press, 1998), 191–228; data from redistricting plans provided by the Georgia Legislative Reapportionment Office.

many districts that contain urban cores, the 5th District was underpopulated. Pursuant to the non-retrogression rule, DOJ would not sign off on a plan that reduced the black percentage. At a minimum, the new plan would have to add roughly equal numbers of whites and blacks as it went about achieving population equality. The Legislative Black Caucus (LBC) had as its goal a 65 percent African-American 5th District. It was widely accepted in the early 1980s that districts needed to be almost two-thirds black for African Americans to be able to elect their preferences.[14] One LBC senator proposed a plan to make the 5th District 73 percent, and in the House one plan had the district at 74 percent black. LBC efforts gained no traction in the House, which minimally increased the black percentage.

The Senate took a very different approach and increased the black concentration to 69 percent of the population. A couple of factors motivated this increase. Republican Paul Coverdell, who was elected to the U.S. Senate in 1992, knew that boosting the black percentage in the 5th District would reduce the black percentage in the neighboring 4th District. Coverdell hoped that a whiter 4th District would elect a Republican. However the coalition of Republicans and African Americans working for a blacker 5th District came up far short of a majority in the Senate, so the plan had to attract white Democrats. Key to securing those needed votes was Senate leader Tom Allgood, whose district in Augusta might have been given a large black majority which would have endangered his reelection. He supported his African American colleague Julian Bond's effort to boost the black concentration in the 5th District in return for less pressure to increase the black percentage in the Augusta Senate district.[15]

The conference committee endorsed a 57 percent black district (54 percent black among those of voting age)[16] which DOJ rejected in light of the alternatives with higher black concentrations. Arguing that it was not guilty of retrogression, the state sought vindication from the district court of the District of Columbia. The week-long trial focused not on the adequacy of the black concentration or on retrogression or its absence. Instead, the verdict hinged on the motivation behind the districting decisions. The state contended that it divided the 4th and 5th Districts on a north-south axis that largely followed the line between Fulton and DeKalb counties. Following the move toward equal population districts, these two counties had each dominated its own congressional district. The state's explanation that it sought to maintain a black population in excess of 20 percent in the 4th District in order to thwart the possibility of Republicans winning that district proved unconvincing.

DOJ noted that because the black population was expanding into south DeKalb,[17] using the county boundary to separate the congressional districts divided a single African American community. DOJ attorneys latched on to testimony provided by then Lieutenant Governor Zell Miller who urged the maintenance of a mountain district. Miller, who came from a mountain county just below the North Carolina line, explained that people in his part of the state had unique interests and needed a member of Congress to represent those interests. DOJ argued that African Americans in Atlanta also constituted a distinct community that should be contained in a single district with a member of Congress to shepherd their interests.

In ruling against the state, the three-judge panel emphasized what it saw as racism underlying the districting decision. The court noted that because the plan was not guilty of retrogression, there was no discriminatory effect. The court, however, concluded that the state failed to prove an absence of a discriminatory purpose and under *Georgia v. U.S.* the submitting authority must prove its plan does not discriminate.[18] The court pointed to the statement by Joe Mack Wilson, who chaired the House redistricting committee, "The Justice Department is trying to make us draw nigger districts and I don't want to draw nigger districts."[19] Wilson told black Representative Al Scott, "If you blacks want anything . . . higher than this 57 percent [black district], you better be prepared to get it from the Justice Department or the courts." Another legislator quoted Wilson as saying, "I'm not going to draw a honky Republican district and I'm not going to draw a nigger district if I can help it."[20] The court asserted in its findings of fact that "Joe Mack Wilson is a racist."

After the Supreme Court refused to review the *Busbee* decision, the legislature adopted a new plan that boosted the black percentage in the 5th District to 65.02 percent and 59.6 percent black among registrants, whereupon DOJ signed off. The litigation and subsequent special session needed to raise the black percentage in the 5th District resulted in a court order that delayed the election cycle for the 4th and 5th Districts. The November 2 election chose 433 members of the House but was primary day in the two Atlanta-area districts. These two districts held their general elections on November 30 and returned white, Democratic incumbents in each district.

In 1986 civil rights hero John Lewis won the district. As Coverdell had hoped, in 1984 a Republican won the 4th District where the black population had been reduced to 13 percent.

DOJ also objected to plans for the state House and Senate. The LBC came up with a plan that had forty-three majority-black House districts although the Caucus set its goal as thirty-six majority-black House seats and twelve in the Senate. The plans adopted by the General Assembly had twenty-nine House and eight Senate districts with black majorities. As with the congressional plan, Africans Americans and Republicans worked together on the state legislative plans. DOJ required only minor adjustments and the 1982 elections saw modest gains with the number of black senators increasing from two to four while the House contingent stagnated at twenty-one.

## THE 1990S

By the time of the next census, DOJ had substantially changed its standards for assessing districting plans. From the time of the initial enactment of the Voting Rights Act (VRA) in 1965 the chief role of Section 5 prevented implementation of *new* discriminatory laws in states having historically low minority participation. While the VRA succeeded in preventing new acts of bias as when DOJ blocked Georgia's 1971 congressional plan, Section 5 was not designed to root out discriminatory practices in place prior to 1964. To deal with existing electoral systems, Congress rewrote Section 2 when renewing the Voting Rights Act in 1982 so that plaintiffs challenging an existing electoral system need not prove intent to discriminate. Plaintiffs could prevail by showing that the plan had a discriminatory effect or result.

### Congress

Georgia legislators approached the post-1990 redistricting committed to creating a second majority-black congressional district. The 1990 census awarded Georgia an eleventh seat and this new district would have a black majority. Doubling the number of majority-black districts would prevent charges of retrogression and legislators anticipated that unlike in the two previous decades their plan would have no difficulty securing approval from DOJ. Shortly before the special session to draw plans for Congress and the state legislative chambers, I met with the Legislative Black Caucus. At that time, the LBC's primary objective was a second district likely to elect an African American. Caucus member Eugene Walker, who chaired the Senate redistricting committee, told his colleagues that to draw a second district with a black majority would require linking the African American populations in three different urban areas since black concentrations in a single urban area was sufficient for only one district, John Lewis's Atlanta district. The plan adopted by the special session of the General Assembly drew a new 60.6 percent black district by linking the black population in south DeKalb (some of the same area at the heart of the 1982 *Busbee* litigation) with black concentrations in Augusta and Macon, using part of the old cotton-growing Black Belt to tie the three urban areas together. The plan split the three urban counties along racial lines in order to bump up the black population in the new 11th District.

Republicans developed their own redistricting operation rather than work with the state's Legislative Reapportionment Office. The LBC had hoped to have a third redistricting program through the American Civil Liberties Union office in Atlanta. When the ACLU did not get its operation up and running, Republicans offered access to their system to LBC members.

There is disagreement over who gets credit for having come up with the initial design, but before the expiration of the sixty-day period given DOJ to review the plan with two black districts someone in the black-Republican coalition discovered a way to draw three majority-black districts. Former state Representative Bart Ladd (R) claims that he gave the plan with three black districts to Cynthia McKinney.[21]

Ladd's account, which may include a few dramatic embellishments, is that he figured out how to link black concentrations in each of two sets of three urban areas together to develop both a second and a third majority-black district. Ladd, a Delta pilot, then flew to Washington where he presented his map to DOJ. He had not drawn a complete map showing the location of all eleven districts but only the feasibility of the three majority-black districts. DOJ was intrigued but told Ladd that he would need to demonstrate how to draw the eight majority-white districts and stay within acceptable population tolerances. Ladd returned to Atlanta where he and others at the Republican redistricting office worked like college students pulling all-nighters before a big exam and completed the task. The three-district plan having been devel-oped on the Republican computer had to be transmitted to the state's reappor-tionment office. At this time data and materials rather than being transmitted electronically were physically taken on floppy disks. File names were limited to eight characters or letters and the name given the three-district plan was "MAXBLACK," which became the name for this proposal and at times more generally applied to other efforts to maximize the number of majority-black seats.[22]

The coalition of some LBC members and Republicans came nowhere close to a majority in either chamber of the Georgia legislature. To force the MAXBLACK plans on the state would require help from DOJ. The careerists at DOJ had long supported increasing the numbers of black officials as indicated by their demands when reviewing Georgia redistricting plans from earlier decades.[23] In the early 1990s, the objectives of the careerists found support among the top tier of appointed officials. Republicans named by President George H. W. Bush to run the Justice Department saw what Paul Coverdell had recognized a decade earlier—concentrating African Americans to create majority black districts left adjacent districts whiter and more Republican. The advantage to the GOP of supporting demands for more black districts was acknowledged in the testimony of Assistant Attorney General for Civil Rights John Dunne quoted in chapter 3.[24]

DOJ's rejection of the state's two-black district plan came in the midst of a growing split within the LBC. The chair of the Legislative Black Caucus, Michael Thurmond, and Eugene Walker, chair of the Senate redistricting committee, favored plans with two black districts. A group led by Cynthia McKinney and civil rights activist Tyrone Brooks, both of whom represented Atlanta districts, and two Albany representatives met with DOJ officials to lobby for the three-district plan. When the representatives of the General Assembly that included the chairs of the two chambers' redistricting committees, Rep. Bob Hanner, white, and Sen. Eugene Walker, met with the DOJ preclearance staff, they were attacked. According to Hanner, at a four-hour meeting with DOJ representatives,

> The Department of Justice was snapping at Gene Walker. A black Department of Justice attorney came down hard on Gene. He also came down hard on Mike Thurmond and the Legislative Black Caucus when they went to defend the second plan. People at the Department of Justice may not have realized that then Cynthia [McKinney] was running for Congress. Therefore Justice came down harder on Gene since they knew he was running for Congress.[25]

The rejection letter from the assistant attorney general criticized the congressional plan. While the state had from the outset been committed to creating a second majority-black district, John Dunne's letter put this in a negative light. "A concern was raised with regard to the principle underlying the Congressional redistricting, namely that the Georgia legislative leadership was predisposed to limit black voting potential to two black majority districts."[26] While Dunne did not demand the creation of a third majority-black district, he criticized the state's plan because it "did not make a good faith attempt to recognize the concentrations of black voters in the Southwest [part of Georgia] and has not yet been able to adequately explain the departure from its own stated criteria in what appears to be resulting in minimization."

A second concern focused on the way in which the more than 60 percent black 11th District had been drawn. DOJ, wanting a still higher black concentration, questioned the decision not to split Baldwin County. "This majority black district not only limits the black percentage of the district but also ignores the community of interest which black residents of Baldwin County share with those in the surrounding counties."[27] The issue here differed from the objection registered a decade earlier where the black population spread out from Fulton into DeKalb counties. Baldwin County's black concentration was miles from other black concentrations in neighboring counties.

The legislature immediately responded to DOJ's objections and increased the black concentration in southwest Georgia's District 2 from 39.4 to 49.1 percent by pulling into the district the black population on the south side of Columbus. Blacks constituted 45 percent of the voting age population and 43 percent of the registered voters in the newly configured district. But since the new map still had not produced a third majority-black district, DOJ issued a second letter denying preclearance on March 20, 1992.

DOJ infuriated legislative leaders by the way it conveyed its evaluation of the second plan. Rather than contacting legislative leaders or the state attorney general's office which had transmitted the plan to DOJ, Justice sent the rejection letter to leaders of the Black Caucus. The state's legal office and its legislative leaders were frantically trying to get a copy of the rejection letter even as a member of the LBC read it at a news conference.

In the second letter, Dunne pointed to a plan adopted by the state Senate but rejected by the House. The Senate plan had attached the black population of Savannah to the 11th Congressional District. DOJ favored this alternative and chided the state because "This configuration was abandoned and no legitimate reason has been suggested to explain the exclusion of the second largest concentration of blacks in the state from a majority black congressional district."[28]

Dunne next turned his attention to southwest Georgia. "In southwest Georgia a review of the proposed remedial plan indicates a similar concern. Although the submitted plan has increased the black percentage in the 2nd Congressional District, it continues the exclusion of large black population concentrations in areas such as Meriwether, Houston and Bibb counties from this district." An interesting element here is the inclusion of these three counties, none of which is in the southwest corner of the state. Bibb and Houston are in Middle Georgia. A decade later portions of these counties were at the heart of a new Middle Georgia district. The emphasis of this second critique was not the development of geographically coherent districts but rather the creation of a third district having a black majority.

Since the rejection of the first plan had not prompted Georgia to meet DOJ objectives, this second letter explicitly outlined what it would take to secure preclearance. Quoting the Dunne letter:

> Several alternative redistricting approaches which created a southwest district with a majority black voting age population by including additional black communities such as the City of Macon and which did not diminish the effectiveness of the minority electorate in the 11th by including Chatham, were suggested to the legislature during the redistricting process. Despite the existence of the alternatives, however, the state refused to recognize potential black voting strength in the state and has failed to explain adequately the choices made during this round of Congressional redistricting.

DOJ demanded that Macon's black population be swapped from the 11th to the 2nd District and that Savannah's African Americans be appended to the 11th District. Making this swap would produce a third majority-black district and all of the major concentrations of African Americans would now live in a majority black district. The three districts managed to corral 61.6 percent of Georgia's black population.

Many white Democrats felt that they had done enough. They had doubled the number of majority-black districts and had created a third district with a heavy black concentration—what would be considered to be a black-influence district under the *Ashcroft v. Georgia* decision of 2003.[29] The legislature faced a time crunch since it received the second rejection letter with only days remaining before its forty-day session ended.

After heated debate, the speaker took the extraordinary step of casting the deciding vote for the plan that created three black districts. In addition to Lewis's 62 percent black 5th District, the 11th District (shown in figure 6.1) which now went from the Atlanta suburbs to Augusta and then ran along the Savannah River to pick up approximately 60,000 citizens of the city, made famous in *Midnight in the Garden of Good and Evil*,[30] was 64 percent black. The other black district, the 2nd in southwest Georgia, achieved a 57 percent black population by including the black neighborhoods of Albany, Columbus, and Macon. To draw this final district, technicians in the Legislative Reapportionment Office went around the edges of the district, precinct by precinct. Majority-black precincts ended up in District 2 while those with white majorities went into a neighboring district. In creating these districts, the legislators and their technicians focused almost exclusively on race in order to boost black populations as high as possible in order to satisfy DOJ demands. DOJ approved this third iteration.

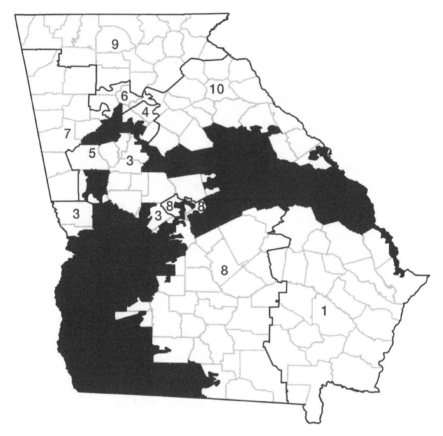

**Figure 6.1   Georgia's Congressional District Plan Adopted in 1992 (majority-black districts shown in black).** *Source*: Prepared by the Carl Vinson Institute of Government, the University of Georgia, July 1992.

The 1992 elections sent three African Americans to Congress. The Democratic field in the 11th District included three black legislators active in the redistricting process along with a white and a black newcomer.[31] Cynthia McKinney, who had urged DOJ to demand a three-black district plan, led the primary with 31 percent of the vote. The remainder of the black vote split, allowing the one white candidate, George DeLoach, to finish second with 25 percent of the vote. Eugene Walker finished third with 22 percent of the vote while Michael Thurmond polled 16 percent. McKinney easily won the runoff with 56 percent of the vote and coasted to victory in the general election with 73 percent of the vote.

Despite having a 57 percent black population, the bulk of the electorate in the 2nd District remained white. The Democratic primary attracted a large field of black challengers including state legislators from Albany and Columbus, a community leader from Macon, and two minor candidates. Incumbent Charles Hatcher, like his predecessors who represented this southwest Georgia district, had served on the Agriculture Committee. In the course of promoting peanut production and other farming interests he devoted less attention to his bank balance and this omission placed him in the midst of the major scandal of 1992. The U.S. House operated a bank into which representatives deposited their paychecks.[32] The bank covered overdrafts at no charge until the receipt of the legislator's next paycheck. Rep. Hatcher had the second highest number of overdrafts at the House bank. In addition to the 819 overdrafts, he had recently divorced his wife and married a young member of his staff.

Even with these problems, Hatcher led the large primary field with 40 percent of the vote. His runoff opponent, African American attorney Sanford Bishop, had fourteen years' service in the Georgia House and most recently a term in the Senate. In the runoff, Bishop retired the incumbent by taking 53 percent of the vote.

While African Americans picked up two additional Georgia congressional districts, their partners in designing the MAXBLACK plan did even better. In 1991 Republicans held only one Georgia congressional district and had never held more than two in the post-Goldwater era of modern Republicanism. With the black population gathered into three districts, Republicans doubled their high point by winning four seats in 1992. Each of these gains came in a district with a substantially reduced black population as shown in table 6.2. Jack Kingston won the 1st District, which lost 50,000 Savannah African

**Table 6.2    Changes in the Racial Makeup of Georgia Congressional Districts Following the 1992 Redistricting**

| District | 1991 | | 1995 | |
|---|---|---|---|---|
| | *% Black* | *Incumbent* | *% Black* | *Incumbent* |
| 1 | 32 | White Democrat | 23 | Republican |
| 2 | 37 | White Democrat | 57 | Black Democrat |
| 3 | 35 | White Democrat | 18 | Republican |
| 4 | 25 | White Democrat | 12 | Republican |
| 5 | 67 | Black Democrat | 62 | Black Democrat |
| 6 | 20 | Republican | 6 | Republican |
| 7 | 9 | White Democrat | 13 | Republican* |
| 8 | 36 | White Democrat | 21 | Republican* |
| 9 | 5 | White Democrat | 4 | Republican** |
| 10 | 23 | White Democrat | 18 | Republican* |
| 11 | New district in 1993 | | 64 | Black Democrat |

*Source*: Author.
* Changed from Democrat to Republican in 1994.
** Incumbent elected as a Democrat but changed parties in 1995.

Americans to the McKinney district making the 1st 9 percentage points whiter. Mac Collins won the 3rd District after Macon's black population went into Bishop's district. John Linder, who had lost with 48 percent of the vote in 1990, inched his vote share up to take the 4th District by a margin of 2,600 votes. His district became substantially whiter when the black precincts in south DeKalb became the northern terminus of McKinney's district.

In 1994, Republicans won three more congressional seats, two of which became whiter in the course of redistricting. A few months after the GOP won a majority of the House for the first time since 1954, the last white Democrat, Nathan Deal who represented the 9th District, changed parties. While the bleaching of neighboring districts to obtain the African Americans needed to create three majority-black districts cannot account for all of the Republican success, the racial gerrymanders certainly helped. Georgia's congressional delegation which had only one African American and one Republican and eight white Democrats prior to redistricting was transformed into a delegation that by April of 1995 had three African Americans, eight Republicans, and no white Democrats.

## State Legislature

As with the congressional districts, a minority of the LBC pushed for MAXBLACK in the General Assembly, which proposed 15 majority-black Senate districts and 51 majority-black House districts. As table 6.1 shows, these objectives exceeded the proposal from the LBC task force which sought 13 majority-black Senate districts and 42 House districts. The plans approved by the legislature had even fewer predominately black districts with 10 in the Senate and 35 in the House.

DOJ objected to plans for both legislative chambers in the same letters in which it rejected the congressional plans. It took two more efforts before DOJ signed off on the 13 majority-black district Senate plan and three more plans to get to 41 African American House districts. Tyrone Brooks, one of the most fervent advocates for the MAXBLACK approach, exulted that, "We got 98 percent of what we were fighting for."[33] With the new plans in place, one additional African American senator and four more representatives won in 1992. The new plans included the first rural districts to send African Americans to the House.

In a reprise of the congressional experience, Republicans made out better than African Americans in the General Assembly. Republicans increased their ranks in the Senate from 11 to 15 and in the House their numbers rose from 35 to 52, one of the largest gains by Republicans in any legislative chamber in the nation in 1992, generally a bad year for the GOP and the last time Georgia voted Democratic for president.

## A MID-DECADE ADJUSTMENT

After the Supreme Court ruled that racial gerrymanders were justiciable in *Shaw v. Reno*, George DeLoach, loser of the 1992 runoff to Rep. McKinney, filed a challenged to the 11th Congressional District. The plaintiffs emphasized the elements that seemed relevant from Justice Sandra Day O'Connor's *Shaw v. Reno* opinion.[34] They pointed out that the district running from the Atlanta city limits into Savannah was longer than North Carolina's 12th District criticized in *Shaw*. They also noted how the district had carefully skirted around white populations in order to maximize the black percentage.

In the Georgia case the court elaborated on the concerns articulated in *Shaw*. In *Miller v. Johnson*, the Supreme Court clarified that it was not the shape of the districts per se that mattered but the degree to which race dominated the motivations of those who created the districts.[35] When, as in the creation of the 2nd and 11th Districts, the legislature elevates race above traditional districting principles such as compactness, contiguity, respect for communities, and adherence to the political boundaries of cities and counties, the plan violates the Equal Protection Clause of the federal Constitution.

The trial court judges and the majority of the Supreme Court found much to criticize in the way that DOJ had dealt with Georgia. The two line DOJ attorneys who oversaw the Georgia submissions had so little recall of the events when testifying that the court found their "professed amnesia less than credible." The court also criticized the cozy relationship between ACLU attorney Kathy Wilde and DOJ. "It is obvious from a review of materials that Ms. Wilde's relationship with the DOJ Voting Section was informal and familiar; the dynamics of that of peers working together not of an advocate submitting proposals to higher authorities." The opinion continued, "Succinctly put, the considerable influence of ACLU advocacy on the voting rights decisions of the United States Attorney General is an embarrassment."

The decision to require the maximization of majority-black congressional districts in Georgia and elsewhere did not evoke criticism from national Democrats since to do so might jeopardize their relationships with black leaders and the African American vote critical to the success of the Democratic Party.

Invalidation of the plan that DOJ had demanded prompted a special session of the General Assembly. The Senate favored a plan with only one majority-black district. The House tried to devise a plan that would retain three majority-black districts.[36] By 1995, growth in the ranks of Republican and black House members made it possible for a coalition of these strange bedfellows to constitute a majority. To prevent that, Speaker Tom Murphy (D) knew that he must support a plan that would retain the support of the black Democrats who adopted the stance, "Three seats, no retreat."[37] Indeed, if black Democrats became alienated, they might support a challenger to Murphy when it came time to renew his tenure as Speaker in 1997. Ultimately the House and Senate failed to resolve their differences on the congressional plan.

When the legislature failed to take corrective action, the trial court came up with a plan. The judges used as their benchmark the last constitutional plan, the one adopted in 1982. Like the 1982 plan, the judge's map had a single majority-black district. Since it is assumed that federal judges will not discriminate against minorities, the court's 1995 plan did not require DOJ approval.

The court plan looked more like traditional Georgia maps. The plan demanded by DOJ had divided numerous counties and was characterized by twists and turns with fingers reaching out to pick up black neighborhoods. In contrast with the 1992 plan that split a dozen counties to create the 11th District and another eight to get a black majority in the 2nd District, its replacements split only six counties, all in the Atlanta metropolitan area as shown in figure 6.2. Fulton County had to be split because its population exceeded what would be tolerated under the one person, one vote standard. The plan split three of Fulton's neighbors whose large populations made it difficult, if not altogether impossible, to keep them whole while combining them with smaller counties and still be within the population limits. The benchmark plan adopted in 1982 had divided only three counties, thus the 1995 plan was a major step back toward the benchmark in terms of county unity.

The failure to have more than one majority-black district prompted yet another suit. In *Abrams v. Johnson*, the United States attorney general and the ACLU argued that the new plan should have at least two if not three majority-black districts.[38] Both the trial court and the Supreme Court rejected that logic. The Supreme Court supported the decision by the district court to use the 1982 plan as the benchmark. Having rejected the two-district plans as unacceptable, DOJ could not now demand their adoption. Nor could the plan that had been ruled unconstitutional be a benchmark against which to assess retrogression. The Supreme Court accepted the district court finding that Georgia's African American population was not sufficiently compact to permit the drawing of a second majority-black district.

The *Abrams* decision addressed the pre-conditions from *Thornburg* and accepted the finding by the district court of sufficient white crossover voting so that racial polarization did not prevent adoption of the plan. The court had the advantage of the results of the 1996 election. While DOJ had argued that the black-preferred candidate could not win in the new 4th District, a district that, according to the 1990 census figures had a 33 percent black voting age population, Cynthia McKinney won handily.

Elections during the remainder of the decade demonstrated the adequacy of the districts drawn by the district court. McKinney and Sanford Bishop in the 2nd District where the black population dropped from 57 to 39 percent

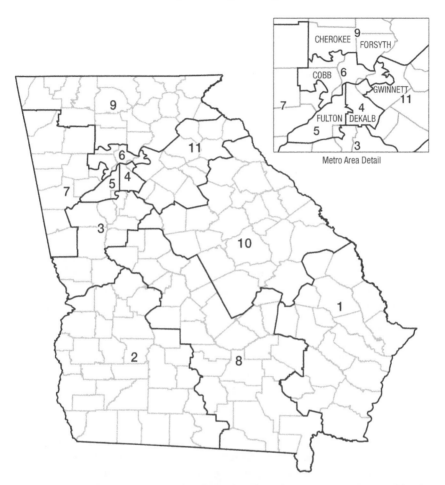

**Figure 6.2   Court-Drawn Congressional District Plan of 1995.** *Source*: Prepared by the Carl Vinson Institute of Government, the University of Georgia, January 1996.

continued to win reelection with little difficulty. Both Bishop and McKinney attracted 30 percent of the white vote and that, in combination with more than 90 percent support from the black community, sufficed to win these majority-white districts.[39]

The General Assembly redrew portions of the House and Senate plans following the invalidation of the congressional plans in *Miller v. Johnson.* An attorney had threatened suit, challenging five Senate and twelve House districts, claiming that like McKinney's congressional district, considerations of race had received priority over traditional districting principles. While the General Assembly could never agree on new congressional plans, self-interest prompted the legislators to modify their own plans so as to stave off further litigation. These new plans reduced black concentrations in the districts held by several party and committee leaders.[40] After eliminating six majority-black districts, the plans used from 1996 to 2001 had eleven majority-black Senate districts and thirty-seven majority-black House districts. Despite reducing the number of majority-black districts, the new plans elected two more black senators, bringing their number to eleven and the number of black representatives increased to thirty-three.

## THE 2001 DEMOCRATIC GERRYMANDER

During the 1990s, Georgia experienced some of the most rapid population growth in the nation. In percentage terms, Georgia grew more rapidly than any other state east of the Mississippi, as its population increased by more than 26 percent. This dramatic population explosion netted two additional members of Congress. Embarking on the new century with thirteen members of Congress, Georgia had its largest congressional delegation ever.

While Georgia had grown dramatically during the decade, the growth was not evenly distributed across the state. North Georgia continued to boom while South Georgia attracted relatively few new residents. Central cities experienced slow growth or no growth while subdivisions sprouted up further and further from the urban core so that four-lane highways sheathed in fast food restaurants, strip malls, and car dealerships crisscrossed what had been rural in 1990.

One response to the population shifts would have increased districts in areas that experienced the most growth. This would have been especially easy when eliminating population deviations for the state House and Senate since the populations for districts in these legislative bodies are much smaller than for Congress. In each state legislative chamber at least one district had twice the population acceptable under one person, one vote.

Despite Republican gains in the legislative and executive branches during the 1990s, Democrats still controlled the governorship and both chambers of the General Assembly in 2001. Since the growth areas tended to be Republican while the less dynamic areas tended to be Democratic, simply rewarding growth with additional legislative seats was unacceptable to Democratic leaders. Recent election returns compounded the challenge for Democrats. Beginning in 1996, Republicans had attracted more votes than Democrats in state legislative contests. If one added up all of the votes cast for Democratic candidates running for the state Senate in 1996 and all the votes for Republicans running for the state Senate, 52 percent of the ballots went to Republicans. Republicans repeated the feat of outpolling Democrats in 1998 and 2000, as shown in table 6.3. Republicans also took small majorities of the

Table 6.3 Percentages of the Votes and Seats Won by the Republican Party in Georgia's General Assembly, 1996–2000

|  | SENATE | | HOUSE | |
|---|---|---|---|---|
|  | *Votes* | *Seats* | *Votes* | *Seats* |
| 1996 | 52 | 39 | 51 | 41 |
| 1998 | 51 | 39 | 53 | 43 |
| 2000 | 55 | 43 | 52 | 42 |

*Source*: Calculated by the author.

votes for House members beginning in 1996 although, as with the Senate, they never came close to winning a proportionate share of the seats. Democrats confronted the challenge of taking a minority of the vote and spinning it into a majority while adjusting for population differences and in doing so minimizing the redistribution of seats to high growth areas. Although the legislators could not have known it at the time, subsequent simulations concluded that plans drawn based on equal populations, contiguity, and compactness would likely have resulted in Republican majorities in about two-thirds of the districts in each chamber.[41]

In an earlier time, the Democrats might have had to yield to the demographic patterns and allowed Republicans a shot at winning majorities. That scenario, however, harkens back to a time when voters chose their representatives. With the computer software available for drawing district lines and the willingness of courts to look the other way, representatives often get to choose their constituents.

Despite demographic and electoral trends running against them, Democrats set out not simply to retain their positions but to expand their ranks in the legislature and Congress. They hoped to reclaim a majority in the congressional delegation dominated since 1995 by Republicans 8–3. The maps drawn in the early 1990s that were ultimately invalidated in *Miller v. Johnson* had provided the testing grounds for the maps produced in the next decade. During the 1990s, Georgia's Legislative Reapportionment Office split counties and used narrow land bridges to unite distant populations that shared a racial characteristic. In 2001, rather than uniting populations of the same race, the technicians brought together distant populations that shared a partisan tie.

Since the early 1970s, Georgia has maintained a professional reapportionment office. The former director, Linda Meggers, began working on redistricting as a graduate student in 1971 and spent her career there. Her technical expertise earned her a national reputation among those who worked with the census to adjust populations after each new decade. During much of a decade, Meggers operated with a skeletal staff and provided assistance to local governments that needed to redraw the boundaries for county commissions and city council districts. As the time for the new census drew near, Meggers increased her staff in preparation for cleaning up the population figures provided by the Census Bureau and gathering and merging political data with the census materials. In previous years, the reapportionment office had worked closely with the Democratic leadership in developing plans. This all changed in 2001 when the reapportionment office was largely bypassed, especially in the development of the blatantly partisan Senate plans.

Another difference was that previous governors took a hands-off approach to redistricting. After all, it was legislators' political futures that the new maps affected and so the chief executive left it up to them. Governor Roy Barnes, a very savvy politician, recognized the potential for a Republican takeover of one or both legislative chambers. He had no interest in becoming the first Georgia governor to have to learn how to lead a divided government. To help with the redistricting, Barnes brought in an outside consultant who drew maps with little input from the reapportionment office or even Democratic legislators. Individual Democratic legislators got to see the proposal for their district but nothing else. Those who objected were warned that if they did not accept this plan they would be even more dissatisfied with the next iteration.

Spinning a majority of seats out of a minority of support was not easy for Democrats since election results suggested that if they had not already become the minority party, they soon would sink to that level. Barnes's consultant turned to several strategies to stretch Democrats' depleted resources. First, they made more efficient use of their party's core constituency. Toward this end, districts that had been packed with African Americans in the 1990s had some of their minority population redistributed. By reducing the black concentrations in majority-black districts, the state risked running afoul of Section 5 of the Voting Rights Act. In reviewing districting plans in the past, the Department of Justice and courts had refused to permit reducing minority concentrations. When retrogression, the reduction of minority concentration occurred, DOJ rejected plans.

In an effort to secure DOJ approval, the state developed evidence showing it could reduce minority concentrations without endangering the ability of minorities to elect their preferred candidates. For decades, an assumption guiding redistricting was that black candidates could only win in overwhelmingly black districts. This belief guided DOJ when it demanded a 65 percent African American 5th District in 1982. Columbia University political scientist David Epstein analyzed the electoral patterns for Georgia legislators from the 1990s.[42] He estimated that in a district in which blacks constituted at least 45 percent of the adult population, their preferred candidate had a 50–50 chance of winning. As the black concentration rose, the probability that blacks could elect their preferred candidate increased. Members of the Legislative Black Caucus found Epstein's analysis convincing and joined in support of plans that reduced black concentrations. African Americans removed from the majority-black districts could then be redistributed to help white Democrats win nearby districts. LBC members recognized that if Democrats lost their majorities in the General Assembly, black legislators would lose the committee chairs they held and have much less influence in shaping legislation. The post-2000 census redistricting plan for the state Senate reduced the black voting age population (BVAP) in majority-black districts by an average of over ten points. Three districts that had been more than 60 percent BVAP emerged in the new plan less than 51 percent BVAP.

More generally, Winburn shows that safe Democratic Senate districts became about 10 percentage points less Democratic in the course of redistricting yet still retained very secure margins in 2002.[43] Safe Democratic House districts became 7.6 percentage points more Republican but still voted almost three to one Democratic in 2002.

Democrats efficiently used their loyalists removed from secure districts. Eleven competitive House districts in the previous plan emerged in the new plan voting 53 percent Democratic in 2002, a gain of more than 11 percentage points over the old districts. In the Senate, six districts that had voted more than 60 percent Republican before redistricting became competitive as Democrats took 48.4 percent of the vote in 2002.

Going back to the county unit days, Georgia had multi-member districts in the House until the 1992 plan. A review of various alternatives as they set out to redraw the lower chamber in 2001 convinced Democrats that no plan utilizing only single-member districts would give them a majority. As a second strategy, Democrats pushed through a plan with twenty-three multi-member districts. Fifteen of these elected two legislators each while six districts elected three and two districts sent four representatives to the House. Most of the multi-member districts were in the Atlanta metro area as Democrats attached smaller Republican populations to predominately Democratic districts, allowing Democrats to win all of the seats in the larger district, as illustrated in chapter 1.

A third Democratic strategy weakened the GOP by pairing some of its members. That this was done to reduce the experience of the opposition party becomes obvious since often adjacent to a district that included two Republicans would be a GOP-leaning district that included no incumbent. Since Georgia law requires that legislators live in a district a year before being elected, Republicans paired with colleagues could not move to a nearby district that had no incumbent. As strategic politicians recognize, winning an open seat is much easier than defeating an incumbent. Pairing eliminated four Republican senators and fourteen representatives.[44]

As a fourth strategy Democrats wasted as many Republican votes as possible by packing Republican districts while stretching their limited Democratic

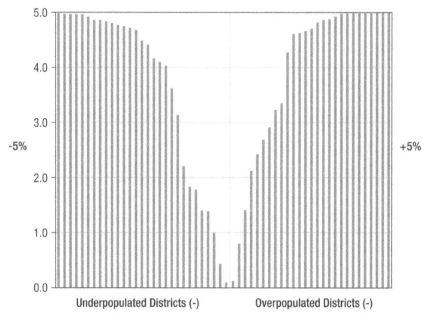

**Figure 6.3  Senate Districts Distributed on the Basis of Population. Deviations from –5% to +5% (each bar represents one district).** *Source*: Plaintiff's demonstrative exhibits *Larios v. Cox*, 300 F. Supp. 2d 1320 (N.D. Ga. 2004).

votes by underpopulating Democratic districts. If a mapmaker sought to draw equally populated districts, the result would approximate a normal curve with a few outliers being under- or overpopulated by 4.5 percent or more. In crafting the new state legislative maps, the creators took pains to ensure that all districts were within plus or minus 5 percent of the ideal population size. They operated on the assumption that so long as the district populations did not deviate by more than 5 percent and minorities suffered no discrimination, courts would accept about anything. As figure 6.3 shows, the distribution of Senate districts was anything but a normal curve and instead had a "U" shape with very few districts coming close to the ideal population and many districts at least 4 percent above or below the ideal. Eighteen districts were overpopulated by at least 4.25 percent and Republicans won sixteen of these, including ten overpopulated by 4.9 percent or more.[45] In 2002 Democrats won seventeen of nineteen Senate districts underpopulated by 4 percent or more. The same pattern characterized House plans.

Looking at a few of the new districts illustrates the consequences of the Democrats' machinations. Senate plans had long, narrow districts that lumped together patches of Republicans. As shown in figure 6.4, District 1, represented by the minority leader in the Senate which had contained most of Chatham and a little bit of Bryan, now extended the entire length of the

**Figure 6.4  Senate District 1 as Adopted in 2002.** *Source:* Plaintiff's demonstrative exhibits *Larios v. Cox*, 300 F. Supp. 2d 1320 (N.D. Ga. 2004).

Georgia coast while also reaching north of Savannah into Effingham County with another arm extended inland toward the southern part of the district to include chunks of Brantley and Pierce counties. In several of the counties, the 1st District contained only barrier islands. As it went through Liberty County it managed to pick up absolutely none of the population.

A second extraordinary bit of mapping transformed the district of minority caucus chair Bill Stephens. In the old map, his district contained all of four counties and most of Cherokee County. These counties were stacked up from

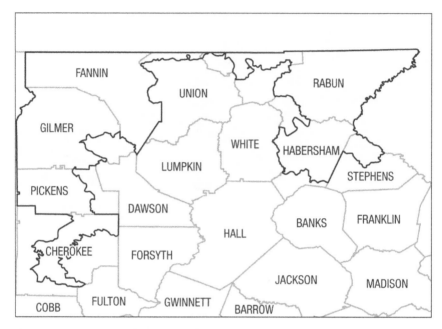

**Figure 6.5 Senate District 51 as Adopted in 2002.** *Source:* Plaintiff's demonstrative exhibits *Larios v. Cox*, 300 F. Supp. 2d 1320 (N.D. Ga. 2004).

north metro Atlanta to the North Carolina border. In the new configuration shown in figure 6.5 Cherokee, one of the state's fastest growing counties which could have constituted a Senate district by itself as its population came within 3 percent of the ideal for a Senate district, was split three ways. Stephens's new district still ran to the North Carolina border but, rather than stopping there, it tiptoed along the state line all the way to South Carolina. It took a narrow path across two of the counties along the state line before ballooning in Georgia's northeast corner to include all of Rabun and parts of two other counties. At one point, the district narrowed to only 740 feet at which point it splashed across a lake.[46] The district defied any conventional notion of compactness or community of interest. Cherokee County voters focus on things such as sprawl and how to navigate traffic as they head toward Atlanta and their jobs. These concerns are completely alien to the mountain folk who live in Rabun, where there are no interstate highways and traffic congestion comes only during the pre-school sale at Walmart. Shortly after release of the map an *Atlanta Journal Constitution* reporter set out to go from one end of the district to the other. It took him almost eight hours and he drove 199 miles.[47]

Shortly after adoption of the maps, I spoke to the Rotary Club in Rabun County on the subject of redistricting. When I opened the floor for questions, the first person to speak was the local state representative who pleaded, "Tell

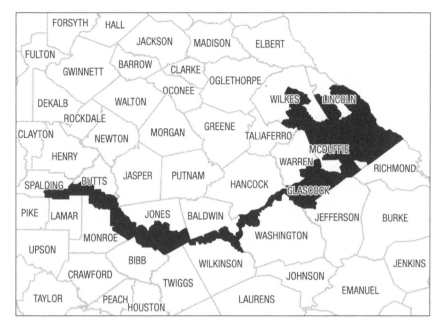

**Figure 6.6 Senate District 24 as Adopted in 2002.** *Source*: Plaintiff's demonstrative exhibits *Larios v. Cox*, 300 F. Supp. 2d 1320 (N.D. Ga. 2004).

these people here that I had nothing to do with those Senate maps!" It was obvious that Representative Ralph Twiggs had heard frequent criticism from his constituents over the Senate maps that denied them a meaningful voice in the Senate by attaching them to the far more populous, distant metropolitan Atlanta end of the district.[48]

A third remarkable Senate district, the 24th, appears in figure 6.6. The map adopted in 1996 gave the 24th five entire counties between Augusta and Athens. When redrawn in 2001, the district had all of only one county— Glascock which with a population of 2,557 was the state's third smallest— and included parts of ten other counties. The new 24th, one of the least compact districts, formed a narrow crescent extending more than halfway across the middle of the state.

To accomplish the pairing, creating multi-member districts and real-location of Democratic loyalists, the new plans split numerous counties. Even counties small enough to fit within a single district did not escape the Democrats' redistricting software. More than a third of the small counties got split between House districts and almost half of the counties that could have been maintained intact in a Senate district got divided.[49]

Democrats manipulated a fourth district in an attempt to save the Senate's most marginal Democrat. Carol Jackson had narrowly escaped defeat in both 1998 and 2000. In an effort to ease her reelection battles, her mountain district which had been composed of eight entire counties in the northeast corner of the state now contained all of her home county (White) and Union and then parts of seven other counties. Critical to making this a safer district was its extension into Gainesville to pick up the only majority-black precinct in this part of the state. Extending Jackson's district into Gainesville resulted in dividing Hall County, which could have been a single Senate district, into four districts. The Republican who had represented Hall before redistricting found himself spread across parts of eight counties.

Georgia Democrats feared that the Bush administration Justice Department would refuse to preclear the plans which so blatantly discriminated against Republicans. Therefore, Georgia did not submit the plans to DOJ but instead took them to the district court of the District of Columbia. In the hearing the Justice Department served as the defendant and, although it found no fault with the congressional or state House plans, it urged the court to reject three Senate districts that had their voting age populations reduced to being barely majority black. The court agreed with DOJ that these districts no longer allowed blacks to elect their preferred candidates and ordered Georgia to increase these districts' black percentages. The Supreme Court reversed the lower court, embracing Georgia's argument for lower black majorities.

As noted in chapter 3, the Supreme Court ruled in *Georgia v. Ashcroft* that a state could either have a limited number of districts with large black majorities or have fewer heavily black districts coupled with a number of districts in which black support could determine the outcome, although it would be unlikely that an African American would win.[50] The Supreme Court pointed to the testimony of U.S. Representative John Lewis who explained that "giving real power to black voters comes from the kind of redistricting efforts the State of Georgia has made."[51] Even the expert retained by DOJ to discredit Georgia's plan acknowledged that African Americans would likely win these districts despite the reductions in black population concentrations. Georgia's plans reducing black concentrations and the concurrence of the Supreme Court in *Ashcroft* are harbingers of the litigation in the next decade discussed in chapter 3 that shifted the test from when the black percentage decreased to whether the plan reduced prospects for minorities to elect their preference.

With the concurrence of the entire LBC except for one senator and one representative, the General Assembly made little effort to increase the number of predominately black districts, adding only one in the House and two in the Senate. LBC expected to increase its ranks by two senators and from four to seven representatives.[52] The number of African American representatives rose to thirty-nine, an increase of three. The Senate LBC contingent declined by one following the defeat of a member surrounded by rumors of corruption.

After his defeat he was convicted in federal court. With the former incumbent in prison, the Republican who had defeated him lost to an African American challenger in the next election.

## COURT PLAN: REPUBLICANS PREVAIL

The *Ashcroft* decision became moot in light of another case. Republicans challenged the legislative districts and in *Larios v. Cox* they prevailed.[53] The court based its decision on the magnitude of the population variations. Governor Barnes and his allies had assumed that since population deviations in their plans stayed within +/- 5 percent of the ideal, they could withstand any legal challenges. While courts might have looked the other way had only a few districts nudged up toward +/- 5 percent deviations, as noted earlier and shown in figure 6.3, many Georgia districts pushed the limits.

When challenged to justify the extraordinary number of districts at the outer edge of the +/- 5 percent deviations, witnesses for the state explained that the plans underpopulated districts in order to protect the representation of South Georgia and Atlanta. The court referred back to *Reynolds v. Sims*, the Alabama redistricting case from forty years earlier, to remind Georgia that giving greater weight to voters in some parts of the state than others violated the Equal Protection Clause.[54] Nor did the court accept Georgia's second justification that it designed the plan to protect incumbents since, as the court pointed out, only Democratic incumbents benefited while many Republican incumbents got paired.

When the legislature failed to redraw the state, the court hired redistricting expert Nathaniel Persily to devise new maps. The new maps held population deviations to ± 1 percent. The court directed the law professor to ignore where incumbents lived. Persily's maps paired a remarkably large number of incumbents so that they unintentionally shared one feature with the Democratic maps that they were to replace. Persily paired sixty-six House incumbents with four House districts actually having three incumbents each. Ironically one of the incumbents who got placed with two of her colleagues had chaired the House Legislative and Congressional Reapportionment Committee, which refused to devise a new map following the *Larios* decision. The new Senate map placed twenty-three of its fifty-six incumbents in districts with colleagues.

With so many incumbents paired, nearby districts had open seats. The court responded favorably to requests from both Democrats and Republicans and made minor adjustments to unpair incumbents when that could be easily accomplished so that the maps used in 2004 had only four incumbent pairings in the Senate and eight in the House.

Under the court's nonpartisan plan Republicans did much better, particularly in the House, increasing their numbers from 75 to 95 thus marking the first time in more than 13 decades that the House had a Republican majority. In the Senate the new districts enabled Republicans to consolidate their majority by increasing their numbers from 30 to 34.

The plans drawn by the court retained 13 majority-black Senate districts while adding three majority-black House districts to increase that number to 41. By 2006 the Senate had a record 12 black senators and 44 African Americans served in the House, and this included the first two African American Republicans.

## CONGRESSIONAL PLAN REVISITED

With both chambers and the governorship in Republican hands, the GOP turned its attention to the Democrats' congressional plan. This map like those for the General Assembly, sought to maximize Democratic holdings. When the maps were drawn, Republicans held an 8–3 advantage. Nationally, Democrats needed only six seats to reclaim a majority in the U.S. House. Governor Barnes, who at this time was being mentioned as a possible Democratic presidential contender, set out to eliminate much of the Democratic deficit. The plan, if it worked as intended, would result in Georgia sending seven Democrats and six Republicans to Congress. The nomination of weak candidates thwarted Democratic ambitions as they won five seats in 2002; two years later they added a sixth seat.

Much like the legislative plans, the congressional map featured strangely configured districts but in this instance the contorted design sought to unite geographically separated Democrats. The strangest looking district was the 13th, nicknamed the "Dead Cat on the Expressway" District because its far-flung features, as shown in figure 6.7, resembled an animal flattened by heavy traffic. The most marginal district, the 11th, resembled something of a combination fishhook and cross of Lorraine as Democrats sought to pull fellow partisans out of urban areas in Bartow, Coweta, and Troup counties while uniting them with black populations in Cobb, Douglas, and Muscogee. Republicans constantly criticized the map for its irregular shape and failure to respect county lines. While the court-drawn map of 1995 had split only six counties, the new map divided thirty-four counties.

In crafting a new plan Republicans had as their primary political objective bolstering Phil Gingrey who, against the odds, had managed to win the 11th District by 4,300 votes. The movement of blacks from Atlanta into Douglas and Cobb counties endangered his hold on the district. The new plan bolstered

## Georgia Congressional, 2002
### District 13

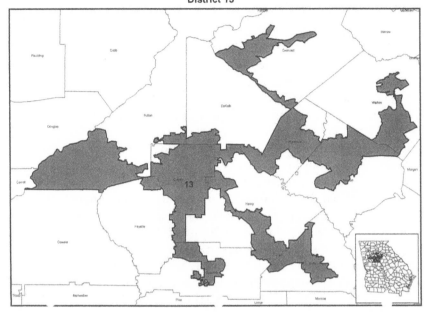

**Figure 6.7    The Dead Cat on the Expressway District Drawn by Democrats in 2001 to Link Distant Black Concentrations.** *Source*: Plaintiff's demonstrative exhibits *Larios v. Cox* 300 F. Supp. 2d 1320 (N.D. Ga 2004).

Gingrey's prospects by giving him a district in which George Bush had polled 71 percent of the vote in 2004 compared with 51 percent in his old district.

A second objective was to dislodge one, or perhaps both, of the white Democratic members of Congress. In designing the new districts, Republicans operated under a self-imposed constraint. In light of their repeated criticisms of the convoluted shapes of the districts drawn by Democrats, they pledged that their new maps would honor Georgia's traditional principles and respect county boundaries to the extent possible. Keeping this pledge should also result in more compact districts.

The new plan did not immediately increase Republican holdings in the congressional delegation. Although competing in more compact, more Republican districts, the two white Democrats, John Barrow and Jim Marshall, won reelection by the narrowest margins of any Democratic House incumbents in the nation in 2006. Barrow, who early in the evening feared he had lost, escaped defeat by 864 votes while his neighbor to the west won by 1,752 votes. Although the white voters added to these congressional districts strongly supported the Republican challengers, the short-term upsurge in Democratic support in 2006 allowed the incumbents to hold on.[55] Had Republicans given greater priority to displacing the Democratic incumbents and split a few more counties or drawn less compact districts, they could have claimed two more seats. Obviously, Georgia Republicans did not approach redistricting with the same partisan vengeance that guided their Texas cousins two years earlier in the redistricting described in chapter 5. Ultimately the 2010 wave election that restored a GOP majority in the House counted Marshall among its victims as he lost by 6 percentage points.

Republicans took care not to reduce African American percentages in the four districts represented by black members of Congress so as to avoid a charge of retrogression. They even increased the black percentage in Sanford Bishop's district from 44.5 to 47.5, a critical element when, in 2010, he narrowly escaped defeat with 51 percent of the vote.

The Republican plan eliminated almost half of the county splits in the Democratic plan that it replaced. Table 6.4 presents three measures of compactness for the Democratic Plan of 2001 and the Republican replacement. Since convoluted districts have longer perimeters, the two plans can be compared on that dimension and for the entire state the new plan reduced total perimeters by 3,100 miles or by more than one-third. The new version of Gingrey's District 11 had a perimeter less than one-third its predecessor while District 13 saw its perimeter shrink by more than 50 percent.

The second measure, Polsby-Popper, which looks at the ratio of the area of the district compared to the area of a circle with the same perimeter as the district, showed only the 4th District to be slightly less compact. While District 13 continued to have a low compactness score of .12, which is four times the value for the previous version of the district. District 11 had also filled only 3 percent of the area of a circle having the same perimeter as the district in the Democratic plan. Under the Republican plan, it filled more than a third of a circle with a similar perimeter. Dramatic improvements occurred in most districts on this dimension. The mean Polsby-Popper score doubled in the GOP plan and increased in all but two districts.

The final measure, Reock, compares the ratio of the area of the district to that of the minimum circle which could be drawn that completely encapsulated the district. Again, the higher the value the more compact the district. Only District 8 failed to show an improvement. District 11, which had been the third least compact on this measure in the Democratic plan, emerged as the second *most* compact in the Republican plan. This measure also showed Districts 12 and 13 having Reock values twice as high under the Republican as compared with the Democratic plan.

**Table 6.4  Measures of Compactness for Georgia Congressional Districts, 2001 and 2005**

| District | 2001 Democratic Plan | | | 2005 Republican Plan | | |
|---|---|---|---|---|---|---|
| | Perimeter in miles | Polsby-Popper Perimeter Score | Reock Dispersion Score | Perimeter in miles | Polsby-Popper Perimeter Score | Reock Dispersion Score |
| 001 | 1,106.76 | 0.12 | 0.39 | 763.77 | 0.26 | 0.49 |
| 002 | 697.12 | 0.26 | 0.44 | 692.98 | 0.29 | 0.46 |
| 003 | 949.72 | 0.15 | 0.46 | 495.02 | 0.21 | 0.54 |
| 004 | 112.97 | 0.25 | 0.42 | 135.93 | 0.23 | 0.45 |
| 005 | 188.24 | 0.09 | 0.26 | 108.48 | 0.26 | 0.49 |
| 006 | 211.99 | 0.12 | 0.36 | 173.88 | 0.29 | 0.46 |
| 007 | 480.31 | 0.07 | 0.33 | 227.78 | 0.24 | 0.58 |
| 008 | 1,054.98 | 0.04 | 0.37 | 713.98 | 0.18 | 0.28 |
| 009 | 872.07 | 0.12 | 0.34 | 371.31 | 0.40 | 0.38 |
| 010 | 487.17 | 0.20 | 0.28 | 614.32 | 0.20 | 0.32 |
| 011 | 1,167.02 | 0.03 | 0.20 | 306.40 | 0.36 | 0.55 |
| 012 | 770.70 | 0.11 | 0.17 | 738.29 | 0.20 | 0.42 |
| 013 | 596.30 | 0.03 | 0.19 | 246.75 | 0.12 | 0.39 |
| Sum | 8,695.35 | N/A | N/A | 5,588.89 | N/A | N/A |
| Min | N/A | 0.03 | 0.17 | N/A | 0.12 | 0.28 |
| Max | N/A | 0.26 | 0.46 | N/A | 0.40 | 0.58 |
| Mean | N/A | 0.12 | 0.32 | N/A | 0.25 | 0.45 |
| Std. Dev. | N/A | 0.08 | 0.10 | N/A | 0.07 | 0.09 |

*Source:* Bryan Tyson, the Republican staffer most involved in his party's redistricting efforts in 2001 and 2005.

## GREEN LIGHT FROM DOJ

The 2011 special session called to redistrict the state marked the first time that the GOP controlled redistricting immediately following a census. Unlike Democrats a decade earlier who desperately used all the items in the gerrymanders' tool kit, Republicans had comfortable majority support in the electorate. They would not resort to extraordinary measures to squeeze out every possible district. Georgia's congressional districts became more compact than the ones drawn in 2005 and somewhat, but not overly, more skewed in favor of Republicans.[56] The GOP had modest goals. They hoped to secure extraordinary majorities with two-thirds of the seats in both legislative chambers. Republicans would continue to be guided by the wisdom enunciated by Paul Coverdell three decades earlier and boost black concentrations, especially in the congressional districts represented by African Americans.

Ever since the redistricting done pursuant to the 1995 *Miller v. Johnson* decision, some congressional districts represented by blacks had lacked black majorities in their populations. The legislature set out to correct that omission as it went about equalizing population while fitting in the 14th District the state's burgeoning population had won. The first column in table 6.5 shows the black percent of the population counted by the 2010 census in the existing districts. Sanford Bishop's 2nd District in the state's southwest corner was 48.41 percent black with only 11,000 more black than white residents. Bishop

Table 6.5   Racial Composition of Georgia Congressional Districts Drawn in 2011

| | | Percent Black | | |
| | 2010 Pop. in 2005 | 2011 Districts | | |
| Districts | Districts | Population | VAP | Registration |
|---|---|---|---|---|
| 1. | 25.31 | 31.24 | 28.95 | 27.96 |
| 2. | 48.41 | 52.28 | 49.46 | 50.11 |
| 3. | 24.52 | 24.08 | 22.40 | 20.47 |
| 4. | 56.09 | 59.04 | 56.41 | 56.74 |
| 5. | 50.31 | 60.45 | 57.41 | 56.62 |
| 6. | 10.28 | 13.44 | 13.00 | 10.76 |
| 7. | 22.38 | 19.26 | 17.81 | 16.56 |
| 8. | 34.93 | 30.41 | 28.53 | 27.01 |
| 9. | 3.34 | 7.19 | 6.60 | 5.93 |
| 10. | 19.39 | 25.72 | 24.12 | 22.49 |
| 11. | 15.60 | 16.66 | 15.58 | 13.92 |
| 12. | 43.25 | 35.48 | 33.30 | 32.79 |
| 13. | 56.82 | 56.96 | 53.93 | 54.29 |
| 14. | Nonexistent | 9.15 | 8.26 | 7.76 |

*Source*: Georgia Legislative Reapportionment Office.

had almost lost reelection in 2010—indeed the AP prematurely called the district for his white, Republican opponent. Due to gentrification and movement of white empty nesters back into Atlanta, John Lewis's 5th District had a bare black majority and like the 2nd District was underpopulated by 60,000.

Figures in the second column of table 6.5 show that the new plan increased the black population percentages in three of the African American districts, boosting Lewis's district by 10 percentage points and giving Bishop a 52.28 percent black district. As typically occurs, the black voting age population is a smaller percentage than the black population so that the 2nd District was just under majority black. However the new 2nd District, which swapped out whites along the Florida line for Macon's black population, was majority black in registration.[57] The south Georgia population swap was designed to benefit both parties, giving Bishop a more secure district while also bolstering Austin Scott who had ousted a Democrat to win the 8th District by 10,000 votes in 2010. This bipartisan gerrymander worked. In the blacker 2nd District, Bishop has consistently polled at least 60 percent of the vote while in the whiter 8th District Scott drew no opponent in 2012 or 2014.

While the new plan bolstered Bishop's position, it targeted the delegation's last white Democrat, John Barrow. The 2005 plan removed Barrow's home in Athens from the district leading him to relocate to Savannah. The 2011 plan cut Savannah with its African American concentration while shifting his district into the Republican suburbs of Augusta and conservative rural counties. These shifts reduced the black population in the 12th District by about 8 percentage points. Barrow survived in 2012 more due to the weaknesses of his opponent than anything else but in 2014, when Democratic turnout went into its usual midterm swoon, Barrow lost by ten points.

McGann and colleagues calculate that the 2011 congressional map was, to use terminology from chapter 1, biased and unresponsive.[58] They estimate that should Democratic candidates get half the statewide vote that would win them only 36 percent of the seats, or five seats, which is what they secured in 2012. To win half the delegation seats Democrats would need about 60 percent of the statewide vote.

The 2011 plans produced fifteen majority black Senate districts and 49 House districts. Unlike in the past, each of these districts had not just a black majority in its population but in its registered voters. As with the congressional designs, the number of state legislative districts with black registration majorities were the most ever. Democrats in the legislature, under the direction of House Minority Leader Stacey Abrams, unanimously opposed the plans contending that bolstering black percentages constituted packing, made biracial coalitions unlikely, and constituted racial segregation. As an alternative, Democrats called for the creation of influence districts having sufficient African American concentrations to make the candidacies of additional white Democrats viable.[59]

When it came to securing federal approval of the plans, the situation in 2012 was similar to 2002 in that the DOJ authorities who would review plans were of the opposite party than the one that drew Georgia's plans. Georgia, like several other states, pursued a two-pronged strategy for Section 5 approval. The plans were sent to DOJ but the state also instituted litigation in the district court of the District of Columbia. DOJ approved all three plans before the lawsuit played out, marking the first time that the state got a sign off on all three of its initial plans.

When these maps were first used, all but two Senate districts elected African Americans. The two with the smallest concentrations of black registrants, each right at 53 percent black, returned senior whites. On the House side, forty-two districts with majority black registration elected African Americans. Joining these members were six individuals from districts not majority black. Excluding the one black Republican chosen from a 26.5 percent black district, the other five had from 38.2 to 48.8 percent African American registrants. Seven districts in which most registrants were black reelected white Democratic incumbents. These districts were from 51 to 61 percent black.

Republicans achieved their goal of a super majority in the Senate winning 38 of the 56 seats. In the House they came up one seat short winning 119. The GOP retained its Senate super majority until a special election in 2017 but never succeeded in securing a 120th House seat before the onset of a Democratic resurgence starting in 2016 that ultimately saw the GOP cache reduced to 105 following the 2018 elections.

Since implementation of the 2011 plans, African American representation has increased. The 2018 election saw Lucy McBath (D) become the congressional delegation's fifth black member when she won the 13 percent black 6th District. Although Georgia's congressional plan was calculated to be the second least responsive (i.e., changes in vote shares were unlikely to result in a partisan switch in a seat),[60] not only did Democrats gain a seat in 2018, but they also came within 433 votes of winning a sixth seat.

African American ranks have increased to fifteen in the Senate and fifty-one in the House. African Americans now hold more than a third of the state's congressional seats and more than quarter of the state legislative seats. The growth in the black delegations has far outstripped increases in the black share of the state's population. Since 1970 Georgia's black population has grown from 26 to 31 percent. The numbers of black legislators have increased from one to five in Congress, 19 to 51 in the state House, and 2 to 15 in the Senate since implementation of the 1974 plans. White Democrats who dominated Georgia politics for generations have become scarce with the last one in the congressional delegation, John Barrow, defeated in 2014. In the legislature whites constitute less than a third of the Democratic caucuses with six senators and twenty representatives.

While Democrats objected to the plans Republicans drew in 2011, unlike in North Carolina and Virginia, they did not go to court in an effort to reduce black concentrations in some districts. They did object when in 2015 Republicans swapped out minorities for whites in two Atlanta suburban districts that Democrats came close to winning in 2014. The objections failed but by 2019 both of the districts had elected a black Democrat.

## CONCLUSIONS

The history of redistricting in Georgia can be viewed through multiple lenses. It could be described as a prolonged assault on white Democrats. A second perspective would focus on changes in the expectations of African American legislators.

As long as the county unit system and the distribution of legislators skewed in favor of rural counties remained undisturbed, white Democrats held all the cards. Only with the onset of the Redistricting Revolution did the first African Americans enter the General Assembly. The requirement for one person, one vote also made Republicans more than occasional visitors representing mountain counties.

Much of the subsequent change came as a result of DOJ demands. After each census beginning with 1970, DOJ rejected Georgia's Senate plans and until 2011 also rejected the state's plans for congressional and state House districts. DOJ used the preclearance provision of the Voting Rights Act to demand the creation of greater numbers of majority-black districts and frequently forced Georgia to increase black concentrations in the majority-black districts it had drawn. The 2011 Republican plan maximized the number of districts with black majorities among registered voters and succeeded in securing DOJ approval.

As long as white Democrats filled most legislative seats, the two disadvantaged groups joined forces against a common enemy. Beginning in the early 1980s and lasting through the 1990 redistricting, the black Democrat–Republican coalition, a coalition that included many of the legislature's most liberal and most conservative legislators, collaborated to take seats from white Democrats. Since the biracial, bipartisan, ideologically diverse coalition had so few seats in the General Assembly, it would have made little progress but for DOJ's veto that provided the leverage to force white Democrats or allow judges to create additional districts with black majorities. White Democrats preferred to maintain districts with black concentrations sufficient to elect a Democrat but too few to elect an African American. Once DOJ required the adoption of plans that cordoned off the most loyal Democrats, Republicans could often win the bleached neighboring districts.

Republicans got more out of these joint efforts than did African Americans. The greatest disparity came following the 1992 redistricting. In that year's election, Republicans picked up three seats in Congress, four in the Senate, and seventeen in the state House compared with African American gains of two congressional, one Senate, and four state House seats. In 1982 neither partner made gains in the state House and each added two Senate seats. Republicans won the 4th Congressional District in 1984, two years before John Lewis won the 5th District.

Although Republicans wanted to renew the partnership, the Legislative Black Caucus cast its lot with white Democrats in 2001. That round also marked the first time that the bulk of the LBC endorsed the state's proposal. In 1981, only one LBC member backed the legislature's congressional plan and for this she got labeled "Aunt Jane," the female equivalent of an Uncle Tom. She was one of two blacks on the House redistricting committee.[61] Ten years later the LBC split with most members supporting the advances offered by the Democratic leadership, but a minority joined the GOP in demanding the MAXBLACK option.[62] In 2001, all but two LBC members signed on with the Democratic leadership's plan.

Part of the explanation for the changing relationship between the LBC and Democratic leadership is that the latter became more sensitive to black concerns. That learning curve came as African Americans increasingly entered the chamber leadership. In 1981, blacks had little formal power in either chamber, although Senator Julian Bond did find allies for his effort to create a heavily black congressional district. In 1991, African Americans chaired and held three other seats on the eighteen-member Senate Reapportionment Committee. Committee chair Eugene Walker also served as Senate majority whip. The LBC was less well positioned in the House, having just two of twenty-five seats on its Legislative and Congressional Reapportionment Committee, although one of its members had just wrapped up a term as gubernatorial floor leader. Those who had joined the legislature's leadership ranks embraced the stand of their party; those who responded to Atlanta's Concerned Black Clergy and the ACLU and supported the MAXBLACK demands had often clashed with the Democratic Party leadership and held no major posts granted by the party.[63]

At the onset on the new century, blacks served as majority leader and assistant administration floor leader in the Senate and chaired the Senate Reapportionment Committee. In the House, African Americans chaired the

Democratic Caucus and served as secretary of the House redistricting committee. African Americans also filled three of the six seats on the conference committee that hammered out differences between the two chambers. From these positions, the LBC could have vetoed the plans.[64] Former Representative Holmes writes of the LBC, "It played an integral role in determining the number and size of multimember districts as well as the minimum black population percentage in Democratic preference vote. . . . Overall, the GLBC had its most successful redistricting session in the history of the legislature."[65] From 1991 to 2001, LBC strategy shifted from MAXBLACK to maximizing Democratic seats.

Redistricting in Georgia also traces the changing expectations about what constitutes a district winnable by African American candidates. In 1982 the LBC, DOJ, and many judges believed that a district needed a 65 percent black population since so few whites would support a black candidate regardless of his or her qualifications. A decade later Cynthia McKinney and her allies urged DOJ to push the black percentages as high as possible but accepted 57 percent for the black district in southwest Georgia.[66] By 2001, the LBC embraced plans lowering black percentages, in some instances to a bare majority of the adult population. In the early 1990s some African American incumbents objected to reducing the black percentages in their districts, fearing that could endanger their reelections, but a decade later incumbents readily accepted the pruning back of their black constituents.[67] Having a large black majority became less of a concern as a sizable minority of whites demonstrated a willingness to vote for African American candidates.

Another consideration behind the shift in LBC tactics, allies, and demands came from their members' advances in the legislature. By the beginning of the new century, senior LBC members had become committee chairs and chamber leaders. All of that would disappear if Republicans achieved majorities, a likely prospect in light of recent electoral and demographic trends. For the first time, the LBC ceased trying to maximize the number of seats likely to elect blacks and agreed to unpack black concentrations in order to improve Democratic prospects in neighboring districts. When DOJ sought to prevent reductions in black concentrations in three Senate districts, the LBC fought its longtime ally. LBC member Robert Brown, vice chair of the Senate Redistricting Committee, testified in favor of reducing black concentrations in Senate districts. "There are other examples of that around the state that I think suggest that there has been some change from that rigid, if there's an African American on the ticket, there's an automatic no vote for whites. So, I think that's changed significantly."[68]

The reunion of the Democratic Party came too late. Packing Republicans into districts at rates pushing the upper limits of what was thought to be the acceptable maximum while underpopulating Democratic districts by like amounts proved fatal. When the court threw out the plans for the General Assembly it acted in line with the adage that "pigs get fat while hogs get slaughtered."

Following the redistricting of the mid-2000s, Republicans had achieved majority status. In 2011, the GOP majority continued the strategy that it had pursued in league with the LBC in 1981 and the McKinney-led rebels a decade later. By maximizing the number of districts dominated by black registrants, Republicans simultaneously maximized the number of districts in which they could hope to win. With their plan in place, Republicans added a congressional seat, two Senate seats, and three more House members. The LBC objected to these plans but did secure five more state House seats, although they made no immediate gains in the congressional delegation or the Senate. The longer term consequences reversed favors, unlike in the 1990s when Republicans continued making gains beyond the initial election. Following the 2018 elections, African Americans held eight more state House seats and one more congressional and Senate seats than in 2011. In contrast, Republicans in 2019 had one fewer Senate seats, eleven fewer state House members, but had gained a congressional seat over their 2011 holdings.

While redistricting gets much of the credit for the transformation of Georgia legislative establishments, two other factors have come into play. The white population of the South, including that in Georgia, has undergone a secular realignment.[69] Redistricting has, at times, provided a catalyst to the partisan changes already under way. The second factor, of course, is the application of the Voting Rights Act by DOJ.

## Chapter 7

# Conclusion

## *Looking to the Future*

One man's gerrymander can easily be another man's nice set of districts.[1]

One party's gerrymander, of course, is the other party's priceless masterpiece.[2]

The Census Bureau began preparations to enumerate the population of the United States well before 2020 with the final piece in place in mid-2019 when the Supreme Court ruled against inclusion of a citizenship question. Although a new census occurs only once a decade, the Census Bureau regularly updates population estimates for states using the American Community Survey and, consequently, by mid-decade it becomes possible to develop projections of which states would gain representation in the next reapportionment and which states will give up seats in the House. At the state and local level, governments also prepare for the census with the goal of a full count in order to maximize their representation in Congress and access to public funding as outlined in chapter 1.

No one studies the census figures or projections of likely gains and losses of House seats more closely than Kimball Brace who heads up Election Data Services. Since the mid-1970s Brace has drawn new districts in more than half the states and creates widely used post-election maps. With each annual release of census estimates, Brace works up projections concerning what the next census will likely mean for reapportionment.

## PROJECTIONS FOR 2020

In December of each year the Census Bureau releases estimates of state popu-lations made at the mid-point of the year.[3] Table 7.1 includes the results of three projections for states that will gain or lose seats based on the estimates as of July 2019. These estimates predict a continuation of the trends discussed earlier in this book. The Midwest and Northeast supply the seats that shift southward and westward.

The first column contains the long-term projection based on population changes from 2011 through the middle of 2019. Projections in the second col-umn rely on mid-range projections of population changes from 2015 to 2019. The third column shows projections based on the most recent year census estimates. Since the rate of population change can vary from year to year, the projections have minor variations. However, there is much consistency in the identity of the likely winners and losers from the 2020 census. The three projec-tions show Texas the biggest gainer expected to add two or three seats. Another southern state, Florida, is in line to add one or seats. Arizona, Colorado, North Carolina, Montana, and Oregon score an additional seat on all three projec-tions. New seats would boost Texas to 38 or 39 members of Congress while Florida would have 28 or 29 representatives. Four to six seats will go to the states of the Old Confederacy. The other winners are all western states.

Several of the projected winners for the 2020 census have histories of add-ing seats. Arizona has grown following each of the last seven censuses and Florida has expanded the size of its delegation following every census begin-ning with 1900. Each of the previous seven reapportionments has awarded Florida with multiple new seats. Texas, the biggest winner as it was in the previous decade, has seen its congressional delegation grow following every census except for 1850 and 1940 and has added three or four seats with each reapportionment beginning with 1982. With eight seats, Colorado's represen-tation will have doubled since the 1960s as the state will have added a seat in four of the six most recent reapportionments.

Of the states projected as winners all except Montana will achieve a level of representation in Congress never previously enjoyed. Montana will reclaim the second seat it had from 1912 until 1992 when it dropped to one.

The projections also show little variation in states likely to lose in the reapportionment sweepstakes. All three projections show California, Illinois, Michigan, Minnesota, New York, Pennsylvania, Rhode Island, and West Virginia each losing a seat. All the most recent projections have Alabama and Ohio losing seats. Should California lose a seat, it will be the first reduction ever in the Golden State's congressional delegation. Following every census California gained representation until 2010. If the projections in table 7.1

**Table 7.1   Projections for Changes in the Apportionment of U.S. House Seats Following the 2020 Census**

| | Time Period Used to Make the Projection | | | Projected Seats as of 2023 | Most or Fewest Seats since Reapportionment of |
|---|---|---|---|---|---|
| | *2011–19* | *2015–19* | *2019* | | |
| *States Gaining Seats* | | | | | |
| Arizona | 1 | 1 | 1 | 10 | ever |
| Colorado | 1 | 1 | 1 | 8 | ever |
| Montana | 1 | 1 | 1 | 2 | 1982 |
| Florida | 2 | 2 | 1 | 28–29 | ever |
| North Carolina | 1 | 1 | 1 | 14 | ever |
| Oregon | 1 | 1 | 1 | 6 | ever |
| Texas | 3 | 3 | 2 | 38–39 | ever |
| *States Losing Seats* | | | | | |
| Alabama | 1 | 1 | | 6–7 | 1862 |
| California | 1 | 1 | 1 | 52 | 1992 |
| Illinois | 1 | 1 | 1 | 17 | 1862 |
| Michigan | 1 | 1 | 1 | 13 | 1932 |
| Minnesota | 1 | 1 | 1 | 7 | 1892 |
| New York | 1 | 1 | 1 | 26 | 1802 |
| Ohio | 1 | 1 | | 15–16 | 1822 |
| Pennsylvania | 1 | 1 | 1 | 17 | 1792 |
| Rhode Island | 1 | 1 | 1 | 1 | 1789 |
| West Virginia | 1 | 1 | 1 | 2 | ever |

*Source*: Compiled by author from Election Data Services press release December 30, 2019.

come to pass, the Northeast will drop four seats while the Midwest will see its delegations reduced by three or four.

While losing a seat will be novel for California, declining representation has become a habit for some of the other losers. Michigan's seats have declined following each of the last five censuses. The string of continuous declines in seats is even longer for Ohio, for which 2020 would be the sixth consecutive loss, while New York is projected to experience its eighth consecutive decline and in Pennsylvania it will be the tenth decade with a loss. Illinois has emerged with fewer seats following every census beginning with 1930 with one exception. West Virginia, which with two seats will become the smallest delegation between Delaware and the Dakotas, had six representatives as recently the 1950s. Alabama was tied with other states for the third largest number of representatives from the South during the 1920s when it had ten members.[4]

For most of the states projected to lose seats, it is not a novel experience. For the large states, other than California, the reductions anticipated in 2022 are less dramatic than in previous recent reallocations. From 1952 through 2012, New York always lost multiple seats with the greatest setback coming in 1982 when five seats went to other states. Pennsylvania lost two or three seats in every reapportionment beginning in 1932 and continuing through 2002 except for 1942. Ohio lost two seats in 1982, 1992, and 2012. Relatively speaking, the hemorrhaging of political influence from populous Rust Belt states has slowed.

States projected to lose seats would drop to their lowest levels in decades. Except for California, all of the other states would drop to their fewest members of Congress since the massive reapportionment in 1932 or earlier.[5] Four states' projected losses would result in their smallest delegations in two centuries. The last time Pennsylvania had as few as the seventeen seats occurred during the 1790s. When Rhode Island loses one of its two seats, it will have the fewest seats since the initial allocation by the Constitution in 1789.

The net gains for the South will increase its dominance in the Electoral College where it already has the largest number of votes. In the 2024 presidential election the South will choose 164–165 electors or more than 60 percent of the votes needed to become president. The South is not as uniformly Republican as it was in the 1980s or in George W. Bush's two elections although the region, except for Virginia, voted for Donald Trump in 2016. With anything approaching that unity, a Republican would need less than a third of the electors from the rest of the nation to secure the keys to the White House.

The fullness and accuracy of the count will determine the allocation of seats for those being distributed right around number 435. Like a college basketball team on the bubble for the NCAA Big Dance, states on the bubble for one of the last congressional seats need to finish strong with a full census count.[6] Table 7.2 shows the estimates for which states would be in line to get the last five seats allocated through reapportionment based on the Census Bureau estimates of population changes from 2018 to 2019 along with the next five states, which would just miss an additional seat. As indicated in table 7.1, there are slight differences in the winners and losers depending on the time period used to predict allocation of the last seats. If reapportionment were conducted based on the population estimates as of 2019, Alabama and Ohio would narrowly retain their seventh and sixteenth seats, respectively. Those retentions would substitute for Texas-39 and Florida-29 shown in table 7.2. It is important to keep in mind that these are *estimates* and the results of the actual census may differ. The margins for allocation of seats are, in some cases, very thin. Under the 2018–2019 estimates, if the actual count in Montana were 2,500 fewer than the estimate, it would not get a second seat. Should an additional 10,000 people be found in Alabama, it would retain

**Table 7.2 Estimates Based on Population Change from 2018 to 2019 of Which States Would Receive the Last Five House Seats and Which Would Narrowly Miss Getting a Seat Based**

| Seat Number | State |
|---|---|
| *Last Five Seats* | |
| 431 | Illinois (17th) |
| 432 | New York (26th) |
| 433 | Texas (39th) |
| 434 | Montana (2nd) |
| 435 | Florida (29th) |
| *Next Seats* | |
| 436 | Alabama (7th) |
| 437 | Minnesota (8th) |
| 438 | Ohio (16th) |
| 439 | California (53rd) |
| 440 | Rhode Island (2nd) |

*Source*: Election Data Services press release December 30, 2019, using the "short term" trend.

its seventh seat. Using the 2019 estimate, Alabama keeps its seventh seat with 18,500 people to spare and Ohio retains a seat by a margin of 12,500. States ranked for seats 436–440 can take hope since in previous decades states projected to lose a seat have outperformed the estimate. Minnesota seemed destined to lose its eighth seat—the same one that is endangered now—a decade ago. On the other hand, projections a decade ago had Missouri narrowly keeping a seat that it lost.

An important factor that could alter the order of states vying for the last seats would be differences in the success of states' efforts to get a full count. Some states have invested heavily in preparing for the count while others, including Texas, have not. Yet a third factor would be the distribution of military personnel. Following the 2000 census, North Carolina edged out Utah for the 435th seat based on the inclusion of North Carolinians serving in the military abroad. Utah, which came up 857 people short of a fourth seat, filed suit asking that its 11,000 young people doing missionary service abroad be counted. Adding these people temporarily out of the country would have allowed it to edge out North Carolina for the last seat. North Carolina's margin came from 18,000 serving in the military abroad. The Supreme Court rejected the Utah bid by a 5–3 vote. The 2020 census changes how some military personal are allocated. Personal stationed overseas will be counted as living in their home state of record while those on temporary duty abroad will be assigned to the state in which they had been living. This change will affect about 15 percent of the military personnel abroad as of April 1, 2020.[7]

Table 7.3    **Continuing Shift in Regional Seats Projected Thru the 2020 Reapportionment**

| Region | 1940s | 1960s | 1990s | 2000s | 2010s | 2020s |
|--------|-------|-------|-------|-------|-------|-------|
| Midwest | 148 | 138 | 117 | 111 | 105 | 101–102 |
| Northeast | 133 | 122 | 100 | 95 | 90 | 86 |
| South | 105 | 106 | 125 | 131 | 138 | 142–143 |
| West | 49 | 69 | 93 | 98 | 102 | 105 |

The Midwestern states are Illinois, Indiana, Iowa, Kansas, Kentucky, Michigan, Minnesota, Missouri, Nebraska, North Dakota, Ohio, Oklahoma, South Dakota, and Wisconsin. The Northeastern states are Connecticut, Delaware, Maine, Maryland, Massachusetts, New Hampshire, New Jersey, New York, Pennsylvania, Rhode Island, Vermont, and West Virginia. The South consists of Alabama, Arkansas, Florida, Georgia, Louisiana, Mississippi, North Carolina, South Carolina, Tennessee, Texas, and Virginia. States in the West are Alaska, Arizona, California, Colorado, Hawaii, Idaho, Montana, Nevada, New Mexico, Oregon, Utah, Washington, and Wyoming.
*Source*: Author.

Table 7.3 reports the regional distribution of seats from the 1940s until the current decade while the last column shows the projected number of seats each region will have after the 2020 census. The Midwest's share of seats, which has shrunk with each decade, will have lost 46–47 seats after the next census down almost a third from its 148 in the 1940s. The Northeast is projected to have lost 47 of 133 seats that it held in the 1940s, a 35 percent decline. These regions were the two most populous as recently as the 1960s but will now be the smallest. The South has grown by more than a third in its House representation since the 1940s and has been the nation's most populous region since 1990. The projections for the 2020s show the South with at least thirty-seven more congressional seats than any other region. The West has more than doubled its House representation since the 1940s. Half of the West's seats come from California. While the growth in California was dramatic prior to 2010, the rest of the region doubled its representation going from 26 seats in the 1940s to 53 after the next census.

Reallocation of seats across regions has political implications. For much of the last generation, the South has been the nation's most Republican region. In previous decades, Republican ranks expanded in southern states allocated additional seats. In 1993, southern states with enlarged delegations had a net gain of seven GOP seats compared with a gain of two in the rest of the region. A decade later all five GOP congressional gains came in states with enlarged delegations. In 2013, however, due to the limitations imposed by Florida's constitution discussed in chapter 5 and litigation in Texas, the four states that added seats had a net gain of only one Republican. But for a lawsuit in Texas, three of that state's new districts would have been drawn to favor Republicans.

The bifurcation of the South into growth and stagnant states suggests that the 2013 pattern may be more likely than the experience of previous decades. Seats added to Florida, North Carolina, and Texas need not advance GOP interests and may instead enlarge Democratic ranks.[8] Loss of a seat in Alabama will come at GOP expense since the Voting Rights Act precludes eliminating the state's one Democratic district.[9] In the short run, the growth states in the South may add to prospects for Republicans in the Electoral College, but in the longer run, Democrats may be advantaged as Florida and North Carolina, both of which voted for Obama in 2008, are toss-up states and Texas will join them once its Hispanic population becomes mobilized.

The Northeast, once a Republican stronghold, has become the nation's most Democratic region with Democrats now holding all congressional seats in New England as of 2020 and all but six from New York.[10] Reapportionment will cost Democrats a seat in Rhode Island and Republicans a seat from West Virginia. Democrats have a trifecta in New York and can probably force a Republican out when the congressional delegation declines by one member. Republicans have relatively narrow majorities in both chambers of the Pennsylvania legislature but Gov. Tom Wolf (D) can veto a blatantly partisan plan. Unless Trump's narrow 2016 victory starts a trend and Pennsylvania remains in the GOP column in presidential elections, Democratic presidential nominees will have slightly fewer electors that they can count on. New York and Rhode Island consistently vote Democratic in presidential elections, and while Pennsylvania went for Trump in 2016, it had stood by the Democrat in the previous six presidential elections. Of Northeastern states losing seats, only West Virginia has usually been in the GOP column.

Illinois, Michigan, and Minnesota have usually voted for Democrats in presidential elections although Michigan narrowly backed Trump in 2016 (10,700 votes) and Minnesota only weakly supported Clinton (44,000 votes). Illinois is safely Democratic and Democrats will redraw the state but Republicans may escape with the five seats they currently hold since the heavy concentration of the Democratic vote in Illinois has limited Democrats' ability to exploit their trifecta.[11] Michigan has a Democratic governor but a Republican legislature. The congressional delegation is evenly divided between Democrats and Republicans. A compromise might result in pairing a Democrat and a Republican in an evenly balanced district. Minnesota also has divided partisan control with Democrats having a 5–3 advantage in the delegation. Its plan might also produce a competitive district.

The political consequences of shifts in the West are likely to be mixed. California, which has not voted Republican since 1988, will have one fewer Democratic elector but Oregon, which has an even longer tradition of Democratic support, can offset that loss. The additional electors for Colorado and Montana are likely to offset one another. Arizona is among the nation's most competitive states. Independent commissions will devise new maps for Arizona, California, and Colorado.

## BOX 7.1   KIMBALL BRACE, REDISTRICTING EXPERT

Kimball Brace is the president of Election Data Services. Redistricting has fascinated him since the early 1970s when he covered the phenomenon as a reporter for NBC and *Congressional Quarterly*.

Since 1977, when he founded EDS, Brace has helped more than thirty states and numerous local jurisdictions through the redistricting process. He has advised both Democrats and Republicans, and state legislators, secretaries of state, local officials, as well as members of independent redistricting commissions.

EDS prepares the datasets that those responsible for drawing new maps rely on. This may involve a tedious matching of census blocks, the smallest unit of analysis for the census, with precincts, the smallest unit for which election data are available. Once the matches have been made, then precinct returns on statewide contests for president, governor, and senator can be merged with census data showing the numbers of individuals classified by age and race or ethnicity. Once these steps have been taken, the mapmakers can ensure that populations are equalized and, in jurisdictions where partisan concerns are present, steps can be taken to protect the interests of one or both parties.

As an expert on issues relating to redistricting, Brace has testified in more than seventy-five cases. His work as a testifying expert has involved both defending maps on which EDS consulted but also as a critic of maps developed by others. He has been qualified as an expert witness on issues relating to the census, redistricting, reapportionment, racial bloc voting, district compactness, contiguity, communities of interest, and demographic databases. The Census Bureau has also tapped into Brace's expertise.

Based on his many years of experience, Brace can advise clients on the likelihood that the decisions they make can be defended if challenged in court.

Among the various activities of Brace's firm are the annual estimates of which states will likely gain or lose seats in the next reapportionment round. These estimates for 2020 are relied on heavily in this chapter. EDS also produces handsome wall maps displaying the results of biennial national elections. His consulting and work as an expert witness also includes issues of election administration.

## THE PREPARATION

Long before the census forms go into the mail, the Census Bureau launches an extensive effort to identify where people live and verify contact information.

In 2020, for the first time, the Census Bureau relied primarily on the internet to collect data. However, as the efforts to provide schooling via online classes during the pandemic underscored, access is far from universal. Those lacking access include not just the homeless but also those living far from the halo of streetlights. To reach the hard to contact as well as to follow up with households that fail to respond online, the bureau hires tens of thousands of part-time workers who will fan out to complete the enumeration through personal contact.

The Census Bureau is not the only entity that prepares well before the numbers get collected. In recent decades the Census Bureau has released the figures needed to carry out the actual drawing of districts late in December of the census year.[12]

The pandemic has derailed the deadlines used in the past. COVID-19 has dissuaded retirees from signing on to go door-to-door to complete the census. In the interest of public health, the Census Bureau has announced that it will not even begin tracking down the almost 40 percent of households that did not respond electronically until August 11. The bureau hopes to finish the count by the end of October, much too late to get data for redistricting to states by the end of the year. The bureau has asked for an extension as the deadline for providing states with the data needed for redistricting so that some might not receive figures until July 31, 2021.[13] By the time that redistricting authorities have the census data prepared and, in most states where not banned, political data merged with the population counts at the precinct level, months will have elapsed. Virginia and New Jersey will hold legislative elections in 2021 and if they do not receive census figures until July it would be impossible to redistrict in time for the 2021 election cycle. Delays in releasing the census figures until well into 2021 would cause conflicts with constitutional and statutory provisions in as many as seventeen states. The Texas constitution requires that redistricting be completed no later than May 31 and in California the adjustments must be done by August 15. States like California with commissions stress that taking the process away from the legislature opened it up for public input, a commitment that becomes difficult to keep in a crunch between late delivery of the data and a legal deadline. Adjustments to district lines may not be completed in some states until early 2022, which gives those disappointed with a plan a short window in which to seek redress in the courts. There may be very little time for candidates to learn their new districts, especially in states like Illinois and Texas that hold early primaries.

The requirement that districts have equal numbers of people can be met using the census data showing the number of individuals and adults by race and ethnicity in each census block. In most jurisdictions, population figures do not fully meet the needs of those who will draw the lines. In jurisdictions where political parties participate in designing new districts, they want to know the partisan consequences of alternative districting plans. To that end, the parties merge the census population figures with information on past voting histories. In order to be positioned to draw the new districts in time for the next round of elections, parties begin gathering electoral data at the precinct level well in advance of the release of the census figures. Some states do the job in-house while other states hire firms like Kimball Brace's Election Data Services.

In many states, parties, especially a party that controls neither legislative chamber nor the governorship, have their own redistricting operations. This requires the acquisition of the software and the technical expertise needed to design districts that will favor a particular party.

Another component to a political party's redistricting strategy is retention of legal talent. Law firms having established relations with one party or the other exist and these law firms developed expertise during previous redistricting cycles in the course of challenging or defending partisan plans. These seasoned litigators stand ready to spring into action to seek an injunction to prevent the implementation of a plan that would harm their party. Attorneys general have the responsibility of defending plans drawn in their states. In some states that office handles litigation, while in other states private attorneys with more extensive experience in defending these kinds of cases get hired.

In 2021, for the first time in half a century, Section 5 of the Voting Rights Act will not be operable. In previous redistricting cycles, all but two southern states plus seven other states, including California and New York, had to get the approval of the U.S. attorney general or the district court of the District of Columbia before implementing statewide districting plans. Plans that reduced the prospects for minority groups to elect their preferences would be blocked. It is possible that some of the covered states will give less consideration to drawing districts for minorities; although that is unlikely, especially where Republicans design the new districts since, as described in chapter 3, drawing districts for minorities usually creates adjacent, whiter districts favorable to Republicans. If a jurisdiction's new plan makes it more difficult for minorities to elect their candidates of choice, it can be challenged under Section 2 of the Voting Rights Act. The minority group could seek an injunction to prevent implementation of the plan, but if an election is on the immediate horizon, it will probably be allowed to proceed. Should a court determine that the minority group has suffered, then it becomes necessary to devise a new plan with the jurisdiction given the first opportunity to make corrections but with the court prepared to step in and complete the process.

Section 5 is not likely to be operable following the 2020 census because in 2013 the Supreme Court found that the conditions, or triggers, that made the section operable were outdated.[14] The Voting Rights Acts adopted in 1965,

1970, and 1975 included standards in Section 4 that determined whether a jurisdiction would be subject to the federal oversight called for in Section 5. Democrats have made addressing the concern raised by the Supreme Court in *Shelby County v. Holder* a top priority. It is possible that if Democrats win the presidency, a Senate majority, and maintain control of the House in 2020, they might rewrite the triggers in Section 4 of the Voting Rights Act. Congress would have to move far more expeditiously than usual to enact new criteria for determining which jurisdictions would have to get federal approval before implementing plans drafted in 2021 and 2022. Even if Congress adopted new triggers, court challenges might delay their application.

In anticipation of the actions taken by legislatures beginning in 2021, the parties and their support groups have become involved in elections for state legislators and governors in 2017–2020. Democrats admit that they did not devote enough attention to creating favorable environments at the state level a decade ago.[15] In preparation for 2020, Democrats vow not to allow Republicans to steal a march on them as the GOP did with spectacular success in Texas in 2002, which resulted in the new plan and dramatic gains outlined in chapter 5.[16] Both parties spent heavily in states where control of a legislative chamber appeared to be in play.

## THE COUNT

Based on Census Bureau estimates made in the middle of 2019, table 7.1 shows the states competing for the last few seats to be awarded. The definition of who gets counted in a state could determine which states get one of those final seats. Everyone living in the United States, whether a citizen or not, should get counted along with those who are serving the nation abroad. A full enumeration is the goal but achieving that can be difficult.

The 2020 count encountered unique challenges. For the first time, the Census Bureau hoped that most of the responses would come electronically rather than through the mail. Households not online or which did not respond were to be visited by census takers. The advertising to fill the ranks of short-term census takers often showed individuals who might be retirees. With individuals older than fifty being more susceptible to the harsher consequences of COVID-19 and with deaths from the virus in the United States exceeding 100,000 as of late May, it became difficult to attract workers to go into unfamiliar neighborhoods to track down heads of households who did not complete forms online.

Securing a full and accurate count of the homeless and those not legally in the country is always challenging. Although the law prohibits the Census Bureau from reporting the name or address of noncitizens to the Immigration and Naturalization Service, many who are illegally in the country prefer to avoid contact with any public official. Some immigrants may hesitate to return census forms because of suspicions about government queries derived from negative interactions with governments in their home country.[17] Even though the Supreme Court blocked the Trump administration proposal to include a question about citizenship, some who are in the country illegally may not have gotten the word and fear that the census includes questions about citizenship.

## RULES FOR THE NEXT REDISTRICTING

As jurisdictions adjust their boundaries to reflect population shifts during the second decade of the twenty-first century, they will continue to need to achieve near absolute population equality in congressional districts. Congressional districts will have tiny deviations or perhaps even the smallest deviations possible except for situations like in Iowa where the state can offer a compelling rationale for small differences in district populations, in other words, no plan can split a county. The second priority will be to do no harm in terms of districts favorable to the election of representatives of minority communities. Section 5 reviews will not be available but minorities can sue using Section 2. Unlike in some past decades when the primary minority concern was that their communities would be split to prevent the election of a representative of the community, the greater concern in the 2020s, like in the previous decade, may be to extend minority group influence by challenging efforts to pack members of the community. Wins in Alabama, North Carolina, Virginia, and elsewhere show that courts have accepted arguments that increased support from white voters means that African Americans can often elect their preferences in districts that are not majority black. Another change from earlier decades is that those who draw districts will have to assess the prospects for minority preferences winning on a district-by-district basis. Setting thresholds for minority districts statewide has drawn rebuke from federal judges.

A related topic likely to end up in court during the 2020s involves combining minority groups for districting purposes. In the past, a condition under which an African American has won despite the absence of a black majority has been when there was a sizable Hispanic district, as in Barbara Jordan's Houston district.[18]

In 2009 the Supreme Court in *Bartlett v. Strickland* held that jurisdictions *must* consider race when redistricting only if a single minority group could constitute a majority of a district's adult population.[19] If a district containing a majority of a single ethnic group cannot be drawn, then a court cannot impose a district that might allow the minority to elect its preference if doing so would contravene state laws.

The Supreme Court has interpreted the first prong of the *Gingles* test (as described in chapter 3) to require that a group constitute a majority of the adult citizen population in an alternative district before a challenge to a plan can succeed under Section 2 of the Voting Rights Act. Although jurisdictions have no obligation to draw districts in which multiple minority groups when added together constitute a majority of the voting age population, all but twenty-five congressional districts experienced an increase in their percentage of minorities between 2000 and 2008.[20] In 205 districts, including most of the Sun Belt, minorities made up at least 30 percent of the population. During the 2020s, plaintiffs are likely to pursue claims that even though a single minority cannot satisfy the first *Gingles* prong, a combination of minorities, such as African Americans and Hispanics, would produce a district in which the non-white, citizen, adult population constitutes a majority. To succeed with that kind of claim, plaintiffs will have to demonstrate that the various minority groups prefer the same candidates (*Gingles* prong 2) and that when the minority groups coalesce behind a candidate, the candidate usually loses to a white bloc vote (*Gingles* prong 3).

Even if the minority populations are too diverse and too scattered to be aggregated into districts dominated by a single group, their growing presence suggests a challenge for GOP mapmakers. Most minority group voters have preferred Democratic candidates in recent elections. For example, the 2016 exit poll showed Hillary Clinton taking 88 percent of the black vote along with 65 percent of the Asian and Hispanic vote and 56 percent of the Other minority vote for a total of 74 percent of the non-white vote nationwide. Republicans attempting to create districts secure for the GOP for the next decade must factor in projections for the growth of minority groups along with increased participation rates. Where Republicans are in charge, they may pack the disparate minorities into one or more districts where the groups can compete to see whether one of their own can win the legislative seat or whether an Anglo will be left to represent the diverse interests. However, as detailed in chapter 5, courts have increasingly cast a jaundiced eye on packing to reduce minority group influence and may force unpacking in response to Section 2 challenges.

While it is appropriate for a jurisdiction to consider the location of minority concentrations, those drawing the districts should consider what are often referred to as traditional factors such as compactness, contiguity, political boundaries, communities of interest, and the location of incumbents. When defending a plan in court, it helps if jurisdictions can demonstrate that they acted in accord with the factors and followed the procedures that they identified as guides for redistricting. Considering factors in addition to where minorities live leaves a jurisdiction better positioned to withstand a *Shaw*-type challenge.

Another way in which to defeat a *Shaw* challenge, at least in federal court, is to emphasize partisan considerations in the legislative record when explaining the placement of district lines. Justifying the placement of lines in terms of partisan advantage remains legitimate in the eyes of federal judges. In 2019 the Supreme Court announced that issues relating to claims of partisan gerrymandering raised political questions that the federal judiciary would not entertain. As explained in chapter 5, state courts have begun to grant relief to claims of excessive partisan gerrymandering, but it remains unclear how widespread that option will be. What role will partisanship play in state court litigation? Will partisan gerrymandering claims succeed only if the bulk of the justices on a state's highest tribunal belong to the party opposite to the one that drew the maps?

If partisans can take advantage of the opposition when drawing new districts, they will almost certainly do so. Democrats and Republicans have invested millions of dollars in state elections with an eye to having their supporters positioned to shape redistricting decisions wherever that may be, in the legislature, the governor's office, or the state judiciary. About three-fourths of the governors who will serve when new maps get drawn are already in office. Hundreds of state legislators who will draw the maps will be elected in 2020. When an incumbent seeks reelection, the result is often a referendum on that individual and if that is the case in the 2020 presidential election, President Trump's popularity will figure significantly in determining what happens in many state political contests. If the president's handling of the COVID-19 pandemic and the civil unrest and demands unleashed by the murder of George Floyd elicits widespread approval, Republican legislative candidates should fare well. If, however, the public finds the president's response to the pandemic, the economic downturn that it spawned, and the civil rights protests unsatisfactory, 2020 could do for Democrats what 2010 did for Republicans.

A cottage industry has developed among political scientists who estimate the national popular vote in presidential elections using data available months before the election. The models almost always include an economic measure and that measure most often uses data from the second quarter of the election year.[21] These models have usually been close to the actual results, although in 2000 and 2016, accuracy in estimating the national popular vote did not predict the resident of 1600 Pennsylvania Avenue.

In addition to the redistricting done by political entities, some states have transferred redistricting responsibilities to independent commissions as described in chapter 1. Some of these commissions consist of elected officials who, if one party holds most of the slots, probably will come up with a partisan plan. In several other states, a commission assumes responsibility if the legislature fails to act. In some of these states the commission consists of political figures and, as occurred in Texas in 2002, their plans may favor one party. In some states a commission designs congressional districts, and like the Iowa Legislative Services Agency, proposes congressional plans that the legislature can reject. Even where political figures retain responsibility for new maps, constraints may limit their tendency to take care of friends and punish political enemies. States like Florida and Ohio have imposed standards designed to prevent the kinds of take-no-prisoners plans adopted in states like North Carolina and Pennsylvania in 2011.

Keeping in mind that the players undoubtedly will change in a number of states, if the redistricting were to be done under the same political circumstances as existed prior to the 2020 election, Democratic trifectas exist in fifteen states with GOP trifectas in twenty-one states. However, of the trifecta states, four on the Republican side and two Democratic states have a single seat and therefore congressional redistricting is not an issue. In several others, like Arizona, California, Iowa, and New Jersey, plans are not prepared by legislators, therefore unified partisan control will not impact the kinds of districts that get drawn. Then, in Florida and Ohio, states with a GOP trifecta, changes in the rules will circumscribe Republicans' ability to advance their fortunes. Nonetheless, depending on what happens in the 2020 elections, Democrats will be positioned to prepare maps in medium and large states like New York (26 seats), Illinois (17 seats), Virginia (11), and Colorado (8). Republicans will be positioned to remap Texas (38 or 39 seats), Georgia (14 seats), Indiana (9), Tennessee (9), and Missouri (8). If Republicans maintain their legislative majorities in North Carolina (14 seats), they may be able to maximize their influence since the Tar Heel governor cannot veto redistricting plans. Political control in large states in which one party exploited its advantage in 2011, like Michigan and Pennsylvania, are currently divided between the parties. Therefore, depending on whether one party benefits from a wave election, the ability of either party to gerrymander to its advantage may be far less than Republicans achieved a decade earlier.

Based on the experience of previous decades, federal judges and the experts hired to assist them will ultimately draw some plans. In some states with divided control, neither side will blink, which will necessitate a court stepping in to provide new districts in time for the 2022 elections. In some other states, the losing party will go to court and, if it succeeds, then federal judges may have to craft new maps even if those drawn in the political process are used for 2022.

Most of the attention devoted to redistricting by the media will focus on partisan battles and implications for minorities, yet other intense struggles will take place largely out of public view. Individual legislators, especially those who represent areas where the population has grown slowly or declined, will play a high stakes game of musical chairs. Lynn Westmoreland (R-GA), formerly head of the National Republican Congressional Committee's redistricting effort, recalls, "I have seen grown people cry when they find that their own career can be over because other politicians are looking out for their own interests."[22] While hearings often fail to attract full attendance, no one willingly misses a session at which district lines are under consideration lest they be dealt an inhospitable district or, worse, no district at all as happened to a Georgia state legislator who missed a meeting to attend the funeral of a relative.

Other battles that have great significance for individual members but are otherwise ignored involve inclusion of specific bits of geography. Even if a legislator retains a district, it may be a pyrrhic victory if friendly precincts have been replaced with those where supporters of the other party live. Legislators may oppose a plan that removes the home of their parents or an area that the legislator has long represented and to which she has close ties. Legislators may fight over areas that include expensive homes or commercial centers, potential sources for critical campaign funds.

In states in which the legislature draws congressional districts, the fate of members of Congress rests in the hands of politicians, some of whom covet the opportunity to go to Washington. In states gaining seats or where retirements have been announced, some of that ambition can be satisfied by the placement of open seats. But in other states a sitting member of Congress may be sacrificed, especially if the member of Congress does not belong to the party that controls the state legislature. Congressional incumbents may be most vulnerable in states that have imposed term limits on legislators since those about to leave the legislature may see in redistricting an alternative to forced retirement from politics.

## CONCLUSION

While a number of questions surround the upcoming redistricting and others will doubtless come up as legislatures, commissions, and courts carry out the process of adjusting for population shifts, one thing remains certain. The process, at least when conducted by a legislative body, will involve politics. Governor Elbridge Gerry used his position to promote his party; in 2021, scores of politicians will follow Gerry's lead and they will have the advantage of sophisticated software and seasoned experts to assist them. Computer software will enable those responsible for drawing districts to honor the traditional districting principles but partisan greed or, as in Georgia in 2001, desperation, may induce mapmakers to push the envelope as they go about placing widely dispersed partisan pockets into a single district.

# Notes

## CHAPTER 1

1. Robert G. Dixon, Jr., "Fair Criteria and Procedures for Establishing Legislative Districts," in *Representation and Redistricting Issues*, Bernard Grofman, Arend Lijphart, Robert B. McKay, and Howard Scarrow, eds. (Lexington, MA: Lexington Books, 1982), 7.

2. Rep. Abner Mikva quoted in Richard L. Engstrom and John K. Wildgen, "Pruning Thorns from the Thicket: An Empirical Test of the Existence of Racial Gerrymandering," *Legislative Studies Quarterly*, 2 (November 1977), 466–467.

3. Sen. John Cornyn (R-TX) quoted in Nicholas R. Seabrook, *Drawing the Lines: Constraints on Partisan Gerrymandering in U.S. Politics* (Ithaca, NY: Cornell University Press, 2017), 57.

4. Yusaku Horiuchi and Jun Saito, "Reapportionment and Redistribution: Consequences of Electoral Reform in Japan," *American Journal of Political Science* 47 (October 2003), 669–682.

5. *Vieth v. Jubelirer*, 541 U.S. 267 (2004).

6. Nicholas R. Seabrook, *Drawing the Lines: Constraints on Partisan Gerrymandering in U.S. Politics* (Ithaca, NY: Cornell University Press, 2017), 7.

7. For a discussion of the Growth South compared with the Stagnant South, see Charles S. Bullock III, Susan A. MacManus, Jeremy D. Mayer, and Mark J. Rozell, *The South and the Transformation of U.S. Politics* (New York: Oxford University Press, 2019), chapter 1.

8. Charles S. Bullock III, Susan A. MacManus, Jeremy D. Mayer, and Mark J. Rozell, *The South and the Transformation of U.S. Politics* (New York: Oxford University Press, 2019).

9. Garrison Nelson, "The Matched Lives of U.S. House Leaders: An Exploration," presented at the annual meeting of the American Political Science Association, New York, NY, August 31–September 3, 1978.

10. What Nelson means by having one leader come from within five counties of another is that by indicating the home counties of congressional leaders on a map and

then counting the counties from the home of one leader to that of another, one would cross no more than five counties.

11. Murphy was first elected from a rural county in 1960 and became Speaker in 1974.

12. For a review of the different districting techniques used following the 2000 census, see Michael P. McDonald, "A Comparative Analysis of Redistricting Institutions in the United States, 2001–02," *State Politics and Policy Quarterly* 4 (Winter 2004), 378.

13. Neither Connecticut's nor North Carolina's governor can veto a redistricting plan. A Tennessee gubernatorial veto of a plan can be overridden by a majority unlike in other states where an override usually requires two-thirds.

14. Alex Tausanovitch, "Voter-Determined Districts: Ending Gerrymandering and Ensuring Fair Representation," Center for American Progress (May 9, 2019). Chen and Cottrell write that "California contributes as many seats to the Democrats through gerrymandering as the top three Republican gerrymanders combined" (Jowei Chen and David Cottrell, "Evaluating Partisan Gains from Congressional Gerrymandering: Using Computer Simulations to Estimate the Effect of Gerrymandering in the U.S. House," *Electoral Studies* 4 [2016], 338–339). In contrast, Wang contends that "election results in California exactly meet the expectations that arise from nationwide districting patterns." Samuel S.-H. Wang, "Three Tests for Practical Evaluation of Partisan Gerrymandering," *Stanford Law Review* 68 (June 2016), 1296.

15. *Arizona State Legislature v. Arizona Independent Redistricting Commission*, 135 S. Ct. 2652 (2015).

16. *Growe v. Emison*, 507 U.S. 25 (1993).

17. Karen Foerstel, "National Parties Mobilize for Battle Over Lines," *Congressional Quarterly Weekly* 59 (March 10, 2001), 554.

18. Tatyana Monnay, "Democrats Prepare to Spend Big to Take Control of 2021 Redistricting," OpenSecrets.org (February 12, 2020).

19. "Eric H. Holder, Jr. Endorses 17 Candidates for Virginia Legislature and NDRC Invests $250,000 ahead of November Elections," NDRC press release (August 15, 2019).

20. Ari Berman, "The Courts Won't End Gerrymandering: Eric Holder Has a Plan without Them," *Mother Jones* (July/August 2019).

21. For an examination of the Growth South versus the Stagnant South and the far better Democratic prospects in the former than the latter, see Bullock et al., *The South and the Transformation of U.S. Politics*. Democrats are hoping to benefit from the same trends in the South that cost them dearly in the 1990s. A generation ago, redistricting plans driven by the U.S. Department of Justice demands that majority-black districts be created whenever possible, coupled with partisan realignment among moderate and conservative whites (see, for example, the discussion of Georgia in chapter 6), facilitated major GOP gains. See the discussion in Nicholas R. Seabrook, *Drawing the Lines* (Ithaca, NY: Cornell University Press, 2017).

22. Jacob Fischler, "Gerrymandering Potential Sways State Legislative Targets," *Roll Call* (January 21, 2020).

23. Alex Isenstadt, "Republicans Fear Drubbing in Next Round of Redistricting," *Politico* (September 5, 2019).

24. Monnay, "Democrats Prepare to Spend Big to Take Control of 2021 Redistricting."

25. "RLSC Launches Major Redistricting Initiative for 2019–2020 Election Cycle," RLSC press release (September 5, 2019) available at https://rslc.gop/./press/. Note that one of these seats was lost in 2019, when Democrats secured a majority in the Virginia Senate and another six are in the nonpartisan Nebraska Senate.

26. Patrick Marley, "Liberal Jill Karofsky Wins Wisconsin Supreme Court Election, Defeating Conservative Justice Daniel Kelly," *Milwaukee Journal Sentinel* (April 13, 2020).

27. Berman, "Courts Won't End Gerrymandering."

28. For a particularly insightful account of this process, see Steve Bickerstaff, *Lines in the Sand* (Austin: University of Texas Press, 2007).

29. Erik J. Engstrom, *Partisan Gerrymandering and the Construction of American Democracy* (Ann Arbor: University of Michigan Press, 2013), 67.

30. Peverill Squire, "Results of Partisan Redistricting in Seven U.S. States during the 1970s," *Legislative Studies Quarterly* 10 (May 1985), 259–266.

31. Gary W. Cox and Jonathan N. Katz, *Elbridge Gerry's Salamander* (Cambridge: Cambridge University Press, 2002), 102.

32. Kerry L. Haynie, *African American Legislators in the American States* (New York: Columbia University Press, 2001); Michael D. Minta, *Oversight: Representing the Interests of Blacks and Latinos in Congress* (Princeton, NJ: Princeton University Press, 2011).

33. David T. Canon, *Race, Redistricting, and Representation* (Chicago: University of Chicago Press, 1999).

34. Several single-state studies appear in Charles E. Menifield and Stephen D. Shaffer, eds., *Politics in the New South: Representation of African Americans in Southern State Legislatures* (Albany: State University of New York Press, 2005). In that volume, Janine A. Parry and William Miller, "African Americans in the Arkansas General Assembly: 1972–1999," find that because of small numbers, blacks had little influence in shaping legislation. Although also relatively small in number, blacks have had greater success in Tennessee, Sharon D. Wright, "The Tennessee Black Caucus of State Legislators," *Journal of Black Studies* 31 (September 2000). Willie M. Leggette, "The South Carolina Legislative Black Caucus, 1970 to 1988," *Journal of Black Studies* 30 (July 2000), reports that blacks had little influence in the South Carolina legislature more than a generation ago; more recently Republicans have dominated both chambers. See also Kerry L. Haynie, *African American Legislators in the American States* (New York: Columbia University Press, 2001).

35. Rufus P. Browning, Dale Rogers Marshall, and David H. Tabb, *Protest Is Not Enough: The Struggle of Blacks and Hispanics for Equality in Urban Politics* (Berkeley: University of California Press, 1985).

36. James W. Button, *Blacks and Social Change* (Princeton, NJ: Princeton University Press, 1989).

37. Frank R. Parker, *Black Votes Count: Political Empowerment in Mississippi after 1965* (Chapel Hill: University of North Carolina Press, 1990), 52.

38. See the discussion in Anthony J. McGann, Charles Anthony Smith, Michael Latner, and Alex Keena, *Gerrymandering in America: The House of Representatives,*

*the Supreme Court, and the Future of Popular Sovereignty* (New York: Cambridge University Press, 2016).

39. Antoine Yoshinaka and Chad Murphy, "The Paradox of Redistricting: How Partisan Mapmakers Foster Competition but Disrupt Representation," *Political Research Quarterly* 64 (June 2011), 435–447.

40. Georgia law requires that a legislator live in the district represented for at least a year before the election. The timing of the new maps prevented either Republican from moving to an adjacent open seat.

41. For a description of various proportional representation systems, see David M. Farrell, *Electoral Systems: A Comparative Introduction*, 2nd edition (New York: Palgrave, 2011), chapters 4–6.

42. Matthew 13:12.

43. Andrew Gelman and Gary King, "A Unified Method of Evaluating Electoral Systems and Redistricting Plans," *American Journal of Political Science* 38 (May 1994), 514–554.

44. The program, Judge-it, is available at: http://gking.harvard.edu/judgeit/.

45. Thomas L. Brunell, *Redistricting and Representation: Why Competitive Elections Are Bad for America?* (New York: Routledge, 2008).

46. Wilbur Ross memo to Karen Dunn Kelley, March 26, 2018.

47. Ann E. Marimow, Matt Zapotosky, and Tara Bahrapour, "2020 Census Will Not Include Citizenship Question, Justice Department Confirms," *Washington Post* (July 2, 2019).

48. Timothy Williams, "Case with Far-Reaching Ramifications and a Question That's Up in the Air for Now," *New York Times* (June 28, 2019).

49. Michael Wines, "2020 Census Won't Have Citizenship Question as Trump Admits," *New York Times* (July 2, 2019).

50. Ross memo to Kelley, op. cit.

51. Katie Rogers and Peter Baker, "Trump Aims to Exclude Immigrants in House Count," *New York Times* (July 22, 2020).

52. "Judge Calls Counting Missionaries Unfair," *New York Times* (March 29, 2001), A12.

53. Peter Bragdon, "Simple Question, Tough Answer: Whom Census Count?" *Congressional Quarterly Weekly Report*, 47 (August 12, 1989), 2146.

54. Mark Monmonier, *Bushmanders and Bullwinkles* (Chicago: University of Chicago Press, 2001),

55. Rhonda Cook, "Georgia Looking to Right Wrongs with 2000 Census," *Atlanta Journal Constitution* (January 30, 2000), C9.

56. "The Knock on the Door," *Economist* (June 13, 2009), 34.

57. For a clear and detailed explanation of how this could work, see Monmonier, *Bushmanders*, 122–123.

58. Ibid., 127.

59. *Department of Commerce v. U.S. House of Representatives*, 525 U.S. 316 (1999).

# CHAPTER 2

1. Chief Justice Earl Warren in *Reynolds v. Sims*, 377 U.S. 533 (1964).

2. Jay K. Dow, *Electing the House: The Adoption and Performance of the US Single-Member District Electoral System* (Lawrence: University Press of Kansas, 2017), 159–168.

3. Since 1912 Illinois had elected twenty-five members from districts and elected at least one member at-large.

4. *Colegrove v. Green*, 328 U.S. 549 (1946).

5. *South v. Peters*, 339 U.S. 276 (1950).

6. Paul T. David and Ralph Eisenberg, *Devaluation of the Urban and Suburban Vote* (Charlottesville: Bureau of Public Administration, University of Virginia, 1961).

7. Nathaniel Persily, Thad Kousser, and Patrick Egan, "The Complicated Impact of One Person, One Vote on Political Competition and Representation," *North Carolina Law Review* 80 (2002), 1319–1320.

8. Recency of redistricting did not prevent substantial population deviations in these two southern states. Florida had redrawn its House districts in 1955, while Georgia with its unique county unit system reallocated seats among counties in a manner somewhat akin to the reapportionment of U.S. House seats after each census.

9. Glendon Schubert and Charles Press, "Measuring Malapportionment," *American Political Science Review* 58 (June 1964), 302–327.

10. *Gomillion v. Lightfoot*, 364 U.S. 339 (1960).

11. *Baker v. Carr*, 369 U.S. 186 (1962).

12. Stephen H. Wainscott, "One Man, One Vote," in *Historic U.S. Court Cases, 1960–1990*, John W. Johnson, ed. (New York: Garland, 1992), 129.

13. *Reynolds v. Sims*, 377 U.S. 533 (1964).

14. Nathaniel Persily, Thad Kousser, and Patrick Egan, "The Complicated Impact of One Person, One Vote on Political Competition and Representation," *North Carolina Law Review* 80 (2002), 1301.

15. *Wesberry v. Sanders*, 376 U.S. 1 (1964).

16. The ideal population for a jurisdiction is the average population per district.

17. Mathew D. McCubbins and Thomas Schwartz, "Congress, the Courts, and Public Policy: Consequences of the One Man, One Vote, Rule," *American Journal of Political Science*, 32 (May 1988), 390.

18. *Avery v. Midland County*, 390 U.S. 474 (1968).

19. *Gray v. Sanders*, 372 U.S. 368 (1963).

20. Population figures from the 1970 census come from *Congressional Directory*, 92nd Congress, 1st Session (Washington, DC: U.S. Government Printing Office, 1971), 94–97.

21. David Butler and Bruce Cain, *Congressional Redistricting: Comparative and Theoretical Perspectives* (New York: Macmillan, 1992), 30.

22. *Karcher v. Daggett*, 462 U.S. 725 (1983).

23. *Vieth v. Pennsylvania*, 195 F. Supp. 2d 672 (M.D. Pa. 2002).

24. If a state's population when divided by the state's number of districts does not produce a whole number, then the minimum population deviation will be one. For example, after the 2000 reapportionment, Florida had twenty-two districts with populations of 639,295 and three districts with populations of 639,296.

25. *Brown v. Thomson*, 462 U.S. 835 (1983).

26. Thomas L. Brunell, "One Person, One Vote Standard in Redistricting: The Uses and Abuses of Population Deviations in Legislative Redistricting," *Case Western Reserve Law Review* 62 (2012), 1072.

27. *Larios v. Cox*, 300 F. Supp. 2d 1320 (N.D. Ga. 2004).

28. *Cox v. Larios*, 542 U.S. 947 (2004).

29. Federal cases involving redistricting are in a very limited class in which three judges hear the trial evidence. Appeals in these cases go directly to the Supreme Court.

30. *Alabama Legislative Black Caucus v. Alabama*, 135 S. Ct. 1257 (2015).

31. In one case, the Supreme Court approved a districting plan that equalized registered voters rather than population. *Burns v. Richardson*, 384 U.S. 73 (1966). Less than twenty years later, the Supreme Court rejected Hawaii's plan based on registration because it differed too much from an alternative plan based on population. David Butler and Bruce Cain, *Congressional Redistricting: Comparative and Theoretical Perspectives* (New York: Macmillan, 1992), 114.

32. James E. Campbell, *Cheap Seats: The Democratic Party's Advantage in U.S. House Elections* (Columbus: Ohio State University Press, 1996).

33. Ronald E. Weber, "Race-Based Districting: Does It Help or Hinder Legislative Representation?," *Political Geography* 19 (2000), 213–147.

34. Ronald Keith Gaddie, Justin J. Wert, and Charles S. Bullock III, "Seats, Votes, Citizens, and the One Person, One Vote Problem," *Stanford Law and Policy Review* 23 (2) (2012), 439. See the concern raised by Alex Kozinski dissenting in *Garza v. County of Los Angeles*, 918 F. 2d 763, 778–788 (9th Cir. 1990).

35. *Evenwel v. Abbott*, 136 S. Ct. 1120 (2016).

36. See, for example, Heather K. Gerken, "The Costs and Causes of Minimalism in Voting Cases: *Baker v. Carr* and Its Progeny," *North Carolina Law Review* 80 (2002), 1411–1467.

37. "Ghost Constituents," *Economist* (April 11, 2020).

38. Sam Roberts, "Census Bureau's Counting of Prisoners Benefits Some Rural Voting Districts," *New York Times* (October 23, 2008).

39. *Fletcher v. Lamone*, 133 S. Ct. 29 (2012), affirming 831 F. Supp. 2nd 887 (D. Md).

40. Stephen Wainscott and John W. Johnson, eds., *Historic U.S. Court Cases, 1690–1900* (New York: Garland, 1992), 127.

41. David Brady and Douglas Edmonds, "One Man, One Vote—So What?" *Transaction* 4 (1967), 941–946; Thomas Dye, "Now Apportionment and Public Policy in the States," *Journal of Politics* 27 (1965), 586–601; Richard Hofferbert, "The Relationship Between Public Policy and Some Structural and Environmental Variables in the American States," *American Political Science Review* 60 (March 1966), 73–82.

42. Ira Sharkansky, "Reapportionment and Roll Call Voting: The Case of the Georgia Legislature," *Social Science Quarterly* 51 (June 1970), 129–137.

43. Allan G. Pulsipher and James L. Weatherby Jr., "Malapportionment, Party Competition and Functional Distribution of Governmental Expenditures," *American Political Science Review* 62 (December 1968), 1207–1219.

44. Roger A. Hanson and Robert E. Crew, "The Policy Impact of Reapportionment," *Law and Society Review* 8 (Fall 1973), 69–94.

45. Stephen Ansolabehere, Alan Gerber, and James Snyder, "Equal Votes, Equal Money: Court-Ordered Redistricting and Public Expenditures in the American States," *American Political Science Review* 96 (December 2002), 767–777.

46. Ibid., 775.

47. Mathew D. McCubbins and Thomas Schwartz, "Congress, the Courts and Public Policy: Consequences of the One Man, One Vote Rule," *American Journal of Political Science* 32 (May 1988), 409–412.

48. Ibid., 411.

49. On the long court battle required to achieve single-member districts in Mississippi, see Frank R. Parker, *Black Votes Count* (Chapel Hill: University of North Carolina Press, 1990), chapter 4.

50. David T. Canon, *Race, Redistricting, and Representation* (Chicago: University of Chicago Press, 1999), shows how the concerns of black members of Congress differ even from those of white Democrats.

51. This paragraph draws on Gary W. Cox and Jonathan N. Katz, *Elbridge Gerry's Salamander* (Cambridge: Cambridge University Press, 2002).

52. Persily et al., "The Complicated Impact of One Person, One Vote," 1333–1334.

53. Ibid., 1337–1339.

54. Ibid., 1340–1343.

55. Charles S. Bullock III, "Reapportionment and Seat Distribution in Multi-County Districts," *Georgia Political Science Association Journal* 2 (Fall 1974), 29–42.

## CHAPTER 3

1. John R. Dunne, Assistant Attorney General, Civil Rights Division, speech presented to the National Conference of State Legislators, Orlando, FL, August 13, 1991.

2. Maurice T. Cunningham, *Maximization Whatever the Cost: Race, Redistricting, and the Department of Justice* (Westport, CT: Praeger, 2001), 142.

3. *Alabama Legislative Black Caucus v. Alabama*, 135 S. Ct. 1257 (2015).

4. On disenfranchisement, see Morgan Kousser, *The Shaping of Southern Politics* (New Haven, CT: Yale University Press, 1974); V. O. Key Jr., *Southern Politics* (New York: Knopf, 1949), chapters 25–29.

5. Key, *Southern Politics*.

6. Recall how Mississippi's heavily black Delta population got cracked as described in chapter 1.

7. *Whitcomb v. Chavis*, 403 U.S. 124 (1971).

8. *White v. Regester*, 412 U.S. 755 (1973).

9. Harrell R. Rodgers Jr. and Charles S. Bullock III, *Law and Social Change: Civil Rights Laws and Their Consequences* (New York: McGraw-Hill, 1972), 25–27.

10. Quoted in Robert Mann, *The Walls of Jericho* (New York: Harcourt Brace, 1996), 448.

11. *Allen v. State Board of Elections*, 393 U.S. 544 (1969).

12. *Georgia v. United States*, 411 U.S. 526 (1973).

13. *Beer v. United States*, 425 U.S. 130 (1976).

14. David C. Saffell, "1980s Congressional Redistricting Looks Like Politics as Usual," *National Civil Review* 72 (July–August 1983), 369.

15. Charles S. Bullock III and Ronald Keith Gaddie, *The Triumph of Voting Rights in the South* (Norman: University of Oklahoma Press, 2009).

16. *City of Mobile v. Bolden*, 446 U.S. 55 (1980).

17. *Thornburg v. Gingles*, 478 U.S. 30 (1986).

18. *Holder v. Hall*, 512 U.S. 874 (1994).

19. *Growe v. Emison*, 507 U.S. 25 (1993).

20. For an enumeration of the number of multi-member districts over time, see Richard G. Neimi, Jeffrey S. Hill, and Bernard Grofman, "The Impact of Multimember Districts on Party Representation in U.S. State Legislatures," *Legislative Studies Quarterly* 10 (November 1985), 446.

21. David Lublin, *The Paradox of Representation: Racial Gerrymandering and Minority Interests in Congress* (Princeton, NJ: Princeton University, 1997), 41.

22. As recently as the 102nd Congress, white Democrats held more than 60 percent of the southern districts 10–50 percent black. Republicans soon demonstrated strength in districts with more than 10 percent black populations. Charles S. Bullock III, "Partisan Changes in Southern Congressional Delegations and the Consequences," in *Continuity and Change in House Elections*, David W. Brady, John F. Cogan, and Morris P. Fiorina, eds. (Stanford, CA: Stanford University Press, 2000), 45–47.

23. John R. Dunne speaking before the National Conference of State Legislatures, Orlando, FL, August 13, 1991.

24. For an analysis of the 1992 election in Texas-29 see Douglas Abel and Bruce I. Oppenheimer, "Candidate Emergence in a Majority Hispanic District: The 29th District in Texas," in *Who Runs for Congress?*, Thomas Kazee, ed. (Washington, DC: CQ Press, 1994).

25. Mark A. Posner, "Post-1990 Redistrictings and the Preclearance Requirements of Section 5 of the Voting Rights Act," in *Race and Redistricting in the 1990s*, Bernard Grofman, ed. (New York: Agathon, 1998), 88.

26. *Shaw v. Reno*, 509 U.S. 630 (1993).

27. *Miller v. Johnson*, 515 U.S. 900 (1995); *Bush v. Vera*, 517 U.S. 952 (1996).

28. *Cromartie v. Hunt*, 34 F. Supp. 2d 1029 (E.D. N.C. 2000).

29. *Easley v. Cromartie*, 532 U.S. 234 (2001).

30. Quoted in Robert A. Holmes, "Reapportionment Strategies in the 1990s: The Case of Georgia," in *Race Redistricting in the 1990s*, Bernard Grofman, ed. (New York: Agathon, 1998), 211.

31. See, for example, Selwyn Carter, "The Impact of Recent Supreme Court Decisions on Racial Representation," in *Redistricting in Minority Representation*,

David A. Bositis, ed. (Washington, DC: University Press of America, 1998), 183–194.

32. In Louisiana's unique electoral system, all candidates, regardless of party, compete in the first round. If no one receives a majority, then the top two candidates face off in a runoff.

33. Charles S. Bullock III and Richard E. Dunn, "The Demise of Racial Districting and the Future of Black Representation," *Emory Law Journal* 48 (Fall 1999), 1209–1253.

34. *Reno v. Bossier Parish School Board*, 528 U.S. 320 (2000).

35. *Johnson v. DeGrandy*, 512 U.S. 997 (1994).

36. *Growe v. Emison*, 507 U.S. 25 (1993).

37. Charles S. Bullock III and Susan A. MacManus, "Voting Patterns in a Tri-Ethnic Community: Conflict or Cohesion: The Cause of Austin, Texas, 1975–1985," *National Civic Review* 79 (January–February, 1990), 5–22.

38. James A. Barnes, "Minority Map Making," *National Journal* 22 (April 7, 1990), 839.

39. James Loewen, "Levels of Political Mobilization and Racial Bloc Voting Among Latinos, Anglos, and African Americans in New York City," *Chicano-Latino Law Review* 13 (1993), 50–60.

40. The congressional district map for the Miami area in the 1990s had a Latino district that wrapped around an extension of a majority black district.

41. For a discussion of the use of 65 percent as a threshold for a minority district, see Kimball Brace, Bernard Grofman, Lisa R. Handley, and Richard G. Niemi, "Minority Equality: The 65 Percent Rule in Theory and Practice," *Law and Policy* 10 (1988), 43–62. *United Jewish Organizations of Williamsburgh v. Carey*, 430 U.S. 144 (1977).

42. *Georgia v. Ashcroft*, 539 U.S. 461 (2003).

43. *Bartlett v. Strickland*, 556 U.S. 1 (2009).

44. Mark Posner, a DOJ attorney, denies both that the department sought to maximize the number of majority-minority districts and that political considerations influenced decisions to deny preclearance. (Posner, "Post-1990s Redistrictings," 97–98.) However the Supreme Court found that maximization drove DOJ decisions at least in Georgia and North Carolina. *Miller v. Johnson*, 515 U.S. 900 (1995); *Shaw v. Hunt*, 517 U.S. 899 (1996).

45. Deposition of John Dunne at p. 122, *Johnson v. Miller*, 864 F. Supp. 1354 (S.D. Ga. 1994), *Aff'd*, 515 U.S. 900 (1995). There is also evidence that the Reagan Justice Department sought to promote GOP fortunes in the course of 1980s redistricting. See Matthew Cooper, "Beware of Republicans Bearing Voting Rights Suits," *Washington Monthly* (February 1987), 11–15. A very different interpretation of Dunne's motivation is that he experienced a conversion as a result of his responsibilities at DOJ and acted solely in order to increase the numbers of minority legislators. See Cunningham, *Maximization, Whatever the Cost*, 123–144.

46. See, for example, David Lublin, *The Republican South* (Princeton, NJ: Princeton University Press, 2004), 104–115; Kimball Brace, Bernard Grofman, and Lisa Handley, "Does Redistricting Aimed to Helped Blacks Necessarily Help

Republicans?," *Journal of Politics* 49 (February 1987), 169–185. At least some southern Republicans recognized as early as the 1970s that creating additional districts with black concentrations would likely work to the advantage of the GOP in neighboring districts. See Richard L. Engstrom and John K. Wildgen, "Pruning Thorns from the Thicket: An Empirical Test of the Existence of Racial Gerrymandering," *Legislative Studies Quarterly* 2 (November 1977), 473. The breakup of multi-member state legislative districts into single-member districts also generally resulted in increased representation by both African Americans and Republicans at the expense of white Democrats. Charles S. Bullock III and Ronald Keith Gaddie, "Changing from Multi-Member to Single-Member Districts: Partisan, Racial and Gender Consequences," *State and Local Government Review* 25 (Fall 1993), 155–163.

47. Quoted in Richard L. Engstrom and Jason E. Kirksey, "Race and Representational Districting in Louisiana," in *Race and Redistricting in the 1990s*, Bernard Grofman, ed. (New York: Agathon Press, 1998), 247.

48. Two dissents to the conclusion that Democrats lost congressional seats because of the affirmative action gerrymanders are registered by Richard Engstrom and the NAACP Legal Defense and Education Fund. See Engstrom, "Voting Rights Districts: Debunking the Myths," *Campaigns and Elections* (April 1995), 24, 46; Engstrom, "Race and Southern Politics: The Special Case of Congressional Districting," in *Writing Southern Politics*, Robert P. Steed and Laurence W. Moreland, eds. (Lexington: University Press of Kentucky, 2006), 91–118; NAACP Legal Defense and Education Fund, "The Effect of Section 2 of the Voting Rights Act on the 1994 Congressional Elections" (1994).

49. Charles S. Bullock III, "Winners and Losers in the Latest Round of Redistricting," *Emory Law Journal* 44 (Summer 1995), 954–955.

50. David Lublin, "Racial Redistricting and Southern Republican Congressional Gains in the 1990s," and Lisa Handley, "Drawing Effective Minority Districts: A Conceptual Model," in *Voting Rights and Minority Representation: Redistricting, 1992– 2002*, David A. Bositis, ed. (Lanham, MD: University Press of America, 2006), 116.

51. John R. Petrocik and Scott W. Desposato, "The Partisan Consequences of Majority-Minority Redistricting in the South, 1992 and 1994," *Journal of Politics* 60 (August 1998), 613–633.

52. Stephen Ansolabehere, James Snyder Jr., and Charles Stewart III, "Old Voters, New Voters, and the Personal Vote: Using Redistricting to Measure the Incumbency Advantage," *American Journal of Political Science* 44 (January 2002), 17–34; Seth C. McKee, *Republican Ascendency in Southern U.S. House Elections* (Boulder, CO: Westview Press, 2010), chapter 3.

53. Lublin, *Paradox of Representation*, 96.

54. David Lublin, "Racial Redistricting," and Handley, "Drawing Effective Minority Districts," 120.

55. David Lublin and D. Stephen Voss, "Racial Redistricting and Realignment in Southern State Legislatures," *American Journal of Political Science* 44 (October 2000), 805.

56. David Lublin and D. Stephen Voss, "Boll Weevil Blues: Polarized Congressional Delegations into the 21st Century," *American Review of Politics* 21 (Winter 2000), 440.

57. For a discussion of the politics involved in drawing the Frost plan for Texas, see J. Morgan Kousser, *Color Blind Justice: Minority Voting Rights and the Undoing of the Second Reconstruction* (Chapel Hill: University of North Carolina Press, 199), 292–316.

58. Donald W. Beachler, "Racial and Partisan Gerrymandering: Three States in the 1990s," *American Review of Politics* 19 (Spring 1998), 1–16.

59. Carol Swain, *Black Faces, Black Interests: The Representation of African Americans in Congress* (Cambridge, MA: Harvard University Press, 1993), 207.

60. Marvin Overby and Kenneth Cosgrove, "Unintended Consequences? Racial Redistricting and the Representation of Minority Interests," *Journal of Politics* 58 (1996), 540–550.

61. Christine Leveaux Sharpe and James C. Garand, "Race, Roll Calls, and Redistricting: The Impact of Race-Based Redistricting on Congressional Roll Calls," *Political Research Quarterly* 54 (March 2001), 31–51.

62. Charles S. Bullock III, "The Impact of Changing the Racial Composition of Congressional Districts on Legislators' Roll-Call Behavior," *American Politics Quarterly* 23 (April 1995), 141–158.

63. Kenneth W. Shotts, "Does Racial Redistricting Cause Conservative Policy Outcomes? Policy Preferences of Southern Representatives in the 1980s and 1990s," *Journal of Politics* 65 (February 2003), 216–226.

64. Winnet W. Hagens, "The Politics of Race: The Virginia Redistricting Experience, 1991–1997," in *Race and Redistricting in the 1990s*, Bernard Grofman, ed. (New York: Agathon, 1998), 324.

65. See, for example, *Busbee v. Smith*, 549 F. Supp. 494 (D.D.C. 1982) and the discussion earlier in this chapter and in chapter 6.

66. Gregory L. Giroux, "New Twists in the Old Debate on Race and Representation," *CQ Weekly* 59 (August 11, 2001), 1972. Representative Bobby Scott (D-VA) who also has a predominantly urban district urged Virginia legislators to reduce the black percentage in his district from 57 to 49 percent in order to beef up the black percentage in the adjoining 4th District.

67. Charles Cameron, David Epstein, and Sharyn O'Halloran, "Do Majority-Minority Districts Maximize Substantive Black Representation in Congress?," *American Political Science Review* 90 (December 1996), 804. See also Lisa Handley, "Drawing Effective Minority Districts: A Conceptual Model," in *Voting Rights and Minority Representation: Redistricting, 1992–2002*, David A. Bositis, ed. (Lanham, MD: University Press of America, 2006), especially p. 68.

68. David Esptein and Sharyn O'Halloran, "A Social Science Approach to Race, Redistricting and Representation," *American Political Science Review* 93 (March 1999), 189.

69. Report of Dr. David Epstein in *Georgia v. Ashcroft*, 539 U.S. 461 (2003).

70. Because of large numbers of non-citizens and low turnout rates even among citizens, concentrations of Latinos need to be higher than black percentages. Leo F. Estrada, "Redistricting 2000: A Lost Opportunity for Latinos," in *Voting Rights and Minority Representation: Redistricting, 1992–2002*, David A. Bositis, ed. (Lanham, MD: University Press of America, 2006), 75. Robert R. Brischetto, "Latino Voters and Redistricting in the Millennium," in *Redistricting and Minority Representation*, David A. Bositis, ed. (Washington, DC: University Press of America, 1998), 50.

71. Bruce E. Cain, *The Reapportionment Puzzle* (Berkeley: University of California Press, 1984), 169.

72. *Georgia v. Ashcroft*, 539 U.S. 461 (2003).

73. Swain, *Black Faces, Black Interests*, 211–212.

74. *Sessions v. Perry*, 298 F. Supp. 2d 451 (E.D. Tex. 2004).

75. Thomas L. Brunell, *Redistricting and Representation: Why Competitive Elections Are Bad for America* (New York: Routledge, 2008), 73.

76. Barnes, "Minority Map Making," 839.

77. *Alabama Legislative Black Caucus v. Alabama*, 989 F. Supp. 2d 1227 (M.D. Ala. 2013).

78. *Alabama Legislative Black Caucus v. Alabama*, 135 S. Ct. 1257 (2015).

79. *Miller v. Johnson*, 515 U.S. 900 (1995).

80. *Virginia House of Delegates v. Bethune Hill*, 139 S. Ct. 1945 (2019).

81. *Personhuballah v. Alcorn*, 155 F. Supp. 3d 552 (E.D. Va. 2016).

82. When the GOP-controlled legislature failed to draw a new map, the three-judge panel that heard the case imposed one. Of the three congressional appellants, only one remained in Congress in 2019. Randy Forbes, whose district was at the center of the case, ran in a neighboring, two-thirds white district where he lost the GOP nomination. The winner in that district lost to Democrat Elaine Luria in 2018. Dave Brat survived 2016 only to lose two years later to Abigail Spanberger (D). Results indicate that Justice Stephen Breyer's assertion that the appellants had failed to show that their reelection chances were imperiled lacked merit. Of course, no members have a "right" to the districts that they currently represent. *Wittman v. Personhuballah*, 136 S. Ct. 1732 (2016).

83. *Bethune-Hill v. Virginia State Board of Elections*, 137 S. Ct. 788 (2017).

84. *Cooper v. Harris*, 136 S. Ct. 2512 (2016).

85. *Thomas v. Bryant*, Case No. 3:18-CV-441-CWR-FKB (N. D. Miss., 2019).

86. *Shelby County v. Holder*, 570 U.S. 18 (2013).

87. Bullock and Gaddie, *Triumph of Voting Rights in the South*.

88. David T. Canon, *Race, Redistricting, and Representation* (Chicago: University of Chicago Press, 1999), especially chapter 5; Christian R. Grose, *Congress in Black and White: Race and Representation in Washington and at Home* (New York: Cambridge University Press, 2011).

89. Grose, *Congress in Black and White*, chapter 6.

90. Ibid., 169–170.

91. Ibid., 83.

92. Claudine Gay, "Spirals of Trust? The Effect of Descriptive Representation on Relationships between Citizens and Their Government," *American Journal of Political Science* 46 (October 2002), 717–733; Susan A. Banducci, Todd Donovan, and Jeffrey A. Carp, "Minority Representation, Empowerment and Participation," *Journal of Politics* 66 (May 2004), 534–556; Katherine Tate, "The Political Representation of Blacks in Congress: Does Race Matter?" *Legislative Studies Quarterly* 26 (November 2001), 623–638.

93. Zoltan Hajnal, "Who Loses in American Democracy? A Count of Votes Demonstrates the Limited Representation of African Americans," *American Political*

*Science Review* 103 (February 2009), 37–57. Although not part of Hajnal's study it is likely that most black voters also back winners in state legislative elections for the same reason that they support winners in congressional elections—they live in districts designed to be heavily minority.

94. See the testimony of Donald L. Horowitz and James F. Blumstein presented during the hearings before the Subcommittee on the Constitution of the Committee of the Judiciary, *United States Senate on the Voting Rights Act*, 97th Congress, 2nd Session, Volume 2 (Washington, DC: U.S. Government Printing Office, 1993), 1307–1364.

95. Bullock, "The Impact of Changing the Racial Composition of Congressional Districts on Legislators' Roll Call Behavior," 141–158.

96. Richard L. Engstrom, "Voting Rights Districts: Debunking the Myths," *Campaigns and Elections* (April 1995), 24, 46.

97. Shotts, "Does Racial Redistricting Cause Conservative Policy Outcomes?," 216–226.

98. Grose, *Congress in Black and White*, 71–82

## CHAPTER 4

1. Figures on the numbers of states in which districting guidelines ban various types of actions all come from National Conference of State Legislatures, "Districting Principles for 2010 and Beyond," June 4, 2019.

2. Richard G. Niemi, Bernard Grofman, Carl Carlucci, and Thomas Hofeller, "Measuring Compactness and the Role of Compactness Standard in a Test for Partisan and Racial Gerrymandering," *Journal of Politics* 52 (November 1990), 1155–1181. Micah Altman, "Districting Principles and Democratic Representation," Thesis, California Institute of Technology, Pasadena, CA (1998).

3. Ernest C. Reock, "A Note: Measuring Compactness as a Requirement of Legislative Apportionment," *Midwest Journal of Political Science* 5:1 (1961), 70–74.

4. Daniel D. Polsby and Robert D. Popper, "The Third Criterion: Compactness as a Procedural Safeguard against Partisan Gerrymandering," *Yale Law and Policy Review* 9:2 (1991), 301–353.

5. Richard H. Pildes and Richard G. Niemi, "Expressive Harms, 'Bizarre Districts,' and Voting Rights: Evaluating Election-District Appearances after *Shaw v. Reno*," *Michigan Law Review* 92 (December 1993), 483–587.

6. Ibid.

7. Stephen Ansolabehere and Maxwell Palmer, "A Two Hundred-Year Statistical History of the Gerrymander," *Ohio State Law Journal* 77:4 (2016), 741–762.

8. Christopher Ingraham, "America's Most Gerrymandered Congressional Districts," *Washington Post* (May 15, 2014).

9. Ibid. In addition to the three worst, others on the list are, in order, PA-7, NC-1, TX-33, NC-4, IL-4, TX-35, and LA-2.

10. *Redrawing the Map on Redistricting, 2012* (Philadelphia, PA: Azavea, 2012), 11–13, informs this and the next paragraph.

11. This paragraph draws on ibid.

12. Michael P. McDonald, "Drawing the Line: Redistricting and Competition in Congressional Elections," *Extensions* (Fall 2004), 16.

13. Ibid., 74.

14. Bruce E. Cain, *The Reapportionment Puzzle* (Berkeley: University of California Press, 1984), 60; Charles S. Bullock III, "Reapportionment and Seat Distribution in Multi-County Districts," *Georgia Political Science Association Journal* 2 (Fall 1974), 29–42.

15. Cain, *Reapportionment Puzzle*, 63.

16. Daniel C. Bowen, "Boundaries, Redistricting Criteria, and Representation in the U.S. House of Representatives," *American Politics Research* 42:5 (2014), 856–895.

17. *United Jewish Organizations of Williamsburgh v. Carey*, 430 U.S. 144 (1977).

18. *Easley v. Cromartie*, 532 U.S. 234 (2001).

19. Thomas L. Brunell, "One Person, One Vote Standard in Redistricting: The Uses and Abuses of Population Deviations in Legislative Redistricting," *Case Western Reserve Law Review* 62 (2012), 1067.

20. Cain, *Reapportionment Puzzle*, 12.

21. McDonald, "Drawing the Line," 15.

22. Ronald Keith Gaddie, "The Texas Redistricting, Measure for Measure," *Extensions* (Fall 2004), 21.

23. Ronald Keith Gaddie and Charles S. Bullock III, "From *Ashcroft* to *Larios*: Recent Redistricting Lessons from Georgia," *Fordham Urban Law Journal* 34 (April 2007), 1014–1015.

24. *Larios v. Cox*, 300 F. Supp. 2d 1320 (N.D. Ga. 2004).

25. Michael P. McDonald, "A Comparative Analysis of Redistricting Institutions of in the United States, 2001–02," *State Politics and Policy Quarterly* 4 (Winter 2004), 390.

26. Andrew Gelman and Gary King, "Enhancing Democracy through Legislative Redistricting," *American Political Science Review* 88 (September 1994), 547.

27. *Larios v. Cox*, 300 F. Supp. 2d 1320 (N.D. Ga. 2004).

28. On the way in which Texas Democrats got divorced from their district cores, see Seth C. McKee and Daron R. Shaw, "Redistricting in Texas: Institutionalizing Republican Ascendency," in *Redistricting in the New Millennium*, Peter F. Galderisi, ed. (Lanham, MD: Lexington Books, 2005), 297–299.

29. National Conference of State Legislatures, "Districting Principles for 2010 and Beyond.

# CHAPTER 5

1. Tom Hofeller, quoted in Rhodes Cook, "Parties in High-Stakes Battle for Right to Draw Lines," *Congressional Quarterly Weekly Reports* 47 (August 12, 1989), 2138.

2. Bruce Cain, "Assessing the Partisan Effects of Redistricting," *American Political Science Review* 79 (June 1985), 326.

3. Peverill Squire, "Results of Partisan Redistricting in Seven U.S. States during the 1970s," *Legislative Studies Quarterly* 10 (May 1985), 260.

4. Paul Clement in "The Supreme Court Takes Another Look at Partisan Redistricting," National Public Radio (March 25, 2019).

5. John Roberts in *Rucho v. Common Cause*, 139 S. Ct. 2484 (2019).

6. Robert Draper, "The League of Dangerous Mapmakers," *Atlantic* (October 2012).

7. Alan Ehrenhalt, "Legislative Districts and Judicial Tinkering," *Congressional Quarterly Weekly Report* 43 (April 13, 1985), 703.

8. Yusaku Horiuchi and Jun Saito, "Reapportionment and Redistribution: Consequences of Electoral Reform in Japan," *American Journal of Political Science* 47 (October 2003): 669–682.

9. For an analysis that discounts the impact of computer-assisted redistricting as a major factor in producing gerrymanders, see Micah Altman, Karin MacDonald, and Michael McDonald, "Pushbutton Gerrymanders? How Computing Has Changed Redistricting," in *Party Lines: Competition, Partisanship, and Congressional Redistricting*, Thomas E. Mann and Bruce E. Cain, eds. (Washington, DC: Brookings Institution Press, 2005), 51–66.

10. For example, Republicans spent $400,000 to win a majority in the Virginia House in anticipation of the 2001 redistricting. Greg L. Giroux, "The Hidden Election: Day of the Mapmaker," *CQ Weekly* 58 (February 19, 2000), 346. The legal problems that prompted Rep. Tom DeLay (R-TX) to resign from the House stemmed from questions about the legality of funds he funneled to win control of the Texas House. Once Republicans controlled the Texas House they adopted a GOP gerrymander for the congressional map. See Steve Bickerstaff, *Lines in the Sand: Congressional Redistricting in Texas and the Downfall of Tom DeLay* (Austin: University of Texas Press, 2007).

11. Not all governors have a role in redistricting. For example, North Carolina's governor cannot veto redistricting plans.

12. David Butler and Bruce Cain, *Congressional Redistricting: Comparative and Theoretical Perspectives* (New York: Macmillan, 1992), 109–110. Anthony J. McGann, Charles Anthony Smith, Michael Latner, and Alex Keena, *Gerrymandering in America: The House of Representatives, the Supreme Court, and the Future of Popular Sovereignty* (New York: Cambridge University Press, 2016).

13. This plan immediately drew challenges from Democrats, and was objected to by the Obama Justice Department and rejected by the courts.

14. Laura Royden and Michael Li, *Extreme Maps* (New York: Brennan Center for Justice at New York University School of Law, 2017).

15. Andrew Gelman and Gary King, "Enhancing Democracy through Legislative Redistricting," *American Political Science Review* 88 (September 1994), 541–559.

16. Morris P. Fiorina, *Representation, Roll Calls, and Constituencies* (Lexington, MA: Lexington Books, 1974), 102–103; Charles S. Bullock III, "The Impact of Changing the Racial Composition of Congressional Districts on Legislators' Roll Call Behavior," *American Politics Quarterly* 23 (April 1995), 151–152.

17. Richard F. Fenno, Jr., *Home Style: House Members in Their Districts* (Boston: Little, Brown, 1978).

18. On the Brat–Cantor contest, see Lauren Cohen Bell, David Elliot Meyer, and Ronald Keith Gaddie, *Slingshot: The Defeat of Eric Cantor* (Los Angeles: Sage, 2016).

19. David Cottrell, "Using Computer Simulation to Measure the Effect of Gerrymandering on Electoral Competition in the U.S. Congress," *Legislative Studies Quarterly* 44 (August 2019), 487–514.

20. Jamie L. Carson and Michael Crespin, "The Effect of State Redistricting Methods on Electoral Competition in United States House of Representatives Races," *State Politics and Policy Quarterly* 4 (Winter 2004), 455–469.

21. David M. Farrell, *Electoral Systems*, 2nd ed. (New York: Palgrave Macmillan, 2011).

22. Gelman and King, "Enhancing Democracy," 552.

23. Ibid., 551.

24. Bryan Tyson, who drew the Georgia congressional plan adopted in 2005 and who has provided technical advice to that state's Republicans during the 2000s, devised a plan that gave his party good prospects for winning ten of the thirteen districts. The Department of Justice would have vetoed that alternative for being retrogressive since it reduced the number of districts in which African Americans could elect their preferred candidates from four to three. Personal communication from Bryan Tyson, August 10, 2009.

25. Fenno, *Home Style*, explains that early in their careers legislators work to expand their base. Once they have gotten sufficient support, they simply seek to maintain that level of support. For a description of how a senior, rural Democrat tried and ultimately failed to adjust to a suburbanizing, increasingly Republican constituency, see Fenno, *Congress at the Grassroots* (Chapel Hill: University of North Carolina Press, 2000), chapter 3.

26. Amihai Glazer and Marc Robbins, "Congressional Responsiveness to Constituency Change," *American Journal of Political Science* 29 (May 1985), 259–273; Christine Leveaux-Sharpe, "Congressional Responsiveness to Redistricting Induced Constituency Change: An Extension to the 1990s," *Legislative Studies Quarterly* 26 (May 2001), 275–286.

27. Carol M. Swain, *Black Faces, Black Interests: The Representation of African Americans in Congress* (Cambridge, MA: Harvard University Press, 1993), 72–73.

28. Claudine Gay, "Legislating without Constraints: The Effect of Minority Districting on Legislators' Responsiveness to Constituency Preferences," *Journal of Politics* 69 (May 2007), 442–456. See also Richard F. Fenno, *Going Home: Black Representatives and Their Constituents* (Chicago: University of Chicago Press, 2003).

29. *Colegrove v. Green*, 328 U.S. 549 (1946).

30. *Gaffney v. Cummings*, 412 U.S. 735 (1973).

31. See, for example, Jonathan Winburn, *The Realities of Redistricting: Following the Rules and Limiting Gerrymandering and State Legislative Redistricting* (Lanham, MD: Lexington Books, 2008).

32. Royden and Li, *Extreme Maps*. A partial dissent comes from Niemi and Abramowitz. "In contrast to results for the 1970s and 1980s, then, contrary to the hypothesis that mapmakers are becoming more skilled at partisan line-drawing, initial results from the 1990s indicate that, on average, partisan control of state

government did little or nothing to enhance partisan gains from redistricting." Richard G. Niemi and Alan I. Abramowitz, "Partisan Redistricting in the 1992 Congressional Elections," *Journal of Politics* 56 (August 1994), 815.

33. Bruce E. Cain, Karin MacDonald, and Michael McDonald, "From Equality to Fairness: The Path of Political Reform Since *Baker v. Carr*," in *Party Lines: Competition, Partisanship and Congressional Redistricting*, Thomas E. Mann and Bruce E. Cain, eds. (Washington, DC: Brookings Institution Press, 2005), 19.

34. *Gaffney v. Cummings*, 412 U.S. 735 (1973).

35. Butler and Cain, *Congressional Redistricting*, 104. "Districting Principles for 2010 and Beyond," National Conference of State Legislatures (June 4, 2019).

36. For a different perspective on the Frost gerrymander, see Seth C. McKee and Daron R. Shaw, "Redistricting in Texas: Institutionalizing Republican Ascendancy," in *Redistricting in the New Millennium*, Peter F. Galderisi, ed. (Lanham, MD: Lexington Books, 2005), 288–292.

37. *Balderas v. Texas*, Civil Action No. 6:01CV 158 (E.D. Tex.), 2001, Slip opinion, 7.

38. Ibid., 9.

39. Richard E. Cohen, "The House on the Line," *National Journal* 32 (April 8, 2000), 1110.

40. Steve Bickerstaff, *Lines in the Sand: Congressional Redistricting in Texas and the Downfall of Tom DeLay* (Austin: University of Texas Press, 2007).

41. Nicholas R. Seabrook, *Drawing the Lines* (Ithaca, NY: Cornell University Press, 2017), 55.

42. McGann et al., *Gerrymandering in America*, chapter 5.

43. Allan Smith, "Democrats Won House Popular Vote by Largest Margin Since Watergate," NBC News (November 21, 2018).

44. Griff Palmer and Michael Cooper, "How Maps Helped Republicans Keep an Edge in the House," *New York Times* (December 1, 2012).

45. Figures on the racial and partisan composition of the districts come from Michael Barone and Chuck McCutcheon, *The Almanac of American Politics, 2014* (Chicago: University of Chicago Press, 2013).

46. Laura Royden and Michael Li, *Extreme Maps Midterm* (New York: Brennan Center for Justice at New York University School of Law, 2017), 2, 25.

47. Jowei Chen and David Cottrell, "Evaluating Partisan Gains from Congressional Gerrymandering: Using Computer Simulations to Estimate the Effect of Gerrymandering in the U.S. House," *Electoral Studies* 44 (2016), 338.

48. Amy Howe, "Justices to Tackle Partisan Gerrymandering . . . Again: In Plain English," *Court* (February 4, 2019).

49. Bernard Grofman and Thomas Brunell, "The Art of the Dummymander: The Impact of Recent Redistrictings on the Partisan Makeup of Southern House Seats," in *Redistricting in the New Millennium*, Peter F. Galderisi, ed. (Lanham, MD: Lexington Books, 2005). Howard A. Scarrow, "Partisan Gerrymandering—Invidious or Benevolent? *Gaffney v. Cummings* and Its Aftermath," *Journal of Politics* 44 (August 1982), 810–821, describes the unsuccessful effort to produce a partisanly fair plan in Connecticut in the early 1970s and how that plan quickly ceased to reflect the partisan makeup of the electorate.

50. Peverill Squire, "Results of Partisan Redistricting in Seven U.S. States during the 1970s," *Legislative Studies Quarterly* 10 (May 1985), 264.

51. Michael Barone and Grant Ujifusa, *The Almanac of American Politics, 1984* (Washington, DC: National Journal, 1983), 382. Indiana has a long history of partisan gerrymandering. In 1852, Democrats designed a plan to win ten of eleven districts while taking only 53 percent of the state vote. Erik J. Engstrom, *Partisan Gerrymandering and the Construction of American Democracy* (Ann Arbor: University of Michigan Press, 2013), 9.

52. Michael Barone with Richard E. Cohen, *The Almanac of American Politics, 2004* (Washington, DC: National Journal, 2003), 1350.

53. The unraveling of the GOP gerrymander in Pennsylvania is but part of a broader problem with Republican plans. Hirsch notes that the Republican advantage in the House following the 2002 elections resulted largely from Republican plans adopted in Florida, Michigan, Ohio, and Pennsylvania. Half of the senators from these states were Democrats and Al Gore won 50.7 percent of the vote in these states. Nonetheless, in 2002, Republicans won two-thirds of the House seats, increasing their numbers from 44 to 51. Hirsch, "The United States House of Unrepresentatives," 201. The benefits achieved by the GOP proved short lived. After the 2008 election, Democrats had majorities of the House delegations from all of these states except Florida and had won thirty-nine of the seats, which gave them 50.6 percent of the seats compared with Gore's 50.7 percent of the 2000 vote.

54. Cain, MacDonald, and McDonald, "From Equality to Fairness," 23.

55. Democrats controlled both California legislative chambers and the governorship and therefore could have drawn a partisan map. They chose not to do so for fear that such a plan might endanger some of the Democrats who had taken Republican seats in 2000. Michael Barone with Richard E. Cohen, *The Almanac of American Politics, 2004* (Washington, DC: National Journal, 2003), 155–157.

56. Seabrook, *Drawing the Lines*, 121.

57. Ronald E. Weber, "Race-Based Districting: Does It Help or Hinder Legislative Representation," *Political Geography* 19 (2000): 213–247.

58. On Cantor's primary loss, see Bell et al., *Slingshot*.

59. Richard F. Fenno, *Going Home: Black Representatives and Their Constituents* (Chicago: University of Chicago Press, 2003).

60. Fiona McGillivary, *Privileging Industry: The Comparative Politics of Trade and Industrial Policy* (Princeton, NJ: Princeton University Press, 2004).

61. Robert M. Stein and Kenneth N. Bickers, "Congressional Elections and the Pork Barrel," *Journal of Politics* 56 (May 1994), 377–399.

62. Anthony Downs, *An Economic Theory of Democracy* (New York: Harper and Row, 1957).

63. Samuel Issacharoff, "Gerrymandering and Political Cartels," *Harvard Law Review* 116 (2002), 628.

64. Robert S. Erikson and Gerald C. Wright, "Voters, Candidates, and Issues in Congressional Elections," in *Congress Reconsidered*, 11th edition, Lawrence C. Dodd and Bruce I. Oppenheimer, eds. (Thousand Oaks, CA: Sage, 2017), 61–88.

65. Morris P. Fiorina, *Representatives, Roll Calls and Constituencies* (Lexington, MA: Lexington Books, 1974); Charles S. Bullock III, "Congressional Voting and the Mobilization of a Black Electorate in the South," *Journal of Politics* 43 (August 1981), 662–681.

66. Norman J. Ornstein, Thomas E. Mann, and Michael J. Malbin, *Vital Statistics on Congress, 1997–1998* (Washington, DC: Congressional Quarterly, 1998), 68.

67. Rahm Emanuel, "A Big Factor in Corruption: Gerrymandering," *Roll Call* (July 25, 2006).

68. L. Sandy Maisel, Cherie D. Maestas, and Walter J. Stone, "The Impact of Redistricting on Candidate Emergence," in *Party Lines: Competition, Partisanship and Congressional Redistricting*, Thomas E. Mann and Bruce E. Cain, eds. (Washington, DC: Brookings Institution Press, 2005), 31.

69. Hirsch, "The United States House of Representatives," 179.

70. Editorial, "Broken Democracy," *Washington Post* (November 10, 2002), B6.

71. Seabrook, *Drawing the Lines*, chapter 5.

72. John A. Ferejohn, "On the Decline of Competition in Congressional Elections," *American Political Science Review* 71 (March 1977), 166–176; Albert D. Cover, "One Good Term Deserves Another: The Advantage of Incumbency in Congressional Elections," *American Journal of Political Science* 21 (August 1977), 523–541; Charles S. Bullock III, "Redistricting and Congressional Stability, 1962–1972," *Journal of Politics* 37 (1975), 569–575.

73. Amihai Glazer, Bernard Grofman, and Marc Robbins, "Partisans and Incumbency Effects of 1970s Congressional Redistricting," *American Journal of Political Science* 31 (August 1987), 680–707.

74. L. Sandy Maisel, Cherie D. Maestas, and Walter J. Stone, "The Impact of Redistricting on Candidate Emergence," in *Party Lines: Competition, Partisanship and Congressional Redistricting*, Thomas E. Mann and Bruce E. Cain, eds. (Washington, DC: Brookings Institution Press, 2005), 36–46.

75. Michael P. McDonald, "Drawing the Line on District Competition," *PS: Political Science and Politics* 39 (January 2006), 91–94.

76. Maureen Schweers, "U.S. House Races: Republican Resurgence After Eight Lean Years," in *Midterm Madness: The Elections of 2002*, Larry J. Sabato, ed. (Lanham, MD: Rowman & Littlefield, 2003), 69.

77. Gary W. Cox and Jonathan N. Katz, *Elbridge Gerry's Salamander* (Cambridge: Cambridge University Press, 2002), chapter 9. See also Susan A. Banducci and Jeffery A. Carp, "Electoral Consequences of Scandal and Reapportionment in the 1992 House Elections," *American Politics Quarterly* 22 (January 1994), 3–26; Antoine Yoshinaka and Chad Murphy, "The Paradox of Redistricting: How Partisan Mapmakers Foster Competition but Disrupt Representation," *Political Research Quarterly* 64 (June 2011), 435–447; Robert S. Erikson and Gerald C. Wright, "Elections, Constituencies, and Representation," in *Congress Reconsidered*, 11th ed., Lawrence C. Dodd and Bruce I. Oppenheimer, eds. (Thousand Oaks, CA: CQ Press, 2017).

78. David R. Mayhew, *Congress: The Electoral Connection* (New Haven, CT: Yale University Press, 1974), 82.

79. Ronald Keith Gaddie and Charles S. Bullock III, *Elections to Open Seats in the U.S. House: Where the Action Is* (Lanham, MD: Rowman & Littlefield, 2000).

80. John R. Petrocik and Scott W. Desposato, "The Partisan Consequences of Majority-Minority Redistricting in the South, 1992 and 1994," *Journal of Politics* 60 (August 1998), 613–633; M. V. Hood, III, and Seth C. McKee, "Unwelcome Constituents: Redistricting and Countervailing Partisan Tides," *State Politics and Policy Quarterly* 13:2 (2012), 203–224.

81. Seth C. McKee, "Redistricting and Familiarity with U.S. House Candidates," *American Politics Research* 36 (November 2008), 962–979.

82. Seth C. McKee, *Republican Ascendancy in Southern U.S. House Elections* (Boulder, CO: Westview Press, 2010), chapter 3; McKee, "The Effects of Redistricting on Voting Behavior in Incumbent U.S. House Elections, 1992–1994," *Political Research Quarterly* 61 (March 2008), 122–132; M. V. Hood, III, and Seth C. McKee, "Trying to Thread the Needle: The Effects of Redistricting in a Georgia Congressional District," *PS: Political Science and Politics* 42 (October 2009).

83. Gary Jacobson designates as quality congressional candidates those who have office-holding experience. Jacobson, *The Electoral Origins of Divided Government: Competition in the U.S. House Elections, 1946–1988* (Boulder, CO: Westview Press, 1990).

84. Thomas L. Brunell, *Redistricting and Representation: Why Competitive Elections Are Bad for America* (New York: Routledge, 2008).

85. *Davis v. Bandemer*, 478 U.S. 109 (1986).

86. *Badham v. Eu*, 695 F. Supp. 664 (N.D. Cal. 1988), affirmed in 488 U.S. 1024 (1989).

87. *Vieth v. Jubelirer*, 541 U.S. 267 (2004).

88. Samuel Issacharoff, Pamela Karlan, and Richard Pildes, *The Law of Democracy*, 2nd revised edition (New York: Foundation Press, 2002), 886.

89. Seabrook points out that under the GOP plan for the 2000s, the party that won a majority of the vote always got the bulk of the seats while under the Democratic plan it replaced only once during the 1990s did the party winning most of the votes get most of the seats (*Drawing the Lines*), 44.

90. *Cox v. Larios*, 542 U.S. 947 (2004).

91. Bernard Grofman, "Crafting a Judicially Manageable Standard for Partisan Gerrymandering: Five Necessary Elements," *Election Law Journal* 17:2 (2018), 117–136.

92. *Gill v. Whitford*, 138 S. Ct. 1916 (2018).

93. *Wisconsin Assembly Democratic Campaign Committee v. Gill*, No. 18-cv-763 (W.D. Wis., 2018).

94. *Common Cause v. Rucho*, 318 F. Supp. 3d 777 (M.D. NC, 2018); *League of Women Voters v. Johnson*, Civil Action No. 3:14cv852 (E.D. Mich., 2018); Simone Pathe and Stephanie Akins, "Federal Court Strikes Down Ohio Congressional Map as Partisan Gerrymander," *Roll Call* (May 3, 2019).

95. Jowei Chen and Jonathan Rodden, "Cutting Through the Thicket: Redistricting Simulations and the Detection of Partisan Gerrymanders," *Election Law Journal* 14:4 (2015), 331–345.

96. *Gill v. Whitford*, 138 S. Ct. 1916 (2018).

97. Emmet Bondurant quoted in Jim Galloway, "N.C. Gerrymandering Fight Has Atlanta Roots," *Atlanta Journal-Constitution* (January 14, 2018).

98. Michael Wines, "Judges Order Michigan to Redraw Gerrymandered Maps for 2020 Vote," *New York Times* (April 26, 2019).

99. McGann et al., *Gerrymandering in America*, 87.

100. Samuel S.-H. Wang, Brian A. Remlinger, and Ben Williams, "An Antidote for Gobbledygook: Organizing the Judge's Partisan Gerrymandering Toolkit into Tests of Opportunity and Outcome," *Election Law Journal* 17:4 (2018), 305.

101. Jowei Chen, "The Impact of Political Geography on Wisconsin Redistricting: An Analysis of Wisconsin's Act 43 Assembly Districting Plan," *Election Law Journal* 16:4 (2017), 1–10.

102. Richard Pildes, "Proportionality Is Not the Baseline in Modern Partisan Gerrymandering Cases," Election Law Blog (March 27, 2019).

103. Nicholas Stephanopoulos and Eric McGhee, "Partisan Gerrymandering and the Efficiency Gap," *University of Chicago Law Review* 82 (2015).

104. Wang et al., "Antidote to Gobbledygook," 311.

105. Jowei Chen and Jonathan Rodden, "Unintentional Gerrymandering: Political Geography and Electoral Bias in Legislatures," *Quarterly Journal of Political Science* 8 (2013), 239–269.

106. Michael D. McDonald and Robin E. Best, "Unfair Partisan Gerrymanders in Politics and Law: A Diagnostic Applied to Six Cases," *Election Law Journal* 14 (2015).

107. Samuel S.-H. Wang, "Three Tests for Practical Evaluation of Partisan Gerrymandering," *Stanford Law Review* 68 (June 2016), 1305.

108. McGann et al., *Gerrymandering in America*, 210.

109. Wang, "Three Tests," 1282.

110. *Lamone v. Benisek*, 138 S. Ct. 1942 (2019).

111. Wang et al., "Antidote to Gobbledygook," 313–314.

112. Grofman, "Crafting a Judicially Manageable Standard for Partisan Gerrymandering," *Election Law Journal* 17:2 (2018), 117–136.

113. Amy Howe, "Justices to Tackle Partisan Gerrymandering . . . Again: In Plain English," *Court* (February 4, 2019).

114. Quoted in Grofman, "Crafting a Judicially Manageable Standard for Partisan Gerrymandering," 120.

115. Quoted in Donald Daley, "The Secret Files of the Master of Modern Republican Gerrymandering," *New Yorker* (September 6, 2019).

116. Olga Pierce and Jeff Larson, "How Democrats Fooled California's Redistricting Commission," *ProPublica* (December 21, 2011).

117. Wang et al., "Antidote to Gobbledygook," 312; Grofman agrees with Wang that no single test is appropriate under all circumstances. Grofman, "Tests for Unconstitutional Partisan Gerrymandering in a Post-*Gill* World," *Election Law Journal* 18:2 (2019), 93–115.

118. Michael D. McDonald, Daniel B. Magleby, Jonathan Krasno, Shawn J. Donahue, and Robin E. Best, "Making a Case for Two Paths Forward in Light of *Gill v. Whitford*," *Election Law Journal* 17:4 (2018), 315–327.

119. Wang, "Three Tests for Practical Evaluation of Partisan Gerrymandering," 1263–1321.

120. David Daley, *Rat F\*\*ked: The True Story Behind the Secret Plan to Steal America's Democracy* (New York: Liveright, 2016), 139.

121. *Rucho v. Common Cause*, 139 S. Ct. 2484 (2019).

122. *Common Cause v. Lewis*, No. 18 CVS 014001 (2019).

123. Michael Barone and Chuck McCutcheon, *The Almanac of American Politics, 2014* (Chicago: University of Chicago Press, 2013), 1400.

124. *League of Women Voters of Pennsylvania v. Pennsylvania*, 178 A.3d 737 (2018).

125. Christopher Ingraham, "Pennsylvania Supreme Court Draws 'Much More Competitive' District Map to Overturn Republican Gerrymander," *Washington Post* (February 20, 2018).

126. Bernard Grofman and Jonathan R. Cervas, "Can State Courts Cure Partisan Gerrymandering: Lessons from *League of Women Voters v. Commonwealth of Pennsylvania (2018)*," *Election Law Journal* 17:4 (2019), 283.

127. *Gill v. Whitford*, 138 S. Ct. 1916 (2018).

128. Some claim that California's 1982 pro-Democratic gerrymander came in reaction to what Indiana Republicans had done. Glazer et al., "Effects of the 1970s Congressional Redistricting," 696.

129. See, for example, David Daley, *Rat F\*\*ked*.

130. Michael Li and Thomas Wolfe, "5 Things to Know about the Wisconsin Partisan Gerrymandering Case," Brennan Center for Justice (June 19, 2017).

131. Chen and Cottrell, "Evaluating Partisan Gains from Congressional Gerrymandering."

132. Donald E. Stokes, "Is There a Better Way to Redistrict?," in *Race and Redistricting in the 1990s*, Bernard Grofman, ed. (New York: Agathon, 1998), 345–366; Sam Hirsch, "Unpacking *Page v. Bartels*: A Fresh Redistricting Paradigm Emerges in New Jersey," *Election Law Journal* 1:1 (2002), 8–11.

133. Daley, *Rat F\*\*ked*, chapter 11.

134. Chen and Cottrell, "Evaluating Partisan Gains from Congressional Gerrymandering," 338.

135. Michael Barone and Chuck McCutcheon, *The Almanac of American Politics, 2014* (Washington, DC: National Journal, 2013), 129–130.

136. This paragraph draws on Pierce and Larson, "How Democrats Fooled California's Redistricting Commission."

137. Daley, *Rat F\*\*ked*, 141–142.

138. Chen and Rodden, "Unintentional Gerrymandering," 239–269, see also Nicholas Goedert, "Gerrymandering or Geography: How Democrats Won the Popular Vote but Lost the Congress in 2012," *Research and Politics* 1 (April–June 2014), 1–8.

139. Chen and Cottrell, "Evaluating Partisan Gains from Congressional Gerrymandering," 334.

140. Kevin A. Hill, "Does the Creation of Majority Black Districts Aid Republicans? An Analysis of the 1992 Congressional Election in Eight Southern States," *Journal of Politics* 57 (May 1995), 384–401; Charles S. Bullock III, "Georgia: A Study of Politics and Race," in *The New Politics of the Old South*, 2nd edition, Charles S. Bullock III and Mark J. Rozell, eds. (Lanham, MD: Rowman & Littlefield, 2003), 53–74.

141. McGann et al., *Gerrymandering in America*, 97–121.

142. This point is made in Devin Caughey, Chris Tausanovitch, and Christopher Warshaw, "Partisan Gerrymandering and the Political Process: Effects on Roll-Call Voting and State Policies," *Election Law Journal* 16:1 (2017), 1–17.

143. Brunell, *Redistricting and Representation*

# CHAPTER 6

1. Kevin A. Hill, "Does the Creation of Majority Black Districts Aid Republicans? An Analysis of the 1992 Congressional Elections in Eight Southern States," *Journal of Politics* 57 (May 1995), 400.

2. John Lewis, testimony in *Georgia v. Ashcroft*, 204 F. Supp. 2d 4 (D.D.C. 2002).

3. Jonathan Winburn, *The Realities of Redistricting: Following the Rules and Limiting Gerrymandering in State Legislative Redistricting* (Lanham, MD: Lexington Books, 2008), 67.

4. The Democratic executive committee in each congressional district decided whether the outcome of the Democratic primary would be decided by popular vote or county unit vote.

5. According to McCrary and Lawson, Mississippi, Maryland, and Tennessee also used variants on the county unit system in the past. Peyton McCrary and Steven F. Lawson, "Race and Reapportionment, 1962: The Case of Georgia Senate Redistricting," *Journal of Policy History* 12 (Summer 2000), 293–320.

6. Charles S. Bullock III, Scott E. Buchanan, and Ronald Keith Gaddie, *The Three Governors Controversy: Skullduggery, Machinations, and the Decline of Progressive Politics in the Peach State* (Athens: University of Georgia Press, 2015).

7. *Baker v. Carr*, 369 U.S. 186 (1962).

8. *Gray v. Sanders*, 372 U.S. 368 (1963).

9. *Toombs v. Fortson*, 205 F. Supp. 248 (1962).

10. Carter's successful effort to thwart an attempt to steal this election is reported in Jimmy Carter, *Turning Point* (New York: Times Books, 1992).

11. *Wesberry v. Sanders*, 376 U.S. 1 (1964).

12. Scott E. Buchanan, "The Effect of the Abolition of the Georgia County Unit System on the 1962 Gubernatorial Election," *Southeastern Political Review* 25 (1997), 687–704; Albert B. Saye, "Georgia's County Unit System of Election," *Journal of Politics* 12 (February 1950), 93–106.

13. Howard Ball, Dale Krane, and Thomas Lauth, *Compromised Compliance: Implementation of the 1965 Voting Rights Act* (Westport, CT: Greenwood Press, 1982).

14. DOJ denies that it ever required 65 percent black districts. But Robert A. Holmes, a political science professor who served in the Georgia House from 1975 to 2008, wrote that "U.S. Justice Department and federal district court rulings have considered a district with a 65 percent black population as the minimum necessary

to ensure the election of a black Congressman." "Reapportionment Politics in Georgia: A Case Study," *Phylon* (1984), 180. Scholars writing later have debunked the idea that DOJ demanded 65 percent black districts. David Lublin, *The Paradox of Representation: Racial Gerrymandering and Minority Interests in Congress* (Princeton, NJ: Princeton University Press, 1997), 45–48; Kimball Brace, Bernard Grofman, Lisa Handley, and Richard G. Niemi, "Minority Voting Equality: The 65 Percent Rule in Theory and Practice," *Law and Policy* 10 (1988), 43–62. Except as noted, much of the discussion of the 1980s round of redistricting draws on Holmes.

15. Robert A. Holmes, "The Politics of Reapportionment, 1981: A Case Study of Georgia," *Urban Research Review* 8 (1982), 2.

16. Holmes, "Reapportionment Politics," 184, writes that whites constituted 54 percent of the district's registered voters.

17. See Kevin M. Kruse, *White Flight* (Princeton, NJ: Princeton University Press, 2005).

18. *Georgia v. United States*, 411 U.S. 526 (1973).

19. *Busbee v. Smith*, 549 F. Supp. 494 (D. D.C. 1982).

20. Quoted in Laughlin McDonald, *A Voting Rights Odyssey: Black Enfranchisement in Georgia* (Cambridge: Cambridge University Press, 2003), 171.

21. Ladd goes on to point out that while he and McKinney are poles apart ideologically, he attended her swearing in as congresswoman when she won the 11th District. Personal interview with Ladd, May 21, 1998. LBC member Robert Holmes has written about the 1991–1992 redistricting from the perspective of a participant observer (Robert A. Holmes, "Reapportionment Strategies in the 1990s: The Case of Georgia," in *Race and Redistricting in the 1990s*, Bernard Grofman, ed. [New York: Agathon Press, 1998]). Holmes attributes the creation of the plan with three majority-black districts to Representatives McKinney and Tyrone Brooks along with ACLU attorney Kathy Wilde (193). Holmes takes credit himself for submitting the three-majority-black district congressional plan (197). The opinion of the federal district court stated that "the necessary kernel of a viable three-district plan—the Macon/Savannah trade—originated with Ms. Wilde." *Johnson v. Miller*, 864 F. Supp. 1354 (S.D. Ga., 1994).

22. Holmes attributes the "MAXBLACK" label to a state legislative plan devised by McKinney and Brooks which provided for fifty-one majority-black House districts and fifteen majority-black Senate districts. Bob Holmes, "Reapportionment/Redistricting Politics in Georgia in the 1990s and 2001–2002: Reflections of a Participant-Observer," in *Voting Rights and Minority Representation: Redistricting, 1992–2002*, David A. Bositis, ed. (Lanham, MD: University Press of America, 2006), 88.

23. Maurice T. Cunningham, *Maximization, Whatever the Cost: Race, Redistricting, and the Department of Justice* (Westport, CT: Praeger, 2001), 142–148.

24. Deposition of John Dunne at p. 122 in *Johnson v. Miller*, 864 F. Supp. 1354 (S.D. Ga. 1994).

25. Personal interview with Rep. Bob Hanner, April 14, 1992.

26. John R. Dunne to Mark H. Cohen, January 21, 1992.

27. Ibid.

28. John R. Dunne to Mark H. Cohen, March 20, 1992.

29. *Georgia v. Ashcroft*, 539 U.S. 461 (2003).

30. John Berendt, *Midnight in the Garden of Good and Evil* (New York: Vintage Books, 1994).

31. The creation of the new majority-black congressional districts in the early 1990s unleashed a pent up reservoir of ambition among African American politicians. For a further discussion of this phenomenon see David T. Canon, *Race, Redistricting and Representation* (Chicago: University of Chicago Press, 1999), chapter 3.

32. John Alford, Holly Teeters, Daniel S. Ward, and Rick K. Wilson, "Overdraft: The Political Cost of Congressional Malfeasance," *Journal of Politics* 56 (August 1994), 788–810; Gary Jacobson and Michael A. Dimock, "Checking Out: The Effects of Overdrafts on the 1992 House Elections," *American Journal of Political Science* 38 (1994), 601–624.

33. Holmes, "Reapportion/Redistricting Politics in Georgia," 91.

34. *Shaw v. Reno*, 509 U.S. 630 (1993).

35. *Miller v. Johnson*, 515 U.S. 900 (1995).

36. James Salzer, "Legislators Will Meet Aug. 14," *Atlanta Journal-Constitution* (July 8, 1995), 13A.

37. Holmes, "Reapportionment Strategies in the 1990s," 213.

38. *Abrams v. Johnson*, 521 U.S. 74 (1997).

39. Charles S. Bullock III and Richard E. Dunn, "The Demise of Racial Districting and the Future of Black Representation," *Emory Law Review* 48 (Fall 1999), 1209–1252.

40. Holmes, "Reapportionment/Redistricting Politics in Georgia," 92.

41. Jowei Chen and Jonathan Rodden, "Unintentional Gerrymandering: Political Geography and Electoral Bias in Legislatures," *Quarterly Journal of Political Science* 8 (2013), 239–269.

42. Expert report of David Epstein in *Georgia v. Ashcroft*.

43. Winburn, *The Realities of Redistricting*, 81, is relied on for this and the next paragraph.

44. Ronald Keith Gaddie and Charles S. Bullock III, "From *Ashcroft* to *Larios*: Recent Redistricting Lessons from Georgia," *Fordham Urban Law Journal* 34 (April 2007), 1014–1015.

45. Ibid., 1013.

46. This was one of twenty-three examples of water contiguity in the legislative plans. Expert report of Ronald Keith Gaddie, *Larios v. Cox*, 300 F. Supp. 2d 1320 (N.D. Ga. 2004).

47. Jim Galloway, "Redrawn District Takes All Day to Tour," *Atlanta Journal-Constitution* (August 11, 2001), A6.

48. Twiggs was accurate in claiming no responsibility for the Senate maps. Until 2004, the norm in the Georgia General Assembly allowed each chamber to draw its own map, which the other chamber then rubber stamped.

49. Winburn, *The Realities of Redistricting*, 76–77.

50. *Georgia v. Ashcroft*, 539 U.S. 461 (2003).

51. Ibid.

52. Holmes, "Reapportionment/Redistricting Politics in Georgia," 107.

53. *Larios v. Cox*, 300 F. Supp. 2d. 1320 (N.D. Ga, 2004).

54. *Reynolds v. Sims*, 377 U.S. 533 (1964).

55. M. V. Hood III and Seth C. McKee, "Gerrymandering on Georgia's Mind: The Effects of Redistricting on Vote Choice in the 2006 Midterm Election," *Social Science Quarterly* 89 (March 2008), 60–77.

56. Anthony J. McGann, Charles Anthony Smith, Michael Latner, and Alex Keena, *Gerrymandering in America: The House of Representatives, the Supreme Court, and the Future of Popular Sovereignty* (New York: Cambridge University Press, 2016), 86.

57. Georgia maintains and reports data on registration and turnout by race.

58. McGann et al., *Gerrymandering in America*, 76.

59. Jim Galloway et al., "Redrawn Districts May Polarize More," *Atlanta Journal-Constitution* (August 28, 2011), A1.

60. McGann et al., *Gerrymandering in America*, 91.

61. Holmes, "Reapportionment Politics in Georgia," 180.

62. Holmes writes that the LBC "split into two factions of almost equal size over the feasibility of creating two majority-Black congressional and one 'influence' (approximately 40 percent Black) district versus three majority-Black districts" (191). Later in the same chapter he reports, "In fact, the majority of its [LBC's] members actually voted to support the two-majority-Black District Congressional Plan to which Justice objected" (208). The LBC chair and several other senior members supported the state plan in meetings with DOJ attorneys. Holmes, "Reapportionment Politics in Georgia."

63. This difference in the relevant constituency of black legislators also occurred in Congress with those in the House leadership more likely to support the Democratic Party position, while members not incorporated into the leadership tended to be more responsive to forces outside the chamber. Nadine Cohodas, "Black House Members Striving for Influence," *Congressional Quarterly Weekly Report* 43 (April 13, 1985), 681.

64. On at least one occasion during the 2001 redistricting session, enough LBC members joined with Republicans so that Democrats had to make changes in the congressional maps. David Pendered, "Black Democrats Revolt Over Murphy's Districts," *Atlanta Journal-Constitution* (September 6, 2001), C8.

65. GLBC refers to the Georgia Legislative Black Caucus. Holmes, "Reapportionment/Redistricting Politics in Georgia," 107.

66. The black concentration in the 2nd District had probably reached its maximum. McKinney helped push the black percentage to 64 percent in the district that she ended up winning.

67. Holmes, "Reapportionment Strategies in the 1990s," 203.

68. Robert Brown testimony in *Georgia v. Ashcroft*, 204 F. Supp. 2d 4 (D.D.C. 2002).

69. Earl Black and Merle Black, *The Rise of Southern Republicans* (Cambridge, MA: Belknap Press, 2002); Charles S. Bullock III, Donna Hoffman, and Ronald K. Gaddie, "Regional Variations in the Realignment of American Politics, 1944–2004," *Social Science Quarterly* 87 (September 2006), 494–518.

## CHAPTER 7

1. Tom Hofeller quoted in Shane D'Aprile, "Preparing for the Ten Year Storm," *Politics Magazine* (January 2010), online edition access at http://www.politicsmagazi ne.com-issues/january-2010/preparing-for-the-ten-year-storm.

2. Richard E. Cohen, "Battle Lines," *National Journal* (December 19, 2009), 28.

3. The discussion of this section draws heavily upon a press release from Election Data Services, December 30, 2019.

4. From the 1912 reapportionment until 1932, Texas had the largest southern delegations with eighteen members while Georgia had twelve. Alabama, North Carolina, Tennessee, and Virginia each had ten legislators.

5. The 1930 reapportionment had an especially great impact since rural legislators in Congress, facing an increasingly urban nation, blocked the reassignment of seats following the 1920 census.

6. For a discussion of the merits of increasing the size of House, see Brian Frederick, *Congressional Representation and Constituents: The Case for Increasing the U.S. House of Representatives* (New York: Routledge, 2010).

7. Election Data Services press release, December 30, 2019.

8. For a discussion of the differences between the Growth and Stagnant South, see Charles S. Bullock III, Susan A. MacManus, Jeremy D. Mayer, and Mark J. Rozell, *The South and the Transformation of U.S. Politics* (New York: Oxford University Press, 2019).

9. While states like Alabama no longer need federal approval of redistricting plans since the scuttling of Section 4 of the Voting Rights Act, in *Shelby County v. Holder*, dismantling of a majority black district would trigger litigation under Section 2.

10. For a discussion of longitudinal trends in party strength see, Charles S. Bullock III, Donna Hoffman, and Ronald Keith Gaddie, "Regional Variations in the Realignment of the American Politics, 1944–2004," *Social Science Quarterly* 87 (September 2006), 494–518.

11. Nate Cohn and Quoctrung Bui, "How the Math of Gerrymandering Works," *New York Times* (October 3, 2017). Anthony J. McGann, Charles Anthony Smith, Michael Latner, and Alex Keena, *Gerrymandering in America: The House of Representatives, the Supreme Court, and the Future of Popular Sovereignty* (New York: Cambridge University Press, 2016), 105.

12. As of mid-2020, there were rumors that, due to the disruption caused by the COVID-19 pandemic, it might be impossible for the Census Bureau to provide states with data for redistricting by the end of the year.

13. Much of this paragraph draws on Hansi Lo Wang, "'We're Running Out of Time': Census Turns to Congress to Push Deadlines," NPR (May 27, 2010), and Max Greenwood, "Census Delay Threatens to Roil Redistricting," *The Hill* (May 15, 2020).

14. *Shelby County v. Holder*, 570 U.S. 529 (2013).

15. Jacob Fischler, "Gerrymandering Potential Sways State Legislative Targets," *Roll Call* (January 21, 2020); A. Berman, "The Courts Won't End Gerrymandering, Eric Holder Has a Plan to Fix It Without Them," *Mother Jones* (July/August 2019).

16. The efforts by U.S. House Majority Leader Tom DeLay to influence Texas state legislative elections in 2002 is chronicled in Steve Bickerstaff, *Lines in the Sand* (Austin: University of Texas Press, 2007).

17. Dan Chapman, "Stakes, Challenges High for Counties Every Georgian, Getting Every Dollar," *Atlanta Journal-Constitution* (January 18, 2010).

18. David T. Canon, *Race, Redistricting, and Representation* (Chicago: University of Chicago Press, 1999).

19. *Bartlett v. Strickland*, 556 U.S 1 (2009).

20. Ronald Brownstein, "The March of Destiny," *National Journal* 41 (December 19, 2009), 18– 25.

21. The models for the 2016 presidential election appear in *PS: Political Science and Politics* 49 (October 2016), 649–679. Results for earlier years appear in the pre-election issue of *PS: Political Science and Politics*.

22. Quoted in Cohen, "Battle Lines," 28.

# Index

Abrams, Stacey, 199
*Abrams v. Johnson*, 182
ACLU. *See* American Civil Liberties Union
ACS. *See* American Community Survey
activism, 27
Adams, Alma, 93
African Americans, 17–18; BVAP for, 187; Clinton, H., and, 217; in Congress, 17–18, 178, 246n63; democrats and, 18, 60, 70, 87–88, 181–82; districts with, 110, *111*, 128, 236n24; for DOJ, 96, 222n21, 243n14; in elections, 81–82; in Georgia, 65–66, 84–85, *85*, 169, 173–80, *178–79*; history for, 201–4; Latinos and, 72, *72*, 79–81, *81*, 130, 133; in Maryland, 138; McKinney for, 246n66; in Mississippi, *20*, 93; in North Carolina, *136*, 136–37; packing, 92–93, 107; in politics, 87, 245n31; ratcheting for, *90*; republicans and, 91–92, 195–96, 229n46; research on, 223n34, 232n93; in rural districts, 53; stacking for, *22*; state legislatures and, 95; for Supreme Court, 112; in Tennessee, 19; Texas for, 88; in United States, 170–73, *171*, 228n22;

in Virginia, 231n66; VRA for, 60–62, *156*, 201. *See also specific topics*
age, 48–50, 187
Alabama, 67; Florida and, 110; *Miller v. Johnson* for, 91–92; population of, 208–9; state law in, 33; state legislatures in, 38; VRA for, 247n9
*Allen v. State Board of Elections*, 64–65
Allgood, Tom, 171–72
American Civil Liberties Union (ACLU), 174, 181, 182, 202, 244n21
American Community Survey (ACS), 28, 29, 205
apportionment, *5–6*, *207*, *209–10*
Arizona, 10, 129, 162
Arkansas, 47
*Ashcroft v. Georgia*, 177
Asian Americans, 80
Atlanta, Georgia, 48, 170

*Baker v. Carr*, 39–40, 49, 60, 109–10, 168
Barrow, John, 85, 195, 199, 201
Bartlett, Roscoe, 117, 138, 151
Barton, Joe, 132
Beauprez, Bob, 16
Bell, Chris, 133
Bentsen, Lloyd, 130

LBC for, 192–93; for Legislative
Services Agency, 161; population
for, *188*; super majority in, 200
Sessions, Jeff, 27
*Shaw v. Reno*, 75, 77–78, 88, 101–2,
153–54, 181
*Shelby County v. Holder*, *77–78*, 91, 93,
215
Shotts, Kenneth, 96
silent gerrymandering, 55
simulations, *152*
single-member districts, 24–25
South Carolina, 85–86
Spanberger, Abigail, 232n82
Spanish, 66–67
Speaker of the House, 8–9
stability, 8–9
stacking, 19, 21, *22*, 24
state courts, 155–58, *156–57*
state law: in Alabama, 33; for courts,
158, 166; for districts, *13*; federal
law and, 12; in Georgia, 224n40;
in Iowa, *161*, 161–62; in North
Carolina, 222n13, 235n11; *Reynolds
v. Sims* for, 55; for vetoes, 222n13
state legislatures: African Americans
and, 95; in Alabama, 38; bias in,
126–27; districts for, 9–15, *11–13*,
183–84; for DOJ, *73*, 73–74; in
Georgia, 245n48; history of, 18;
House of Representatives and,
2; MAXBLACK proposal for,
244n22; National Conference of
State Legislatures, 101; recruitment
in, 9; research on, 124, 126;
responsiveness for, 124–26; state
house, 169; state senates, 168–69; in
Texas, 114; voting for, 127–28
state prisons, 50–51
state seat allocations, 3–4, *5–6*, 7–8
state senates, 38, 168–69
Stenholm, Charles, 116–17
Stephens, Bill, 189–90, *190*
Steyer, Tom, 14
suburbanization, 138, 236n25

Supreme Court: African Americans
for, 112; appeals for, 226n29;
citizenship for, 27, 216; Congress
and, 32, 62; DOJ and, *82–83*, 182;
Equal Protection Clause for, 97,
169; federal law and, 166; Hawaii
for, 226n31; Illinois for, 128;
Kennedy challenge from, 150–55,
*152*; law from, 19; Maryland for,
51–52; *Miller v. Johnson* for, 181;
minimalist approach for, 42–43;
Pennsylvania for, 149–50; politics
and, 148–50; population deviations
for, 34–35, 45–46; population for,
129; reapportionment for, 101–2; for
Redistricting Revolution, 167–68;
Scalia for, 3; Texas for, 16, 50;
VRA for, *76–77*, 91–92, 214–15;
Wisconsin for, 151. *See also specific
cases*
surveys, 108–9
Swain, Carol, 89
swing ratio, 124–26, 133

Tea Party, 14, 133–35, *134*
Tennessee, 17, 19, 39, *109*, 222n13
Texas: for African Americans, 88; Bush,
G. W., for, 1–2; democrats in, 159;
Florida and, 206, 210–11; Georgia
and, 117, 164, 247n4; *Georgia v.
Ashcroft* for, 90; gerrymandering
in, 235n10; Latinos in, 78; non-
citizens in, 49; politics in, 12, 15,
130–33, *131*; republicans in, 123–24,
147; state legislatures in, 114; for
Supreme Court, 16, 50; Tennessee
and, 17; VRA for, 75–76
Thompson, Myron, 91
*Thornburg v. Gingles*, 68–69, 182
Thurmond, Michael, 175
transparency, 163
Trump, Donald, 15, 26–28, 125, 208,
211
Twiggs, Ralph, 191, 245n48
Tyson, Bryan, 236n24

# About the Author

**Charles S. Bullock III** is the Distinguished University Professor of Public and International Affairs, the Richard B. Russell Professor of Political Science, and Josiah Meigs Distinguished Teaching Professor at the University of Georgia.

CPSIA information can be obtained
at www.ICGtesting.com
Printed in the USA
BVHW081800030321
601249BV00002B/5